EX LIBRIS

Loretto in the Rockies

Loretto in the Rockies

By

SISTER M. CELESTINE CASEY, S.L., A.M.
Director of Journalism
Loretto Heights College

and

SISTER M. EDMOND FERN, S.L., A.M., Ph.D.
Director of Classical Languages
Webster College

DENVER, COLORADO
1943

NIHIL OBSTAT:

THOMAS F. SCHMUCKER, C.M., S.T.D.
Censor Deputatus
Denveri, die 19 Januarii, 1943

IMPRIMATUR:

✟ URBANUS IOANNES VEHR
Archiepiscopus Denveriensis
Denveri, die 22 Januarii, 1943

The Most Reverend Urban J. Vehr, D.D.
Archbishop of Denver

Sister M. Pancratia Bonfils—1880

To the Memory of
MOTHER PANCRATIA BONFILS
and
To All Those
Who Have Ever Lived
At Loretto Heights

Foreword

LORETTO IN THE ROCKIES

is an inspiring story of a pioneer school in the West—a story vividly told of the struggles and trials of a small band of Sisters of Loretto from the far-away Southland who braved the hardships of early Western life to establish the very first convent school in the Rocky Mountain region.

As year by year the story unfolds, joys and sorrows, lights and shadows color the pages of the book. Here appear the names of the daughters of Colorado and other parts of our country from the first high school graduates of the nineties to the college women at the end of the first golden cycle.

The writers of *Loretto in the Rockies* have done a splendid piece of research through records yellow with age and dusty papers still carrying the valued information. They have interviewed many of the senior sisters who have brought forth from memory's treasure chest much of ancient lore. From these sources have been drawn threads that have been woven into a beautiful tapestry which will remain forever a sacred memorial to Loretto Heights.

Enlivened by clever anecdotes and enriched by a sincere philosophy of life, the simple story of fifty years of convent school happenings makes this book a valuable contribution to Catholic biographical and historical literature.

SISTER MARY VIVIAN EDELEN

Director of Social Sciences and
Registrar of Loretto Heights College

Preface

It was long a matter of amazement to me that so many of our gifted writers had left untouched for fifty years the story of Loretto Heights, the story of wonder and glorious achievement, the story vibrant with human interest for the people of the West. How could they be content to let it remain in obscurity?

Having had the good fortune of being a daughter of one of the pioneer families of Colorado and also of having been taught, for ten years, by the Sisters of Loretto at old St. Mary's Academy when it stood in all its stateliness on the present site of the Denver Public Market, Fifteenth and California Streets, the thought came to me—Why should I not write the story of Loretto Heights? Well, why not? Why not attempt to put in permanent form the thrilling story, which through the years had accumulated rare anecdotes? The history of Loretto Heights with its interesting local happenings should be released to an eager and friendly people—our people of the Golden West.

In addition to my own desire to do this gigantic work, I was urged on by those who recognized that Loretto Heights had a story which would be a contribution to the Catholic history of Colorado and the surrounding states.

In 1935 with the favorite tools of a Western miner—a pan, a pick, a spade, and a hammer—I went into action. I began investigating the sources of incidents and other data told by casual visitors who related intriguing events which took place in the years now fast receding. When the first glimmerings of sparkling flakes appeared in my mining pan, I felt the promise of a great reward. The more I shifted these flakes from side to side the more real they became as material to be used. Delightedly I washed the surplus from my findings, and, following the trail, I made larger and more valuable discoveries as I turned over spade after spade of rich material. I threw away my pan now and took firm hold of my pick and hammer.

During eight full years of searching through heavy tomes of forgotten writers and prying open memory's treasure chests, belonging to our senior sisters, numerous samples rich in content came tumbling out—all mine for the taking. Dates, verified and re-verified, episodic recollections, meticulous observations, esteemed opinions, obtained through adroit interviews, not to mention valuable gleanings from newspapers, turning yellow with age—all these gave me stories of those first graduations, addresses of the popular speakers of the day, as well as real estate announcements releasing important facts concerning various purchases of sections of the property at Loretto Heights. This information lured me on to further efforts in compiling this story, *Loretto in the Rockies.*

Suddenly I began feeling like a millionnaire who unexpectedly strikes it rich. The tiny flakes of gold, floating around in my pan, had by this time turned into large nuggets; all around me was gold, for the wonderful year of the Golden Jubilee was passing and hoarded treasures were being increased. Digging deeper and ever deeper, I now found the grade hard and true, like the gold of the wisemen. Finally I turned the beam of my miner's searchlight upon that wealth of material and I saw that my collection was valuable and fine.

From hundreds of neglected sources this story rich in romance and adventure had in 1940 really begun telling itself. Then in the summer of '42, Sister Mary Edmond of Webster College, former president of Loretto Heights College, from February, 1930 to August, 1934, and director of the classical department for fifteen years, was sent to collaborate on the final setting of the book.

Here, then, we present the narrative of the struggles and sacrifices of our pioneer sisters who have gone and of a few still with us, who were associated with the early community and shared the hardships and deprivations that sometimes brought the night. But the nights at Loretto were never without hope for the oncoming days—days filled with Colorado sunshine; days enriched with magic sunrises, rolling hills abloom with myriad-colored wild flowers, meadow larks and bluebirds bursting their throats in zestful song, fragrant and healing air, and people with faith in themselves and in one another.

Accounts of these days and the data concerning them are conscientiously reproduced here in *Loretto in the Rockies.*

Sister M. Celestine Casey, S.L.

Octave of the Epiphany, 1943.

Loretto in the Rockies is the result of an idea which Sister M. Celestine cherished for years and of the research which she cheerfully undertook as a basis of the history she had in mind.

My contribution in helping to bring this volume to the reader was a comparatively easy task—simply a matter of putting into place, nugget by nugget, findings which had already been secured; of making use of veins filled with rich ore; and, passing over the shale and mica schist and other nonessentials, of seeking the recurrence of the lode.

I am grateful for the opportunity of tracing the history of fifty years which centers around this foundation of the Loretto Society; of studying the faith and courage of the founding sisters and their equally valiant successors, who succeeded, with God's grace, in keeping unswervingly to the work they had undertaken in spite of obstacles which might have weakened hearts less brave.

Some of the Sisters of Loretto who helped to make history in Denver and at Loretto Heights were friends "loved long since and lost a while": beloved teachers, a saintly mistress of novices, and revered superiors. The names of Mother Pancratia Bonfils and Mother Praxedes Carty deserve to be held in loving remembrance by the sisters and students at Loretto. One was the foundress; the other by her business ability, when Mother General of the Loretto Society, restored financial security to the foundation.

To be instrumental, even in a small way, in preserving the memory of these noble Lorettines is a means, perhaps, of making some return for part of the cost of the education which these earlier teachers passed on to those students who were to continue their work in Loretto schools.

SISTER MARY EDMOND FERN, S.L.

Acknowledgments

Appreciative thanks are given to all who assisted the writers in bringing to completion *Loretto in the Rockies*: Mother M. Edwarda Ashe, Superior General of the Sisters of Loretto at the Foot of the Cross, and her Council for reading the book in manuscript and offering valuable criticisms; Mother Olivette Norton, Superior General when this book was first taking form, for her interest which extended to the last chapter; Sister M. Antonella, archivist at Loretto Motherhouse, for releasing important information; Sister Frances Marie Walsh, superior of Loretto Heights College, and the community, for loyal co-operation and material support; Sister Mary Vivian, registrar of the college; Sister Mary Dolorine, dean from 1918 to 1934; Sister Rose Margaret, custodian of the library files; Sister Francis de Sales, dean of studies; Sister Frances Therese, dean of women; Sister M. Cecille, moderator of Alumnae Association; Sister Mary Florence, director of public relations; and Helen Bonfils Somnes, good friend of Loretto Heights College, for financial assistance in publishing this volume.

Acknowledgment is also made to the officials of the United States Weather Bureau, Denver, for verifying the statement in Chapter I, namely, that on March 19, 1888, the snowfall was the heaviest of the year, 3.6 inches; to the clerks of Littleton Court House, seat of Arapahoe County, who courteously gave data concerning the property at Loretto Heights; to officials at Loretto Motherhouse and Loretto Heights College for financial releases; and to the Arapahoe Abstract and Title Company, Littleton, for financial statements, furnished by Miss Catherine Maloney.

Valuable information was secured from the *Denver Times* of November, 1888, and September, 1889; the *Denver Catholic Register,* the *Denver Republican,* the *Rocky Mountain News,* the *Denver Post,* and from the State Historical Museum; also from the First Assistant Post Office Department, Washington, D. C.; and the United States Post Office in Denver, through the courtesy of Mr. J. O. Stevic.

The following books were consulted in writing this history: *History of Colorado* by William M. Byers; *History of Colorado* by Wilbur Fiske; *History of Colorado* by Frank Hall; *Loretto Annals of the Century* by Anna C. Minogue; *The Life of Reverend Charles Nerinckx* by Reverend W. J. Howlett; *The Life of Reverend Charles Nerinckx* by Right Reverend Camillus Paul Maes, Bishop of Covington; *Life of Bishop Machebeuf* by Reverend W. J. Howlett; *The Pinnacled Glory of the West,* edited and published by Very Reverend Hugh L. McMenamin; *Yesterday,* Golden Jubilee Book of Sisters of St. Joseph, Denver; *Religious Orders of Women in the United States* by Elinor Tong Dehey.

For many local happenings and events the writers were dependent upon the Yearbooks of Loretto Heights, the Annals of '14, '15, '16, especially; the annals of the community; the registrar's files; the *Pancratian,* the academy school paper; and the *Heightsonian,* the college paper; and numerous scrapbooks of newspaper clippings.

Table of Contents

Illustrations

Important Data

Concerning Loretto Heights Academy, Pancratia Academy, and Loretto Heights College

March 19, 1888—Mother Pancratia Bonfils, Sister Bartholomew Nooning, Sister Agatha Wall, and Sister Victorine Renshaw selected the site for the new academy, Loretto Heights.

November 14, 1888—First forty acres bought from R. M. Morse, $16,000.

September 25, 1889—Five more acres bought from same party, $2,250.

January 23, 1890—Ground broken and building begun.

September 21, 1890—Corner-stone laid.

November 2, 1891—Twenty sisters and fifty-one girls moved to the new Loretto Heights Academy.

November 16, 1891—More girls came, increasing the enrollment to ninety.

December 10, 1891—Dedication of Loretto Heights Academy by the Most Reverend Nicholas C. Matz, Bishop Denver, on Feast of the Holy House of Loretto.

March 1, 1892—Mother Pancratia Bonfils was transferred to Montgomery, Alabama.

June 15, 1892—First graduating exercises of Loretto Heights Academy.

August 15, 1893—Sister Aimee Hynes and Sister Dolorine Morrison pronounced Perpetual Vows as Sisters of Loretto.

September 17, 1918—College founded by Mother Clarasine Walsh, Sister Dolorine Morrison, and Sister Vivian Edelen.

* * * * *

October 24, 1928—Ground broken for Pancratia Hall.

September, 1929—Corner-stone laid, Pancratia Hall.

September 7, 1930—Pancratia Hall occupied by academy students.

September 18, 1930—Pancratia Hall dedicated by the Most Reverend J. Henry Tihen, Bishop of Denver.

June 1, 1941—Pancratia Academy formally closed; to be used hereafter for *college* purposes.

Map of the Grounds

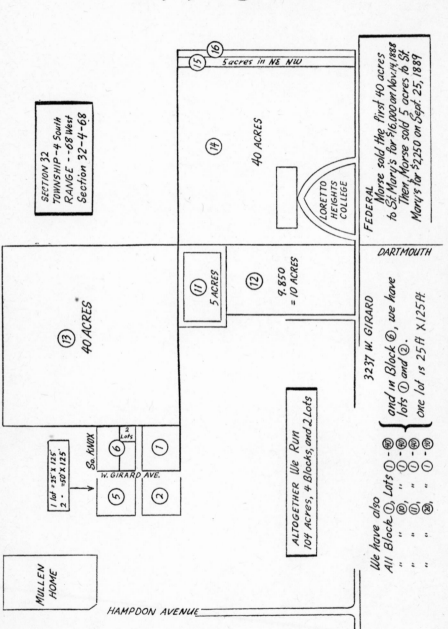

Map of the Grounds at Loretto Heights.

Chapter I

THEY SELECT THE SITE

It was on a March day, the feast of St. Joseph, eighteen hundred eighty-eight, that two Sisters of Loretto, a stiff mountain breeze swaying their long graceful veils, stepped to the center of the rounded top of Sheridan Heights, just seven miles southwest of Denver. They were selecting a site for a new building.

Their school, St. Mary's academy, had outgrown itself. More room was needed—and Sheridan Heights looked better to Mother Pancratia Bonfils and her companion, Sister Bartholomew Nooning, than property in north Denver which they had almost decided to purchase. The Sheridan view appealed to the aesthetic sense of Sister Bartholomew who was well educated in the fine arts.

However, before making a definite decision with regard to the site, the Sisters arranged to bring two other Sisters, whose opinions they valued, to view the location in order to ascertain whether others would discover what *they* had found in this tract of virgin soil.

Accordingly, on the afternoon of that same day, March nineteenth, Mother Pancratia Bonfils and Sister Bartholomew Nooning returned, in the midst of a snow storm, with Sister Agatha Wall and Sister Victorine Renshaw. Fortunately for them a Mr. Sullivan had offered to take them out in his two-seated runner. In weather like this, everyone used sleighs, for carriages were useless outside the city limits. Although a week before a robin had been seen, the Sisters in setting out on the trip had to draw their shawls close about them. How they did skim over the snow, the deepest snow that winter.

There was snow, snow everywhere, falling in large crystals as if inviting the sisters to visit them atop the hill. With their cheeks glowing and breath etching mystic designs in the frosty air, these four pioneer Lorettines, in actual age about thirty-eight or nine and in religious life more than twenty-four years, clambered out of the runner sleigh, sinking ankle deep in woolly, fluffy flakes of snow. Here they were, over seven miles from St. Mary's—practically out in the country.

They tramped around and around, their view unbroken for several miles by any habitation of man, except by Fort Logan, which lay to the southwest of them, snuggled up to the neck in a snowy coverlet soft as lamb's wool. That was the military post where General Custer used to meet his men, and this very ground on top of Sheridan Heights served as a drilling field for his soldiers. Down there, not very far, maybe three miles, on the other side of Platte River, lay what was once the first town in Colorado, Montana City, where gold and silver were taken wholesale out of the little creek flowing through the village. History oozed out of every place at which the sisters looked that afternoon in Passion Week of 1888.

O-oooooooo! And the four Sisters of Loretto drew in long, lung-filling breaths of pure mountain air, fanning to flame that adverturous spirit which had dominated the early sisters of St. Mary's, one of whom was Mother Pancratia herself.

"And, Mother Pancratia, do you see those little black huts toward the Platte River? Those must have been the hiding places for the scout and messenger, Kit Carson; do you suppose he is there now watching us and wondering what we are doing up here? Oh, this is so exciting! Let's take it, let's buy this land; it's so full of wonder! Look, we can see for miles and miles around us!"

"Now, Sister Agatha, do not get too excited. Though this looks like God's own country out here, let us not be carried away by this scene of fairyland; we have many things to consider. Sister Victorine, what do you think of this as a location for our new academy? We'd surely never be cramped for space and we could call the site the Heights."

"I love the location, Mother Pancratia. Couldn't we call it *Loretto Heights?* Don't you think that name would be quite suitable?"

"Yes, I do, Sister Victorine. What do you say, Sister Bartholomew?"

"Well, all you have to do to get my vote is just to take a look at those mountains there to the west. Can't you see his majesty, the sun, stalking up and down behind those ranges—he's surely putting on a display for us this afternoon. While it's snowing here, look away out there at the lakes of flaky gold, bubbling between those peaks, and—say, just take a look above us. Did you ever see any better hint from Almighty God than that smile of His, warm and reassuring, abreakin' through the skies? Some day I'm goin' to paint this scene. Mother, I'd like you to buy this whole countryside. That's how I feel about this location."

"Sisters, this snow scene on these heights is indeed beautiful; imagine what the place will be like in a few weeks when this winter picture is replaced by a summer's growth of grassy plains, interspersed here and there with fields of grain, corn, and alfalfa; and, climaxing the whole, our new academy. Let us pray that God will bless our project and help us in this great undertaking.

"The people of Denver are proud of what we have already done for their daughters. If we succeed in securing this property, we can bring our boarders out here and keep the day students at St. Mary's. With more room and additional teachers, we can give all our pupils better training.

"You know, Sisters,"—and Mother Pancratia scanned the snow-clad valleys and mountains—"this section of the state must have been a vantage ground for the Arapahoes and Cheyennes. Now I understand something that I did not know twenty-five years ago when the Indians used to surprise us at St. Mary's. From this height they could view the whole valley on every side; pivoting right here, they beheld the vast panorama of the plains to the north and south; there to the west, Sister Bartholomew, they had the magnificent sight of your Rocky Mountains; and down there, about three miles east from here, was the site of Montana City where today are West Evans avenue and the Platte River.

"You remember they called that little town Montana City, Sister Agatha; you were very young in those days, and I, though even then a Sister of Loretto, was barely fifteen. My, how terribly frightened I became when those Indians took a notion to peer through our windows, back in those early days, just after I came to Denver, and some of you were here earlier than I. We never knew when they would push themselves right into the middle of our kitchen —we really had little more than a kitchen—"

"Well do I remember, Mother Pancratia," interrupted Sister Bartholomew, "the first time you tried your hand at making biscuits, the Arapahoes must have smelled those browning biscuits away out here and followed the scent all the way to St. Mary's. You recall, don't you, that just as you were pulling the pans out of the oven, there stood a huge Indian, grunting, it seemed to me, miles down his throat—'*Huh! me hungry!*'"

"Oh, what did you do then, Mother?" asked Sister Victorine.

"She fed him, of course," Sister Bartholomew answered, "and earned there and then the title of 'White Angel,' the title we still give Mother. Those days held many terrors for us, yet every one of us loved them."

"But tell us more of Montana City," urged Sister Victorine. "It was down there on the Platte. Let me see— that would be at a distance of about six miles south of our convent on Fifteenth and California, wouldn't it?"

"Yes, Sister Victorine, that was the distance; but at that time they did not call those streets Fifteenth and California; they named all streets as briefly as possible—they were *E* and *F* streets. Poor Montana City survived only one winter. The twenty or more log cabins which Jason Yonker and others of the *Lawrence* party threw together, were used for only a short time. That was in 1859, so they told me, just five years before our good friend, Father

Machebeuf, brought our first Sisters from Santa Fe to Denver.

"But, Sisters, forgive me. Here I have been reminiscing and living over again those early days; I have been forgetting that the snow is now almost four inches deep. You must be getting cold. Look, the driver can scarcely keep the horses from bolting. We'd better go. Just as soon as we get back to St. Mary's, I shall write to Mother Superior and tell her of this wonderful location."

Always a woman of action, Mother Pancratia, encouraged by her companions, wasted no time in communicating with the Motherhouse in Kentucky for the necessary permissions to buy the property and enter into negotiations for the erection of the new school. When these were secured, she consulted real estate men and the architects, F. E. Edbrooke and Company. On November 14, 1888, the first forty acres of the present campus were purchased from B. M. Morse for $16,000 by St. Mary's Academy, in the name of the Loretto Literary and Benevolent Institution. The following year, September 25, 1889, five more acres were purchased from the same Mr. Morse for $2,250.

Chapter II

THE PRESS SHOWS INTEREST

As soon as the Sisters had decided on the location for the new school, interest in the place quickly developed. The girls of St. Mary's Academy had many a picnic out on Sheridan Heights. The following excerpt taken from the monthly paper, *Convent Echo,* published by the pupils of St. Mary's, September, 1889, describes one of these outings:

On September 20, the girls of St. Mary's academy, Denver, enjoyed a delightful day at Mt. Loretto, Loretto Heights. Early on that bright September morning we started off on the Circle railway. Mother sent our lunch out a few hours later, and all day long we rambled over the beautiful country surrounding the site of the future Loretto home. At nightfall, we returned to our loved St. Mary's, laden with geological specimens and charming wild flowers. But the best gleanings of our day's wanderings at Mt. Loretto were the bright red roses painted on our cheeks by the pure fresh air in which we had revelled all day long.

One sees from this that Mt. Loretto, as those at St. Mary's daringly called the new property, served as a picnic ground for the pupils of the city school. While negotiations for purchasing the site and plans for the building were being completed, this locality became more familiar. On Saturday, January 23, 1890, scarcely two years after Mother Pancratia and Sisters Bartholomew, Agatha, and Victorine had selected the location, ground was broken for the new academy to be known in future as Loretto Heights.

Through the untiring efforts of the Sisters of Loretto and particularly of the Mother Superior, Mother Dafrosa Smythe, of the Motherhouse of Loretto, Kentucky, sufficient funds were raised to begin the building. The plans for this great venture were carried out under the supervision of Mother Pancratia Bonfils, who for almost twenty-five years had been more intimately and continuously connected with the progress of the Loretto Order in Colorado than any other Lorettine. She it was who, recognizing the necessity of a larger and more modern building, furthered whole-heartedly this educational movement by conceiving the idea of the new school and bringing it to a reality in Loretto Heights Academy.

This building program was of such importance to the general public that the editors of the *Denver Republican* carried a cut and a full-page description of the building under date of May 20, 1890.

ST. MARY'S WALLS RISE
Sketch of the Splendid Building of the Sisters of Loretto
A Structure That Will Be a Credit to the City
Final Estimates Made

The basement walls for St. Mary's academy, being built by The Sisters of Loretto, are about completed. Only thus far has the contract been let for that magnificent structure, of which a very accurate cut is given. The site is a little east of north of Sheridan post, and a half a mile distant. It is being built on what is known as Mount Loretto—a rising ground that overlooks the entire surrounding country, and gives a magnificent mountain view.

Taking this accompanying cut as a guide, a detailed description of the building will be given.

LORETTO HEIGHTS ACADEMY

In the first place there are three entrances—one at each end of the building opening into a corridor that extends the entire length of the building, 220 feet. The third entrance is the main one and opens into a tower, 30 feet square. Set in a grotto over the arch at the main entrance is a statue of heroic size of the Virgin Mary.

Inside the arch and before the main doors of the entrance are reached is a vestibule with marble floors. The broad steps to the various entrances are all of red stone; that, in fact, being the material used in the whole building. In outward appearances it will be made of red Colorado sandstone in the rough, dressed and carved thus making a combination at once beautiful and attractive.

The two wings of the building are each 52 x 100 feet in size; and the measurements of the width of the central portion is 65 feet. The tower from the ground to the top of the cross is 165 feet. There are also three floors and an attic story aside from the basement floor.

Commencing with the basement, the various floors will be divided about as follows: One wing of the basement will be used for a calisthenic hall, the balance of the floor being used for the Sisters' dining rooms, private dining rooms, toilet rooms, kitchen, serving rooms, stores, pantries, and bathrooms.

On the first floor is the main hall running the entire length of the building, and laid with tile. From this will open the waiting and recreation rooms, parlors, study, library, museum, laboratory, class rooms, and reception rooms.

On the second floor will be large and small music rooms, the Sisters' dormitory, infirmary, community room, toilet rooms, dormitory and dressing rooms for the students.

On the third floor are to be study rooms, children's infirmary, girls' dormitories, and clothes closets, private bedrooms, oratory room in the tower, and locker rooms.

On the attic floor are to be private bedrooms, the Sisters' dormitories, and an exhibition or lecture hall taking up the whole right wing, 52 x 100 feet in size.

In the tower and just above the attic floor is space reserved for a chime of bells. If the chimes are put in at the completion of the building they will be the first in the West.

Above the belfry tower and 100 feet from the ground is an observatory which is shown in the cut by a railing between the heavy square stone pillars. In this, it is proposed to put a telescope.

The building will contain many other rooms. There will be 86 principal rooms in the building. The interior finish is to be of hard wood. Extending from wing to wing in the rear of the building and on every floor is a broad veranda connecting by stairways with the veranda beneath it, and so onto the ground. This will be found of greatest convenience and help in case of fire.

The architecture is of Romanesque style. F. E. Edbrooke and Co. are the architects, and they estimate the cost at $175,000. The building will be heated with steam, and lighted by electricity from a private plant.

This news story is for the most part correct. However, one acquainted with the building would question the statement: "There are also three floors and an attic story aside from the basement." A reporter of some fifty-two years ago might have thought that the fifth floor, because of its dormer windows, was an attic floor. An attic, as the term is now understood, would not contain, as the reporter described this floor, "private bedrooms, sisters' dormitories, and an exhibition or lecture hall, taking up the whole right wing, 52 x 100 feet in size."

In order to understand the interest and appreciation with which the people of Denver and vicinity viewed the magnitude of the building under erection, it is necessary to recall that at the time when Loretto Heights was under construction, Denver did not have the magnificent public school buildings which are the city's pride today.

A story in the May, 1890, issue of *Convent Echo* stated that the great school on Loretto Heights was rising. The work on the new building progressed rapidly, and on September 21, 1890, the corner stone was laid. For this important ceremony Mother Dafrosa Smythe, the Mother Superior, came from the distant Motherhouse in Kentucky. Mother Dafrosa visited the new academy under construction on Loretto Heights and expressed herself as well pleased with the site and the progress of the work.

Red sandstone, hauled in wagons from quarries in Manitou, Colorado, a distance of about seventy-five miles, was the material used for the outer walls—the same red sandstone which the casual tourist views today in the fantastic shapes and forms of the *Garden of the Gods*. There, nature through the ages left its imprint on the stone; here, as the building arose, the horny hands of the master masons carved in bold relief, high on the facade—SISTERS OF LORETTO—the name of those resolute religious women who were to direct, under God, the education of the daughters of the West. Below this title was placed in a niche a statue, heroic in size, of our Lady of Grace, symbol of the fundamental educational principles which were to guide the Sisters, while the words—FIDES, MORES, CULTURA— carved over the arch just above the main entrance, remind both teachers and students of the purpose for which their institution exists.

Impressive ceremonies were witnessed at the laying of the corner stone, Sunday, September 21, 1890, at which the Most Reverend Nicholas C. Matz, Bishop of Denver, assisted by several clergymen, officiated. The Reverend Hugh L. Magevney, S. J., one of the faculty of the Sacred Heart College in the "Highlands" of Denver, was the orator of the day.

Hundreds of those who were present at the ceremony were conveyed by a special train, which left Denver at 2:40 p. m. and made the return trip at 6:40 that evening, the railroad officials making a rate of one fare for the round trip.

The Colorado Catholic, at that time the weekly paper of the diocese, in its issue of September 26, 1890, ran this news article:

It was a splendid sight when the corner-stone of Loretto Heights academy was laid with all the rites of the Catholic Church. The gorgeous vestments of the clergy, the uniformed soldiery from the nearby military post, Fort Logan, the master masons, synonyms of power, in their shirt sleeves, and below, the upturned and expectant faces of an attentive throng—all this skirted by several hundred vehicles of various description.

These vehicles surrounded the half completed walls of the new temple of learning and religion and fringed the open space on the platform about the dignitaries of the Church. Strangest of all sights, the tall shafts of the building derricks pointed their long fingers heavenward toward a benediction that came from a warm and sympathetic Colorado sky.

The Denver Times, September 22, 1890, gave a full description of the ceremony which had taken place the afternoon before. The news story of *The Times*, vibrant with local color, is still intriguing to the reader removed by more than half a century from the scene, especially if that reader has a living interest in the early history of this foundation.

It was a perfect day, just such a one for the consecrating of a fitting monument to the heroic zeal of a band of noble women. A soft wind came softly over the green fields and brown heather. Over to the west, the angels of the Rockies; to the south and east, the great landscape; and to the north, the smoke of the city. But here, all was peace.

At 3:30 p.m. Bishop Nicholas Matz, assisted by Reverend Fathers Persone, McDevitt, Guida, Francis, Malone, and Magevney, began the solemn ritual of the Church while the massive block of granite was lowered slowly into its resting place for some centuries to come. The customary deposits of all data relating to the erection of the edifice, current coins and daily journals having been made, the Bishop gave the signal and the stone was lowered. After its base had been sprinkled with water blessed for the occasion, mortar was spread well and true. Then Bishop Matz stepped forward and made the sign of the holy cross in the wet bed, and the great block swung into place amid a respectful silence. The chant was continued and the walls were encircled by the priests while they consecrated it to the glory of the Creator.

The corner-stone is a highly finished block of Colorado granite bearing on its eastern face this inscription: "O.S.J. and O.S.M." (O Suffering Jesus, and O Sorrowful Mary). While upon the northern face, looking toward the city, appears a cross and the familiar motto, "A.D. 1890."

The procession moved with stately steps around the red stone walls and finally arrived at the stairway leading to the platform. This, they again mounted while the hats of the multitude were raised and every one felt the cool air running through his hair, and the locks of the little girls from the school streamed out just as they will do many days to come like yesterday, when they romp before their completed home and gaze with wondering and innocent eyes at the vapors of corruption and deceit that roll up from the great city yonder.

The spectators had been waiting, and Bishop Matz had taken his seat with the pastoral staff in his hand. Now, the military band played an air, and the Reverend Father Magevney advanced to the front of the platform to deliver his address. Walking quickly, and with the easy confidence of an orator to the edge of the platform, he held up his hands and spoke in ringing tones:

"My friends, this scene today is expressive of the tribes of the children of Israel coming out of Egypt and entering the Holy Land, those wanderers of the desert. And again, it is expressive of God's zeal for His own. It was those who had done His bidding, and a reminder of the love that we who love to walk in His ways shall forever enjoy. The going out of Egypt of the children of Israel into the land of promise brought a benediction upon their heads, and unexpected riches of God's grace were showered down upon these children of heaven as the prophets of God led them on to their glorious rest.

"We have today something in a remote imitation of this leading into the land of promise, we have today eloquent significance of this parallel, taken from and put into practice of every-day life by the good Sisters of Loretto. They came into this land when it was nothing but a waste. They crossed these plains stretching from us to the east when dangers and perils of every description assailed adventurer and soldier alike, to fulfill their promise that they would carry the teachings of God into this land. My friends, we celebrate that event today, and most high and noble Bishop and Fathers.

"No wonder in looking around I see all denominations and every sect represented here, looking on this sight with admiration at the great work done by these noble women. Let me thank you all for this appreciation; and, especially, let me thank the military band for beautifully and fittingly contributing to the happy effect of the grand event. Indeed, this occasion is an opportunity of showing that we can appreciate the unselfish and devoted lives of those noble sisters that seem to go up in a very prayer to the throne of God.

"We can never undervalue their unselfish devotion to the training of our young American girls into true and noble women, for it is the preserving of all her virtues that makes woman what she is when her beauty smiles resplendent. This is educational in the truest sense of the word, and this is the religion that the Sisters of Loretto give your daughters. They have these living examples of the sisters' unblemished lives before their young minds. Prayers not only fall from their lips, but shine out from their eyes and their whole lives devoted to the glory of God, as shown by the very motto upon this corner-stone. Their motto is that all is done for the suffering Jesus and the sorrowful Mary.

"Look around in this great country of ours and see how few there are who have the courage to work for the cause of God, and the very least that we can do in appreciation of this life is to contribute to their work with our approbation. They want you to have the knowledge that they are trying to rear these American girls of ours to be good women. The least you can do then, is to give them your moral support.

"Their object is to devote their lives to these young girls who will some day become our women. There is no need of telling you that there is no use of making laws that will be effective in raising to us pure men, and to have politics that will secure good virtuous effects unless these men have good and holy mothers. There was never a man, however base and degraded, who did not think his own mother was holy and beautiful and true. The true mother rearing her children in the way of God is a very apostle in the kingdom of heaven.

"Let me thank you on the part of these good sisters for your attendance here, and your kind attention. Let me ask you in their name that you will hold in your memory a high place for this academy, in a way that speaks of admiration by allowing your girls to come to this academy."

Father Magevney's address was the finale of an eventful day for the Sisters of Loretto, who, naturally, were the most interested auditors in that throng. As the ceremony was being brought to a conclusion, the westering sun bathed the walls of the edifice and all the spectators in a golden glory. The artist soul of Sister Bartholomew thrilled to the radiant scene into which she read a message from the most high God; the valiant heart of Mother Pancratia was humbly grateful for the so far successful issue of her plans for a wider educational field. She believed that the building program of the Sisters should provide not only for the needs of the present but also of the future; in this, time proved that she was a woman of vision. The Sisters of St. Mary's community, when kneeling in prayer that night, turned grateful hearts to God and rejoiced that the work so well begun was half done.

Chapter III

MAINLY HISTORICAL

The Sisters of Loretto of St. Mary's Academy, whose educational work in Denver God had visibly blessed during a quarter of a century, were faithful and loyal daughters of their religious mother, the Loretto Society, known as the Sisters of Loretto at the Foot of the Cross. This community of Sisters had its origin, and still has its home center, amid the beautiful wooded valleys of central Kentucky. Its motherhouse, novitiate, and junior college are all located at Loretto, sixty miles south of Louisville.

Reverend Charles Nerinckx, a Belgian refugee of the French Revolution, having suffered for many years untold hardships in his native land and being impeded there in the exercise of his priestly functions, offered himself as a missionary to the Most Reverend John Carroll, first Bishop not only of Baltimore but indeed of the United States. After arriving in this country, Father Nerinckx spent a few months at Georgetown University endeavoring to improve his English. In 1804 he was sent by Bishop Carroll to the distant, scattered missions in Kentucky. When the zealous priest had labored for some years with apparently little fruit, both he and his co-worker in that vast territory, the Reverend Stephen Theodore Badin, were convinced that to secure lasting results they must provide schools for the religious instruction of the children.

Just about this time Miss Mary Rhodes, a young lady who had received a good convent-school training in her native Maryland, was visiting her brother, Bennet Rhodes, who lived on Hardin's Creek near St. Charles, Kentucky. Seeing that there were no schools for the children of the vicinity, she offered to teach them the rudiments of secular education and give the religious instruction of which they were so much in need.

Father Nerinckx accepted her generous offer and the school was started in an abandoned, dilapidated cabin. Miss Rhodes was soon joined by two equally zealous young girls of the neighborhood, Miss Christina Stuart and Miss Nancy Havern. The satisfaction and peace which these three teachers derived from their self-imposed, gratuitous service aroused in them the desire of devoting themselves permanently to this work as members of a religious teaching community.

At their request, Father Nerinckx, the pastor of St. Charles congregation, of which they were members, wrote a simple rule to be a guide for their daily life and sought and obtained from the Most Reverend Benedict Joseph Flaget, the first Bishop of Bardstown and Kentucky, the ecclesiastical approbation of their work.

Although from a human standpoint there was nothing to lure them in this arduous life, these three young girls, with no thought of the future or the final outcome of their undertaking, inaugurated the work which was to prosper and expand beyond the lowly log cabin near Hardin's Creek, where they made their humble beginning in Catholic education, the first enduring venture of its kind west of the Alleghanies.

Father Nerinckx in his journal gives the details of the rather unexpected manner in which this religious community of teachers came into existence. Of their poverty and dependence on Providence he wrote:

Great difficulties, hardships, and labors were met at every step, but such is the lot of every pious undertaking. The nuns increased, the house grew, and the schools continued, yet they had nothing to depend on but the sole providence of God and the gracious protection of the Blessed Sorrowful Mother Mary. The revenues of the school were very low, and many could pay nothing as some were very poor, and some were orphans, and the work of the sisters brought in but little, so Providence and the Blessed Virgin were the principal benefactors of this great undertaking.

The date of the foundation is authentically established. Father Nerinckx in the second chapter of his *Rules of the*

Society and School of Loretto, Kentucky, printed in London in 1820, says of the place and time:

A small spot of land, of about 50 acres unmeasured, indifferent for natural conveniences, bought by Sister Anna Rhodes for $75 for the Society, about the chapel of St. Charles, on Hardin's Creek, County of Washington, Kentucky, United States of America, called *Little Loretto,* was begun on the 25th of April, 1812.

The work, begun under circumstances thus related, was watched by the people of the countryside; some criticized, others praised. To many of the young girls who were observing the progress of the little school, the life and purpose of the newly-founded sisterhood had a direct appeal. On the very day that the first three postulants, Mary Rhodes, Christina Stuart, and Nancy Havern, received the simple novice garb from the hands of Father Nerinckx, in the parish Church of St. Charles, others sought admission to their life of self-denial and hard labor.

In time, better accommodations and housing were provided for the sisters and their pupils. The work continued to prosper. The number of sisters increased steadily and other schools were opened in various parts of Kentucky.

Then, in 1823, at the request of the Most Reverend Louis William V. Dubourg, first bishop of St. Louis, twelve sisters left Loretto on May 12, to open a school in Perry County, Missouri. This, the first foundation outside the State of Kentucky, was the beginning of that westward trail which the Lorettines were to follow in establishing the greater number of their houses.

Other Loretto schools were established in different centers in Missouri. Later, in 1846, at the request of the Jesuit Fathers who were missionaries in southeastern Kansas, four Sisters of Loretto were sent from St. Genevieve, Missouri, to take up the work of education among the Indian girls of the Osage tribe. The story of the labors of these first sisters and the equally zealous women who later were sent to this mission field, especially of Mother Bridget Hayden, the superior of the group, to whom God had given

First Communion Class in Old Cathedral—1885

First Orchestra, '92 — Glee Club, '25 — Glee Club, '41 — Orchestra, '40

a heart and talent suited to this work, forms one of the most interesting pages in the history of the sisterhood.

A few years later, in 1852, the Most Reverend John Baptist Lamy, first Bishop, and later Archbishop, of Santa Fe, asked for and obtained sisters for the instruction of the young in his newly appointed field in distant New Mexico. When Bishop Lamy requested teachers for his Spanish mission, he felt that in justice he should make known the actual conditions in his Vicariate to the higher superiors at the Motherhouse; but these, nothing daunted, showed by their ready acceptance of this altogether new work that the characteristic spirit of their holy founder, Father Nerinckx, still lived.

In those days the journey over the "traders trail" was dangerous even for stout-hearted men, for the long trek through arid plains was filled with perils and hardships. Yet, with courageous hearts six sisters left the Motherhouse on July 27 for that distant Santa Fe mission. Sickness forced one of their number to return; Mother Matilda Mills, the superior of the little band, died of cholera and was buried at Independence; other sisters though attacked by that dread disease recovered sufficiently to continue the route. Under such difficulties the journey was finally completed, and the four remaining sisters arrived, three months after setting out from Loretto, on Sunday, September 26, amid the joyous acclamations of that hospitable people, of the ancient town of Santa Fe.

In his *Life of Bishop Machebeuf*, the late Reverend William J. Howlett wrote of the coming of the Sisters of Loretto to Santa Fe and of their work in that region:

Enlightened religion has done much for New Mexico, and a great portion of the credit for its spread must be given to the Sisters of Loretto in their well-named Academy of Our Lady of Light and its dependencies in various parts of the Territory.

Bishop Lamy and Father Machebeuf in preparing for the Sisters of Loretto and bringing them to New Mexico, builded better than they knew at that time, for humble, painful and unpromising as that beginning was, it was fruitful in consequences for good, and no less than twelve other establishments owe their origin to it directly or indirectly.

One foundation made from the Santa Fe house is closely connected with this story of *Loretto in the Rockies*. Father Machebeuf, who had been associated with Bishop Lamy for several years in Santa Fe, had been sent as a missionary to Colorado. After laboring for some time in the widely scattered missions, he began to devise ways and means of providing for the religious education of the youth of Denver. It was natural that he should turn for help to the Sisters of Loretto, whose zeal he had witnessed in Santa Fe. Father Machebeuf entered into correspondence with the Mother Superior at Loretto and received the promise of sisters for the coming school year.

This promise was fulfilled when three sisters from Santa Fe accompanied Father Machebeuf to Denver, at that time little more than a rude mining camp but even then giving indications of its future importance as the gateway between the middle states and the West.

This first band of sisters, Mother Joanna Walsh, Sister Ignatia James, and Sister Beatrice Ryan, reached their new home, June 25, 1864, after traveling the distance from Santa Fe to Denver in a stagecoach. When this little group arrived, they were taken to the house which Father Machebeuf had previously provided, a large two-story frame residence formerly occupied by Governor George W. Clayton.

Sister M. Joanna Walsh, first superior of St. Mary's Academy, wrote to Sister M. Vitalis Forshee, the first high school graduate not only of St. Mary's Academy but in Colorado to receive a diploma, an interesting account of the long, tiresome journey from Santa Fe to Denver. This letter, now an important historical document, is preserved in Sister Joanna's collection of letters in the archives at Loretto Motherhouse. After a detailed account of many incidents along the way, their passing through the Garden of the Gods, their arrival in Denver, taking up residence, and opening school are described:

After a long ride, the driver quite unaccountably slackened pace. He had the good taste to let his passengers enjoy a transient view of the wonderful Garden of the Gods. One could not help being impressed. The ground was literally carpeted with flowers of various hue. There they had been for ages spread out in panoramic beauty and "born to blush unseen," till the speculators of the 19th century invaded their precincts. But still more affecting was the sight of its monuments, never touched by sculptor's chisel. Mail time being limited, our reverie came to an end, and with neither stop nor halt we arrived at the site of our new home.

The coach halted at the church. The Vicar General, Father Machebeuf's residence was close by. And what an unpretentious one it was! But it spoke volumes of his missionary spirit of self-sacrifice and that of his faithful companion, our good and holy Father Raverdy. We received a hearty welcome, but so fatigued were we that we were unable to enjoy it. Lunch was quickly prepared; so our first repast was partaken of in the humble dining room of our future Bishop. We were then escorted to our field of labor where we could look down on the nucleus of the magnificent city you behold today. The ladies had been busy preparing beds, and, our need of rest being unmistakable, they proposed a nap. One of them led us to our little dormitory and then left us to enjoy the first sleep since leaving Santa Fe. I suppose we could have slept for twenty-four hours, but, near six o'clock, one of the ladies returned, prepared tea, and came to waken us. The first salute on opening our unsatisfied eyes was, "O, shall we be ready for Mass?" She was, as you may suppose, greatly amused at the error of our imagination and gently replied: "You have been asleep only so many hours, so it is only 6 o'clock of the same day."

After seeing to our comfort she left us to ourselves, a pleasure we had not enjoyed for almost a week. We said supper prayers where we were, but by the time for night prayers, after parading through the apartments, we selected a little room for our oratory. There we knelt before a frameless picture of the Crucifixion, standing on our trunk —we had but one—and supported against the wall. We tried to pray most fervently, but how we missed the presence of Our Blessed Lord in the Sacrament of His Love! And for some time we had to suffer that privation; for we were poor, and the house was unfurnished till the immediate opening of school.

Father Machebeuf, though very poor himself, had managed to buy a home for the sisters, located on a plot of ground at *E* and *F* streets, known today as Fifteenth and California, on these terms: an immediate payment of $2,000 and his personal note for $2,000, to be paid within sixty days. This residence, a large one for the time, was considered one of the best in Denver. Sister Joanna, in the letter mentioned above, spoke of the house and the debt which had been incurred:

Our property (on 14th and California Streets) had been purchased by Father Vicar General, but we had to assume the debt. This, as you may suppose, was a tremendous weight on our shoulders, since we had never before owed a cent to anyone. We, therefore, anxious to commence the liquidation of the debt, held a council; and the decision of the three 'sages' was to remit installments from each week's proceeds, reserving only what was necessary for the expenses of the establishment. We adhered faithfully to this plan, but sometimes our open calculations were too limited.

Sister Joanna and her two companions were called upon to make sacrifices in those early days when priests in Denver were few and their mission stations many. When the great feast of the Assumption was at hand, the sisters assembled to plan for the celebration of Our Lady's day:

On the eve of the Assumption a consultation was held since we realized that we were to be deprived of Mass on this great feast of Our Blessed Mother, Father Vicar General and Father Raverdy having gone to visit other points. Moreover, we had not had retreat or even ordinary Confession, and our little altar was poorly furnished with what is only absolutely necessary and we had nothing to add to it. The minutes of the consultation were:

1. Resolved, that in default of exterior decorations, we turn the drift of our thoughts to the intensifying of our fervor in the interior preparations we are making for the renewal of our vows;

2. Resolved, that after dismissing the day scholars, we take the boarders for a walk, in search of some wild flowers from the prairies around us.

We returned joyfully from our expedition into nature's spacious garden, and, proud of our acquisition, arranged all for the altar. Having no Mass the next morning, the boarders before retiring were promised a nap. We woke by rule time, said morning prayers, made our meditation, then lit the candles, and, kneeling at the feet of Our Blessed Lord, renewed our holy vows. We longed to receive Him into our souls, but there was no priest within leagues to put us in possession of that treasure. During the day we thought of the fine celebrations in the different houses and the dear ones pronouncing the same solemn words as ourselves; yet we were happy in our prairie wilds, hundreds of miles away; happy because holy obedience placed us there; and the Sacramental Presence of Our Gracious Lord compensated for the lack of all the world beside.

The Civil War was still raging when the Sisters of Loretto took up their residence in Denver in June, 1864. While the members of the little community were quite conscious of the disturbed condition of the country in the East and South, they were often alarmed, as is learned from the same letter, by the warfare which was being carried on near them:

Though there was sameness in our daily duties, yet we could not complain of monotony, as from time to time we used to hear of war events, battles lost, battles gained, urgent proclamations for thousands of new recruits, guerillas, mail coaches robbed and burned—thus cutting off communication with any of our houses. Finally, ''Richmond is taken'' came flashing on the wires, news joyful to some of our boarders, sorrowful to others.

But I must not pass over another species of warfare. Fearful Indian depredations were committed in various places not far distant, and fears were entertained that the Indians in full force would fall upon Denver any day or night, though families from the vicinity were flocking in for safety. They did not, however, attack the city; but imagine how we felt as we turned our eyes toward 15th street and beheld a company of those fierce warriors, mounted on elegant horses, riding, I think, four abreast, and one in front waving triumphantly a human scalp placed on the end of a long pole. Do not blame those poor savages. In their eyes it was just retaliation, for, as usual, they had been defrauded of their rights.

That first Colorado winter brought added suffering to the Sisters and their charges:

Winter anticipated our preparations, Mother Joanna continued, and, with the reception of our boarders, we were not prepared for its rigors. Our little dormitory was cold, had never seen a fire; for there was no way of making one. We secured ourselves of the best we could at night, availing ourselves of anything that could serve as an addition to bed covering, yet on awakening each one found a lump of ice before her mouth, our breath having frozen as it was exhaled. The cold was intense. Almost daily we heard of persons being frozen to death, limbs amputated, etc., so it was the providential care of our good God that saved us. Father Vicar General and Father Raverdy were not much better off than we, only they were more accustomed to the climate.

Shortly after their arrival in Denver, as shown by the files of the *Rocky Mountain News,* July 13, 1864, Vol. 6, No. 13, the Sisters of Loretto issued the first Bulletin Announcement for the opening of St. Mary's Academy, Denver:

ST. MARY'S ACADEMY

For Young Ladies
Under the care of the Sisters of Loretto
Denver-Colorado-Territory

The situation of the Academy, on California Street, is healthy and pleasant; the grounds for recreation are ample and retired.

The pupils will always be under the mild and efficient care of their instructors.

Children of every denomination will be admitted into the institution.

For the sake of order the boarders will be required to observe the general rules and regulations of the School.

The course of instruction will embrace the various elementary as well as all the higher branches of a finished education.

The scholastic year is divided into two sessions of five months each; the first regular session beginning on the first Monday of September, and the second on the first day of February.

N. B.—This year the Academy will be opened on the first day of August.

TERMS

	Per Session
Board	$120.00
Tuition, Elementary branches	15.00
Tuition, Higher branches	20.00
Washing	20.00

French or Spanish languages, extra charges.
Music on Piano or Guitar, extra charges.
Use of instruments, extra charges.
Drawing and painting, extra charges.
Embroidery and different kinds of fancy work, free of charge.
All payments must be made in advance.
All boarders are required to furnish their own bedding, also table furniture, etc., etc.
No deduction will be made for absence or withdrawal, unless occasioned by sickness or dismissal.

A DAY SCHOOL
will be annexed to the institution
TERMS—to be paid in advance:

Primary branches, per month	$3.00
Higher branches, per month	4.00

Languages, music lessons, etc., will be the same as for the boarders.

All communications relative to the institution should be addressed to the Superioress of the Sisters' Academy, Denver, Colorado Territory.

REFERENCES

Right Rev. J. B. Lamy, Bishop of Santa Fe, N. M.; Right Rev. J. B. Miege, Bishop of Leavenworth, Kansas; Very Rev. J. P. Machebeuf, V.G., Pastor of Denver.

This foundation, the first of a series established by the Sisters of Loretto in Colorado, was called St. Mary's Academy, a school always dear to the heart of Father Machebeuf. From the beginning it prospered. As the pupils increased in number, another frame building was added in a short time to the Clayton purchase. This in turn being outgrown, the first wing of the new brick building was erected. With the passing of the years, this wing was added to, again and again, until in 1880 an imposing edifice, facing California Street, occupied the greater part of the property extending a full block from Fourteenth to Fifteenth.

St. Mary's Academy continued to increase in attendance to such an extent that even with its various additions it could no longer furnish suitable accommodations for its boarding and day students. The crowded conditions caused Mother Pancratia and the other sisters to give serious consideration to a plan for erecting an academy exclusively for boarding pupils, on a scale large enough to care for their needs at that time and allow for future growth. The location, it was felt, should be beyond the city limits, away from the distractions of the city and its expansion. The site was selected, as related in Chapter I, on a March day, the feast of St. Joseph, 1889; and the building, a year and some months later, was well on its way.

In this brief resume of the humble beginning of the Loretto Society and its subsequent westward expansion as an educational order, one perceives that those first brave sisters laid the foundation more firmly than they ever realized. The work which was begun in that lowly log cabin in 1812, near the running brook, amid the virgin forests of Kentucky, has continued to grow until now foundations flourish in many states—from Lake Michigan on the north to the Gulf of Mexico on the south; from the Ohio on the east to the great Pacific on the west; yes, even beyond the Pacific, across the international date line, where west becomes east, on into the far-flung mission lands of China, where the fields are white for the harvest.

Thither six Sisters of Loretto went in 1923, following the call of the missions to distant China. Since that time these six and the other sisters who since then have been added to the number have devoted themselves to the Chinese of Hang Yang, not only to the children in their school but to all who in any way stand in need of their aid.

Ten years later, September, 1933, eight Sisters of Loretto opened a school in Shanghai for girls, who, for the most part, are Eurasians. During the past five years of war in China, the sisters in both these foundations, like so many other religious communities of women laboring in that stricken country, have turned aside from their ordinary occupation of teaching, to minister to the sick and wounded, regardless of creed or nationality. In their self-denying life in that foreign land, the Sisters of Loretto are carrying out, in their quest for souls, the sacred injunction of their holy founder, Father Nerinckx: "Gain souls at whatever cost."

Chapter IV

THE DREAM COMES TRUE

Work on the new academy had been going on steadily. The interest of the sisters in the construction deepened as they watched their hopes and plans take form first in the blue prints of the architect and later, as floor was added to floor, in the main central section which was buttressed by massive wings and crowned by an imposing tower.

The contractors had promised to have the building ready for occupancy on July 1, 1891; however, it was not until four months later, November 2, feast of All Souls, that nineteen sisters and fifty-one girls took possession of the school.

It must have taken some planning at the Motherhouse to assemble a faculty for the various departments of the school about to be opened. Records show that a number of the sisters were selected from St. Mary's Academy, while others were drawn from the Motherhouse and Santa Fe. On the evening before the sisters were to bid farewell to their associates at St. Mary's, they gathered in the parlor where they found at hand piano, harp, and other musical instruments. An impromptu musical program was given, and their sweet voices blended in familiar songs. The most touching strain that night was "Some Day I'll Wander Back Again."

Departures sometimes sadden those who leave; but at St. Mary's there was scarcely any sadness—if any existed, it was not manifested. Those who were leaving were full of natural enthusiasm over the work awaiting them at the new foundation on Loretto hill, which, overlooking the Platte and Bear Creek valleys, lies north of and almost opposite the military post of Fort Logan, and faces North Federal Boulevard, now called South Federal Boulevard.

After breakfast, on the day they were to take up residence at Loretto Heights, each of the Sisters and girls tied into a bundle her own mattress, pillow, sheets, and blankets, so that when those seventy bundles arrived at the new building, each would have her own bedding, and less confusion would result in getting ready for the first night in new surroundings. The van into which these bundles were packed left St. Mary's about nine in the morning. At three in the afternoon, Sisters and girls boarded the Circle train which conveyed them within two miles of the building on the hill. Walking the remainder of the way, they arrived about five o'clock.

At last they were there at the new home—Sisters and girls—full of happy anticipation now that the dream of years was realized. The group parted, all going in different directions—the Sisters to devote themselves to the immediate preparations for the comfort and needs of their charges; the girls, filled with eager curiosity to inspect the building.

The sisters were astonished when they discovered that neither light, heat, nor water had been connected for the contractor had promised Mother Pancratia with a great deal of emphasis that she need not worry—everything would be in full working order by the morning of November 2. However, in those days, too, contractors were sometimes remiss in the fulfillment of pledges. It might have been expected that Mother Pancratia, experienced in the building of other academies and their units in Colorado, should have been suspicious of predictions easily made but not so readily carried out.

Feeling quite sure that the new abode would be in readiness, and fearing lest the severe storm which the Weather Bureau had scheduled for the early part of that first week in November, the sisters trusted the promise given by the builders and hurried their departure.

For some time after their arrival the sisters were busily engaged trying to set things in order. Great was their amazement when six o'clock came and they realized that the van containing the bedding and food had not arrived. They waited anxiously, hoping that it would arrive any minute—seven o'clock—eight o'clock—and yet it had not come. The van had left St. Mary's at nine o'clock that morning, and now it was almost nine at night. The distance was only seven miles—what could have happened to the supplies and furnishings with which the driver had set forth from St. Mary's at nine o'clock that morning?

It had been easy enough to take care of the girls for the first hour or two, for, enthusiastic and excited, they were fully occupied in investigating the marvellous new building and enjoying the view of the mountains cameoed against a glorious sunset. But now it was nine o'clock—it was dark. There was no light except that of candles; no water, and every one was thirsty; no heat—and the November evening was chilly. There was no food either. Mother Pancratia had arranged that the van would bring the necessary supplies. Until darkness was upon them, no one had been disturbed by the inconveniences which now seemed to crowd upon them. The sisters who naturally should have been worried about the lack of heat, light, and water had been busy attending now to this and then to that.

When the distressed superior understood the situation, she put her head down on a table and wept aloud—

"Why did I do this? Oh, why?"

The sisters tried to console her, telling her that everything would be all right—the van was sure to come.

"But the girls! Suppose the van does not come at all tonight? Here we are stranded and seven miles from St. Mary's!"

To that hungry family the distance seemed, just then, not seven miles but seventy. Although Mother Pancratia had been with these western girls for many years, she was yet to learn much more of their sterling qualities. Were they not daughters of pioneers? She would have no cause to worry about them—but her tender heart was suffering.

Suddenly there was a shout from the girls who were crowded at the front entrance. The van was coming! It was really there. Each girl snatched a candle, lit it, and, leaning far out from the windows, the lights in their eager young hands, showed the way to the men who were unloading the van, while the sisters helped to bring in the bedding and, yes, the food. The moving-in was spectacular and dramatic.

Soon bread, butter, and ham were ready for supper—a ten o'clock supper at that. What an innovation for the convent girls who were used to being served their evening meal promptly at six. Now their hunger was appeased; but there was neither water nor tea—nothing at all to drink, and the ham which they had eaten only added to their distress.

Whenever asked about the lack of water on that night, Sister Jovita, one of that group of sisters, would invariably remark: "I was more concerned about the bedding that I did not get to use after my great care in packing it that morning at St. Mary's. You know we had taken such precautions to have our own mattresses and everything we needed, that it was a great surprise, when we awoke the next morning, to find that scarcely anybody had slept in her own bed. I tell you, Sisters, Mother Pancratia straightened out the bed question in no time. Every one was so good natured that it did not take her long to do it. Those pioneering days were happy ones!"

Next morning coffee was prepared at a house some distance down the boulevard. For some time the scarcity of water on the campus was a real hardship. Finally, the waterman began to make regular supply trips; but the Sisters never tasted a drop until the girls had been supplied —with them the girls always came first. Even after the artesian well was in operation, the water problem continued; the rods were often out of order, and, while repairs were going on, there would be a "dry spell" of greater or less duration.

This group of Sisters and girls experienced for two weeks the thrills of prior occupancy. Then on November 16, 1891, additional pupils arrived, increasing their number to seventy. Those first days and weeks were laborious ones for the sisters, filled with hardships and privations—they were pioneer days in the real sense of the word.

The names of those first Sisters at Loretto Heights are of deep interest to their numerous friends in the city of Denver as well as to the thousands of alumnae scattered over the United States from New York to California. Fifty years are not so long in passing, yet, after that lapse of time, unless records have been faithfully kept, reliable information is difficult to secure. As far as available data now show, the sisters who went to Loretto Heights Academy on that eventful day, November 2, 1891, were Mother Mary Pancratia Bonfils, Sister Mary Columba Gallavan, Sister Mary Bartholomew Nooning, Sister Mary Rosetta Clements, Sister Mary Ignatia Tobin, Sister Mary Menodora Wynn, Sister Mary Paschal Doyle, Sister Mary Gregoria Mc-Laughlin, Sister Mary Linus Maier, Sister Mary Jovita Mills, Sister Mary Eudocia Chacon, Sister Mary Antoinette Logsden, Sister Mary Eutropia Toolen, Sister Mary Agatha Wall, Sister Mary Walburga O'Sullivan, Sister Mary Chrysostom Sullivan, Sister Mary Cassilda White, Sister Mary Sidonia McCauley, Sister Mary Vincenta Gonzales, and Sister Mary Vida Jackson.

Of that first community only two are living in 1942—Sister Mary Linus Maier, Vicaress General of the Loretto Society, from whom a great part of these interesting details has been gathered; and Sister Mary Chrysostom Sullivan, who is still actively engaged in her zealous religious life at the historic Bethlehem Academy in Kentucky.

Ranking first among the seventy students who came out to the Heights for its opening year were two young ladies, who made up the graduating class, Misses Katherine Casey and Olive Fort. The former had spent all her school days at St. Mary's; therefore, it cost her a struggle to make the change in her senior year. Miss Fort had studied at St. Mary's only during her high school course. For both these girls there was adventure in transferring to the splendid new academy, the most admired school at that time in all Colorado.

Katherine Casey is now Sister Mary Menodora, a Sister of Loretto, teaching at Loretto Academy, Las Cruces, New Mexico; and Olive Fort is Mrs. Frank B. January of 3234 Abell Avenue, Baltimore, Maryland.

Chapter V

DEDICATION OF BUILDING AND
FIRST SCHOOL YEAR

During the first days and weeks in their new surroundings, the sisters were carrying a heavy schedule—the classes had to be organized and taught, and between times some kind of order had to be brought out of the chaotic conditions which reigned throughout the building. When all had settled down into a comparatively regular life, the sisters began to plan for the dedication. This took place quite appropriately December 10, 1891, on the feast of the Holy House of Loretto, to which their founder, the Reverend Charles Nerinckx, was so devoted that he named the first foundation of the religious community, which had been established under his guidance, "Little Loretto."

So solemn and devotional are the blessings of the Church for such occasions that it would seem that Jesus, Mary, and Joseph actually walked that morning with the Most Reverend Nicholas Matz, successor to the revered and apostolic Bishop Machebeuf, and his assisting priests. Leaving the chapel where the opening ceremonies had taken place, the Bishop and clergy went in prayerful procession from room to room, from floor to floor of the new academy. The sisters, too, participated in that impressive ceremony prescribed by the Church.

To the friends of Loretto, the dedication was an inspiring sight; to the casual on-looker, it savored somewhat of a walking "marathon" because of the distance traversed in going through the eighty-six rooms, in ascending and descending the four flights of stairs leading to the various floors, and then out and around the building. When this circuit was completed, the procession re-entered through the main vestibule and returned to the chapel where a Pontifical Mass was celebrated. The convent choir sang Mozart's "Twelfth Mass" and Rossini's "Laudamus Te."

The Denver Republican, under date of December 11, 1891, in its news story of the dedication ceremonies gave the names of the clergymen of Denver and other cities who assisted or were present for the occasion:

The clergy assisting the Most Reverend Nicholas Matz, the celebrant, were Reverend Father Robinson, vicar general, archdeacon; Reverend Father Persone, S.J., deacon; Reverend Father Howlett, subdeacon; Reverend Father O'Ryan, master of ceremonies; other priests in the sanctuary that day were Fathers Guida, Phillips, Malone, Carrigan, Magevney, Pantanella, Francis, and Wilbs—all of Denver; also Father O'Leary, the first chaplain of Loretto Heights academy; Reverend Father Jeauvenceau, Santa Fe; Reverend Father Fitzgerald, Colorado Springs; and Reverend Father Carmody, Cheyenne, Wyoming.

Bishop Matz gave the address for the occasion. His text was "Suffer the little children to come unto me for of such is the kingdom of heaven." The Bishop recalled the influence of the Church on education through the ages and her great care of the young, noting that even in the midst of persecution, the children were never lost sight of. After a brief resume of the development of educational institutions in other lands, the Bishop continued:

In whatever direction we turn our eyes we find institutions established by the Church for the education of our youth. Look at our own United States. Everywhere there are schools. And right here in Colorado we have ten or eleven institutions of different sisterhoods established for the work of education, charity, and care for the fallen and friendless. Among these stands most prominently the Sisters of Loretto who have labored in our midst for a quarter of a century. We are celebrating today, perhaps, the crowning of their material labors. I think that there is not a finer institution in the United States than this and I have visited some of the finest institutions in the land. All honor to these faithful and devoted sisters who have sacrificed so much for the advancement of education here in Colorado.

The Bishop urged the parents to patronize the educational institutions in their own state and discontinue their patronage of out-of-state schools and colleges; only by their support of schools in their own state could the Catholics build up a worth-while educational system of their own.

The Denver Republican carried a complete report of the ceremony. When the reporter who had been covering the story for his paper gave a parting look at the new building, he was struck by the air of solidity and indestructibility which the massive gable-ends, flanking the central part of the structure, with its great tower, gave to the edifice. He commented on this as well as on the solidarity of various parts of the interior—the tile floor of the imposing main corridor, its oak panelling, and the hard woods found throughout the various rooms and corridors.

Figures varying from $200,000 to $300,000 have been given at different times as the cost of the main building of Loretto Heights; but the figure, $190,572, has been authenticated. As prices are now, one would be inclined to doubt this last quotation. The only explanation for the comparatively low cost is that materials and labor must have been much cheaper in those days when standards of living were not what they are today.

With the dedication ceremonies singing in their hearts, the Sisters of Loretto were encouraged to go forward; they felt that their pupils and the people of Denver and vicinity were supporting their broad educational endeavor. Full of enthusiasm, they made preparations for their happiest Christmas since that first Colorado Christmas spent in the two-story white frame house, the first St. Mary's on E and F Streets, twenty-seven years before.

Christmas vacation over and the pupils back to continue their studies, Mother Pancratia and her teachers began the New Year with high hopes and courage. A broad, well-planned course of studies was being carried out even during this first year. The practical and the artistic were incorporated in the curriculum which offered good solid courses in grammar, arithmetic, English literature, rhetoric, French, Spanish, German, algebra, geometry, geology, botany, zoology, physics, ancient and modern history, and an intensive study of religion. Preparatory to these high school subjects, there was a strong elementary school department. Speech lessons and singing, piano, violin, harp, also an orchestra—all these subjects kept the pupils usefully employed. A picture of the orchestra during that first year is in Chapter XVII. For many reasons this picture is treasured by the students forming the group and valued by their relatives.

Our Lady of Loretto and her faithful spouse, St. Joseph, patrons of the Loretto Society, were taking special care, during that year, of the new Colorado foundation. The beautiful trees now gracing the campus are evidence of their interest. At certain times, after the snows melted, water was released from the reservoirs in the mountains. Dashing like a torrent over hills and through valleys, it would eventually find sanctuary through the irrigation ditches and their outlets on the parched grounds surrounding the building. When news of the coming of the water was heralded, the sisters, assisted by some of the generous pupils, formed a bucket brigade along the ditch and carried water to the thirsty roots of the young trees. Many a recreation hour was spent in work such as this.

As the year passed, gradually the inconveniences caused by faulty lighting and water systems were of less frequent occurrence, but the mode of traveling to Denver for the purchase of supplies remained a problem. The Denver firms in those days made no delivery to out-of-town customers, even to so large a family as the one residing at the Heights. The sisters finally purchased a horse and buggy—those were "horse and buggy days"—and two of the sisters made trips at stated intervals to the city for necessary supplies. No thought or notice was given to the fact that the sisters drove their own buggy and many of them became skilled in the art of driving. Today a horse and buggy is a rarity on the streets of Denver; it would excite attention at the present time to see a Sister of Loretto driving through the streets as in days of yore.

In the early spring, Mother Pancratia and the directress of the school, Sister Walburga, were already planning for the exhibition to be given at the close of the year. It was an "exhibition" for which they planned—such terms as graduating or closing exercises were not current in those days—and exhibition meant just what the word still signifies, a showing or setting forth of school work, artistically presented, especially literary productions and beautiful Spencerian penmanship, with here and there shaded and ornamental drawings. There was also work in embroidery, china painting, pastel, and oil painting—each piece the pride and joy of both the instructor and the student who executed it. The girls took great delight in preparing their work for the exhibit in anticipation of the joy of accomplishment which would be theirs on that final day when the work of months was viewed by admiring and appreciative parents, relatives, and friends.

It was for such an exhibit that "the invited guests," as *The Denver Republican* stated, "arrived early, most of them driving down from the city, although a goodly number came on the trains. Before the exercises the guests were shown the art exhibit of the school. The evidences of culture in art are many, and the display is a creditable one, alike to scholars and teachers."

Reporters in the "gay nineties" must have been not only gatherers of news and writers of entertaining features but also trained society editors. In this same "story" of June 16, 1892, the reader is given a full description of the sweet girl graduate:

On the afternoon of June 15, the hum of mental industry which ordinarily emanates from the stern temple of Catholic learning erected on Loretto Heights was hushed, and instead of young ladies deeply absorbed in study, were scores of the same robed in fancy costumes of white, with corsage bouquets, transparent fans, swan-white gaiters and all that kind of thing designated to make your winsome young women all the more fascinating. It was graduation day at the school. . . .

The commencement exercises were to begin at three o'clock in the afternoon, but long before that time the "exhibition" hall on the first floor was filled with relatives and friends of the students, while guests crowded the broad corridors leading to the hall. There were no elevators in those days—but the climb up the many flights of stairs did not daunt the devoted relatives and friends who toured the building on that warm June day. With eager expectation they packed the assembly hall; here they rested enjoying, before the exercises began, the beauty of the spacious stage decorated with cut flowers and potted plants.

The medals, laurels, and other prizes were all there, artistically displayed; five upright pianos were arranged in segments for the musical recital. The program presented that afternoon showed the standard which had been attained in music and art. Fortunately, *The Denver Republican* carried this program which the interested reader will find in its entirety on page 294.

Bishop Matz addressing the graduates said:

It is my pleasant duty to present you with the honors of graduation from this institution. The laurels and medals you wear are more honorable than those ever presented on the Grecian field. And the culture you have received from these dear Sisters is more abiding than all the skill of the charioteers.

After congratulating the graduates, Misses Katherine Casey and Olive Fort, who had the honor of being the first students to be graduated from Loretto Heights, the Bishop concluded the ceremony by bestowing on them the full crown of laurel wreath. The sub-graduate, Miss Nellie Stockbridge, was given a half wreath of laurel, a sign that she had successfully completed three years of her academic course.

Awards were made that day for proficiency in art, music, and sewing as well as for religion and deportment.

At the close of the exercises, Reverend William J. Howlett addressed the students adding his congratulations to those of the Bishop. His words referring to both Loretto Heights and St. Mary's are of interest:

Two days ago I witnessed a little exhibition. . . . I heard the praises of old St. Mary's sung in every key and old memories were the principal things of thought and speech. The strong and growing daughter (Loretto Heights) was not entirely forgotten, however, but was referred to as sitting in the midst of Colorado's fairest desert, surrounded by the blooming cactus and flowering soapweed.

Old St. Mary's had its beginning and bore the cross.
The new St. Mary's (Loretto Heights) seems in its beginning to wear old St. Mary's crown.

Your teachers are striving to instruct you properly
in Christian ways and need no recommendation from me
today. These days, I foresee, will be sweet with memories;
and the names of the pupils of this new St. Mary's will be
pleasantly and lovingly recalled as those of the old. May
God bless all of you.

Father Howlett, who addressed the graduates and students on that first commencement day at Loretto Heights,
was associated with the Sisters of Loretto for many years;
first as rector of the Denver Cathedral in 1886, then later
as pastor of St. Ignatius, now Sacred Heart Cathedral, in
Pueblo; and as chaplain during the last twenty-three years
of his life at the Motherhouse in Kentucky. Father Howlett
will be remembered in Colorado, not only for his years of
priestly service in Denver, Leadville, Pueblo, and Loveland,
but also, in later years, for his contributions to Catholic
literature. Besides being the author of the *Life of the
Reverend Charles Nerinckx,* founder of the Society of the
Sisters of Loretto at the Foot of the Cross, and the *Life of
Bishop Machebeuf,* apostle and first bishop of Colorado, he
was a frequent contributor to Catholic periodicals, especially to the *Colorado Catholic* and the *Denver Register.*

Father Howlett's words on that day of graduation,
while not in the nature of a prophecy, have proved true
down through the years. Reminiscingly sweet and almost
sacred have been the thoughts of the sisters as they revert
to the names of those dear girls who were on the roll call
in that memorable year of '91 and '92.

One of the greatest regrets to the students saying farewell on that June day was the fact that Mother Pancratia
was not there to say Godspeed, especially to the graduates.
She who had planned the erection of that center of learning
and culture, who had worried and prayed over it, who had
watched it take form, section by section, in Colorado red
sandstone—she was not there at that first graduation in
the new academy, then the pride of the West. In the early
spring, about March 1, Mother Pancratia had been trans-

ferred to Montgomery, Alabama, to replace another sister who had been missioned elsewhere.

Obediently, though it doubtless cost her a struggle, Mother Pancratia, who had come to Denver when scarcely sixteen, who had endured the privations of the pioneer sisters, who had worked so hard for the establishment of Catholic schools and academies in this thriving city of the plains, who had given her best days to this work, traveled back across the country to the southland.

Like the great Teacher, this humble Lorettine was absent at the scene of triumph on that graduation day, when in the natural order of things one would have expected to find her there. Another had been sent to take her place; she was at a new mission, just one of the many. In this manner does God try His elect. In the case of Mother Pancratia this must have been especially true.

Chapter VI

THE FINANCIAL CRISIS

While the first school year at Loretto Heights Academy was drawing to a successful close, financial clouds were appearing on the horizon, were even lowering over the school so recently launched. When the Sisters of Loretto and Mother Pancratia entered into plans for the new building, not a great deal of thought was given to the monetary side of the enterprise. In fact there seemed to be no reason to be concerned about the debt which would be incurred. The sisters planned that the sale of the property which they owned in West and North Denver would liquidate whatever liabilities would be theirs. For this reason they entered into the building program with a feeling of financial security.

About the time that the first school year was nearing completion, the property in West Denver and the lots in North Denver were appraised at $285,000, a sum which would almost cover both the actual cost of the new building and the acreage of the first purchase at Loretto Heights. In March, 1892, a reliable firm in Denver estimated the new academy and its acreage at $295,000 and advised, quite earnestly, that the superiors at the Motherhouse should take advantage of the market and sell the real estate owned in the city.

One should not suppose that there was a lack of business acumen in the sisters in charge at the Motherhouse or at the Heights. Likely, they anticipated even greater future values for Denver-owned property, though, to one now studying the situation, it would seem that the logical thing to have done was to sell all the property in Denver, or at least the North Denver lots.

Before the higher superiors at the Motherhouse, upon whom the responsibility rested, had come to any decision

with regard to the sale of the property, the country was
being gripped in the initial stages of the panic of '93. The
main cause of this depression was the repeal of the Sherman Act which had provided a monthly market for the sale
of 4,500,000 ounces of silver. The annulment of this bill,
which had been passed in 1890, affected not only the state
of Colorado but all the silver-producing states of the West.

Property in Denver depreciated immediately, and as
a result the Sisters of Loretto felt the full force of the
slump. In March, 1892, the sisters had been offered $25,000
for two blocks in North Denver, *A* and *B*, in section 68;
in the summer of that same year, this property was valued
at $5,000, a price which could not possibly be considered,
even though they were in dire financial straits.

However, the sisters were not wholly abandoned; helpful hands were extended to them and to Mother Pancratia
at this trying time. The Denver firm of McPhee and Mc-
Ginnity, through its senior partner, informed Mother
Pancratia that, although there had been difficulties, on account of the scarcity of money in the country, in negotiating
a loan for Loretto Heights from the New York and other
eastern corporations, yet they were now ready to secure
the necessary financial aid.

Mr. Charles D. McPhee had shown, for twenty years,
an active interest in the welfare of St. Mary's Academy,
by giving the sisters practical business advice. As soon
as Loretto Heights had been established as a country boarding school, this good friend extended the same interest to
the affairs of the new institution, considering its material
success secondary only to that of his own family and dis-
claiming any obligation on the part of the sisters beyond
that of co-operation.

Mr. McPhee and his business associates felt quite safe
in assuming the responsibility of securing this loan, especially since the property which the sisters owned in
Denver and at the new foundation was a sufficient security
for entering into the deal. Even under the fluctuating conditions of the real estate market, the firm had evaluated the
property owned by the Sisters of Loretto at $580,000.

Fully aware of the precariousness of the times, which appeared even more threatening on account of the debt incurred by her project, Mother Pancratia, courageous in this as in all dangers, was ready to carry on as superior of the institution which was in great financial straits. But strange are the ways of Providence and wonderful His opportunities for merit. While occupied with plans for meeting some of these money obligations, Mother Pancratia received orders from her higher superiors, in March, 1892, to go to a new mission.

As builder and first superior of Loretto Heights, no one could be more familiar than she with the relation of the situation to conditions of the country, with her own obligations, and with the indebtedness of the building for which she had suffered, worried, and rejoiced so much— yet, at the moment when aid was at hand, Mother Pancratia was transferred to another school.

Mother Ann Joseph Mattingly, a woman experienced in many affairs, was appointed to take up the work as superior at Loretto Heights. Under her supervision that first year was brought to a close, and the opening of the second year was approaching. While the superior and the sisters were hopeful, yet they faced reality. In the economic panic which had seized the country, the most experienced financiers became cautious, since on all sides business was toppling.

Facing Mother Ann Joseph was a tremendous financial burden. She understood conditions and tried every available means of stemming the tide and saving the credit of the community. She was in a difficult position. Humbly and generously she listened to the praise showered upon her predecessor, Mother Pancratia, and agreed that the praise was well merited. Thoughtless friends of the former superior voiced their criticism of her removal. To these criticisms Mother Ann Joseph's reply was always the same, namely, that Mother Pancratia and she were bound by the same rule of obedience—one had left Loretto Heights by order of higher superiors, the other had come for the same reason. Therefore the new superior was confident that the good friends of Mother Pancratia would lend her a helping hand in the hour of need.

Such a modest appeal was more than the great men of the West could resist. They set about in their big-hearted way to make amends for the cool reception they had given Mother Ann Joseph. The community of Loretto Sisters, who had felt keenly the departure of Mother Pancratia, rallied loyally to the aid of her successor.

Though the debt was heavy and the outlook for the school and sisters was indeed dark during the time that Mother Ann Joseph was in charge, from March, 1892, to June, 1894, all worked together in the spirit of Christ at Loretto in the Rockies. During those years of extreme poverty for the sisters, Mother Ann Joseph did her best to meet, at least in some small way, the demands of creditors. All learned to do without; the bare necessities of life sufficed those pioneer sisters who, strong in faith and hopeful of better days, devoted themselves zealously to the task at hand and to the practice of cheerful fortitude and endurance.

Denver merchants from whom the sisters purchased supplies were truly magnanimous in the credit which they granted the hard-pressed community. Although these firms themselves were in straitened circumstances, knowing that the sisters would pay as soon as possible, they were patient and forbearing. On the other hand, a number of other Denver merchants refused to serve the school in its hour of need. Business was business with them. The sisters censured no one; but to the present day the Denver firms which then served the Sisters of Loretto are remembered daily in the prayers of the community for benefactors.

Religious communities other than the Sisters of Loretto at the Heights and at St. Mary's Academy were affected by the depression at that time. Other religious orders, both men and women, who had come to Denver and surrounding towns to bring Catholic education to the inhabitants of Colorado, suffered similar distress. The Jesuit Fathers arrived in Colorado in 1884, twenty years after the

Lorettines, and settled at Morrison, a mountain town about fifteen miles from Denver. Four years later, their college, when transferred to Denver, was called Sacred Heart; and again, at a much later date, April 19, 1921, its name was changed to Regis. The early history of this school parallels in many ways that of the Heights.

The Sisters of Charity of Leavenworth came to Denver in 1873, nine years after the Sisters of Loretto. They, too, suffered during this panic of '93 in their efforts to keep open the doors of St. Joseph's Hospital. In November, 1883, the Sisters of St. Joseph of Carondolet arrived to open the school in St. Patrick's parish in North Denver. Their story resembles that of many of the other foundations in those pioneer days. In *Yesterday,* their Golden Jubilee booklet, Helen Heald gives a graphic description of their living quarters: "They found a little three room cottage containing four wooden bedsteads, two mattresses, a kitchen and parlor stove awaiting them. No light, heat, or provisions had been prepared, so there was only one thing to do—retire." The obscurity of darkness hid from the public eye the many hardships endured by those pioneer sisters.

Another religious order answering the call of the western mission in Colorado were the Sisters of Mercy in St. Louis. Four sisters and one postulant offered themselves with a generous heart for the distant mission when Bishop Machebeuf made known the needs of his Vicariate. They arrived in Denver in February, 1882, but after a few days they determined to locate in Durango. "Seven years later," Elinor Tong Dehey writes in *Religious Orders of Women in the United States,* "the metropolis of Denver was chosen for the future work of the Sisters of Mercy in the diocese of Denver, and the Motherhouse of the community was transferred there." A group of teaching sisters began the work at St. Joseph's school the same year. In 1889 Mother Mary Baptist inaugurated the establishment of Mercy Hospital, and it was finished two years later. These sisters, too, as their history must show, suffered from the effects of the panic of '93, in establishing themselves in Denver in those harrowing times.

In 1888 the Friars Minor, or Franciscan Fathers, opened St. Elizabeth's Church; and on May 12, of the same year, three Franciscan Sisters came to take charge of the school of that parish. Prior to that date, the Sisters of Loretto had taught this school for several years in a little frame house. The Reverend F. Bender was then in charge of the parish.

Still later, in 1891, the Sisters of Charity of Cincinnati arrived in Denver and took over the Logan Street school for boys and girls in September of that year. This school had been taught by the Sisters of Loretto when it was begun in the historic "White House," which formed a part of the property of St. Mary's Academy on California Street. After the school had increased its enrollment, it was transferred to temporary quarters above a store on 15th and Stout Streets, next to the old Cathedral. Having tramped up and down the rickety steps in this building for several years, the boys found themselves and their school transferred to an imposing structure at 18th and Logan.

In this location the Sisters of Loretto taught only one year. The new Loretto Heights Academy which was opening in the fall of 1891 had made great demands on their teaching personnel and the Sisters of Loretto were replaced at the Cathedral school on Logan Street by the Sisters of Charity.

The Franciscan Sisters, who opened St. Anthony's Hospital, came to Denver in '93, the very year of the panic. These heroic women must have endured untold hardships during their first difficult years. In 1894 the Redemptorist Fathers took over the pastoral charge of St. Joseph's Church. Each of these foundations had its own experiences during the "hard times." Their annals would make interesting Colorado history. The Lorettines were involved more deeply than the other religious communities, perhaps, on account of their recent heavy building program.

Mother Ann Joseph, who had been a member of the second band of Lorettines whom the saintly Bishop Mache-

beuf had brought from Santa Fe in 1865, had early learned
her lesson in endurance. She and her valiant community,
setting aside all thought of self, taught their young charges
the personality of Christ. Sometimes, however, heavy
clouds obscured the way; but the sisters, full of faith, kept
bravely on, knowing that their work, if it was God's work,
would eventually succeed.

Chapter VII

NEVER A DULL MOMENT

Meanwhile the students at the new country boarding school were following a well-arranged program, work alternating with play. As was shown on a preceding page, many of the subjects taught at that time in the high school courses were on the college level. The successive directresses, Sister Winifred Leahy, Sister Walburga O'Sullivan, Sister Mary Kevin Coffey, and Sister Roberta Jarboe —all women of high scholastic standing—took their duties seriously and saw to it that the students were diligently faithful in their quest for knowledge.

During the two years that Mother Ann Joseph discharged the office of superior, the enrollment fluctuated between fifty and seventy. Some of the best families in Denver were having their daughters educated in this school. The following students, who later became distinguished members of society, belonged to the roster of those years: Georgie Weinberg, the McFarland twins, Ella, May, and Catherine Mullen, the McPhee girls, Katherine Casey, the Seeks, the Montagues, Alice Duffy, Blanch and Gertie O'Neil, Nellie Stockbridge, Marvie Miller, the McAdams, Beckers, McKinleys, and many others.

But all the days at the new school were not always devoted to hard study. While receiving a solid education, these daughters of the early West were given many opportunities for enjoyment. One of their popular amusements was the riding club. The illustration in a preceding chapter of this book gives an idea of their jaunty riding habits and their prancing steeds. Off they would go to the mountains, well supplied in picnic fashion, for their pleasant outing. Morrison was one of the favorite haunts on these trips.

Several times during the school year, the girls of the orchestra, thirty or more in number, would pile their in-

struments into a big tallyho, having in mind the abandoned
Jesuit college in Morrison as their journey's end. After
an enjoyable picnic lunch, they arranged themselves on the
former college campus to which they had been invited and
played their favorite airs.

A desire of entertainment and fun did not always
lure the girls to the mountains. Denver, too, held many
attractions for the appreciative young ladies. The well-
known *Mountain and Plain Festival,* resembling the *Mardi
Gras* of New Orleans and the *Veiled Prophet* of St. Louis,
ranked first among the annually anticipated pleasures. The
large floats of the *Mountain and Plain Festival* representing the leading industries of the state, mining and farming,
had a special charm for the girls. A student of Loretto
Heights Academy was sometimes chosen Queen of the festival, and, as a consequence, the whole student body felt itself
especially honored.

The privilege of attending interesting plays at the
theater and of eating lunch in the city was a real treat for
the girls at boarding school. When good plays and operas
were brought to Denver, they were shown in the Tabor
Grand Opera House, one of the historic land marks today,
made famous by the well-known H. A. W. Tabor. The
older academy girls were always given the opportunity of
attending the worth-while programs.

Now the Swiss Dairy was a favorite place for lunching
when the students had several hours to spend in the city.
Sometimes the Sisters who chaperoned the girls would
lunch with them at this place. The girls considered that
occasions like these were real events in their lives. When
Sister Bartholomew and Sister Columba, who often accompanied the students on these trips, remained with their
charges for lunch, they liked nothing better than hot rolls
and "steamboat" coffee, for them the best part of the meal.
The proprietors of the Swiss Dairy, considering it an honor
to have the sisters, served them gratis.

These two sisters, Sister Bartholomew and Sister
Columba, often related many interesting stories of "ye

olden days.'' They did much of the buying for the community and had many unique encounters on their shopping tours. One day as they were returning from a heavy shopping trip, laden with their purchases, the street car stopped to take on two negro passengers out of whose pockets pistols protruded. These formidable looking characters, their eyes rolling shiftily from side to side, seated themselves opposite the sisters, who were almost frightened to death. Sister Columba turned to speak to Sister Bartholomew but seeing Sister Bartholomew's nose, which was already crooked, suddenly snap farther to one side, her voice failed her. And Sister Bartholomew ever after maintained that Sister Columba's eyes were so crossed that she could not tell whether she was looking at her companion or at the armed darkies. At all events neither of them was able to talk until the dusky riders suddenly left the car.

The sisters were never more glad to see their horse, ''Daisy,'' and the buggy waiting for them at the end of the Englewood line. Patiently the old mare plodded up the steep hill to the Heights, with the frightened occupants and their groceries in the vehicle behind her. When the sisters were safe within their own walls their tongues were loosed; vividly they described with all the details their ride home from Denver.

Later they heard that the darkies had boarded the street car for the sole purpose of holding up the passengers, but, when they saw the sisters, they were ashamed to alarm ''them religious ladies.''

Occasionally children's epidemics, measles and chicken pox, broke out among the girls, and, of course, the inevitable colds. At these times the sisters isolated the victims in an unoccupied wing of the building, which served as a temporary infirmary, and nursed them back to health. The interest and attention which the students received in the class rooms and the kindly ministrations heaped on them in the infirmary elicited grateful appreciation from the pupils and formed a bond between students and teachers which later developed into feelings of deep loyalty and love. The infirmary had such a charm for many of the girls that it required clear insight on the part of the sister infirmarian to distinguish the sick from the well. Usually, however, the feigned sickness was easily recognized.

Life at Loretto Heights in that second year of the panic was far from monotonous. While the girls were pursuing their studies and enjoying many pleasant diversions, the superior, Mother Ann Joseph, and her community of sisters, planned to keep their students happy, even though they themselves had weighty problems on their minds. Loans which had been negotiated under the former superior were now due and the convent's bank account was utterly depleted. Ways and means for meeting the financial burdens kept the sisters inwardly anxious and perplexed.

In the meantime care was given to the cultivation and improvement of the cactus-covered campus. A second planting of trees had been made and alfalfa was growing in abundance. Whenever the slender means permitted, men having a knowledge of farming and cattle were employed; these were supervised by those sisters who had some experience in such matters. The usual hazards of new enterprises accompanied the attempted improvements; sometimes the rainfall was frequent; again there were long periods of drought which blighted the crops. Grasshoppers ate what was left of the alfalfa, and, to add to the gloomy picture of farm life, mosquitoes were active in annoying both man and beast.

The one hope in those trying days of experiments in agriculture was the almost never-failing kitchen garden. Close to the building, near the artesian well, corn, beets, potatoes, beans, and melons grew in abundance. Though the garden seemed like a mirage in a desert, it was a substantial reality and kept the table well supplied with the necessary green things.

From time to time kind friends donated cows, horses, and finally a few hundred chickens. The second crop of alfalfa furnished food for both animals and fowls. The sisters felt that they were indeed extending their farming interests when twelve or fifteen pigs were installed in fine new sties. These in turn, when killed and cured, became quite a resource for the kitchen and table.

The pigs were always a source of interest to the pupils of all grades. One lovely day in early fall, so the story goes, these animals staged a spectacular drama. It seems that they had as it were a sort of celebration. Perhaps they had fed on fermented corn—but whatever the cause was, after feeding time, the pigs became quite gay. In their hilarity they burst their boundaries and went forth on a tour of investigation.

Soon big pigs, medium-sized pigs, and baby pigs came grunting their way up the steps of the west porch, knocking one another over as they tumbled through the doors and into the corridors and class rooms. In a short time there was an uproar everywhere; the children went delirious with laughter as they scrambled to the tops of their desks in their efforts to give place to the intruders. The tots in the primary room were sure that one of the baby pigs had laughed and laughed when it came into the room.

Though the sisters endeavored to get order out of this confusion, they also were enjoying the antics of the unusual visitors. At length the hired help, now aware of the strange flight, appeared suddenly and took command of the paraders. The hitherto hilarious pigs, by this time over their unwonted joviality, went rather resentfully, ambling and shuffling, out of the building. Their exit was more dignified than their entrance had been.

The students had a difficult time readjusting themselves to the comparatively tame class room routine—the analyzing of simple, compound, and complex sentences, the translation of Latin, French, and Spanish, the vain effort to prove that certain angles of congruent triangles are equal; the distinguishing of Napoleonic wars from the great Roman victories. The directress, Sister Roberta Jarboe, finally consulted with the superior, Mother Ann Joseph, and they both decided that classes would be dismissed for the afternoon. A picnic tramp over the hills would be a pleasant surprise for the entire academy.

On the next day the girls recalled with pleasure the visit of their funny little friends. They even wrote delightful essays and verses about their peculiar visitors. One of their rhymes went like this:

O come again, my dear little pig,
And visit me in class;
Do for me that funny jig
That no one could surpass.

You made me quite hysterical,
For all that I could see
Were fancy-stepping piggy feet
Give way to bended knee.

Do come again, my little pig,
And teach me how to do it;
And never, never grow up big,
For if you do, you'll rue it.

Chapter VIII

MOTHER PRAXEDES BECOMES SUPERIOR OF LORETTO HEIGHTS

Thirty years had now come and gone since the Sisters of Loretto had made their first humble beginnings in the field of Catholic education in Colorado, in the historic "white house," the first St. Mary's Academy on California Street. The community at Loretto Heights had continued to weather the financial storm although the outlook still remained forbidding; the school had had its third commencement or "exhibition"; members of three graduating classes had received the symbolic laurel wreaths, and vacation was now at hand when Mother Ann Joseph informed the sisters that Mother Praxedes, a woman of rare executive ability and understanding heart, had been appointed superior of the institution.

Mother Ann Joseph spoke highly of Mother Praxedes as a deeply religious woman who had been in charge of several Loretto schools and communities in the Southwest and was now coming from her latest responsibility, the superiorship of Loretto Academy at Florissant, Missouri. Mother Ann Joseph knew her well; their acquaintance dated back even to the old days in Santa Fe.

In her young womanhood Mother Praxedes, née Susan Carty, had come from Ireland. After working in the business world for several years, she decided with characteristic shrewdness that by entering a religious order she could accomplish much more for others and at the same time sanctify her own soul. With whole-hearted enthusiasm she commenced her novitiate at the Loretto Motherhouse, but after a few months her health began to fail. The superiors wisely decided to transfer the young novice to the novitiate in Santa Fe where she could continue her training and at the same time have a better chance of recovering her health.

Accordingly, in 1875, this young religious was one of a party who made the caravan journey over the "Santa Fe Trail" to the far distant Spanish town where, on account of the difficulties of traveling in those days, a second novitiate had been established. There, amid surroundings strange and almost foreign, the novice entered with high heart and courage into the work of training herself for her future life, not dreaming that she was to become one of God's "shock troopers" in the Southwest and elsewhere. Even during her novitiate Sister Praxedes gave evidence of a deep religious spirit, winning amiability, and alert efficiency—qualities which distinguished her throughout the remainder of her life.

Shortly after completing the year of canonical training, the young religious was entrusted with responsible charges in various houses of the Society. In 1880 she was appointed superior at Las Cruces, New Mexico, where a heavy debt had been incurred for a new building. Here and in other parts of the Southwest, the name of Sister Praxedes became a household word. Having become known for her resourcefulness and successful administration, Sister Praxedes was later transferred to Loretto Academy at Florissant, Missouri, over which she presided until her appointment as the successor to Mother Ann Joseph at Loretto Heights.

Only once had Mother Praxedes seen the beautiful new building to which she was now assigned. Sister Dolorine Powers, the superior at St. Mary's, had taken her out from the city house where, in passing through Denver, she was a guest. At her first view of the Heights with its magnificent background of the Rocky Mountains, she stood spellbound at the foot of the hill. "Do we own that building!" she exclaimed. "Yes," answered Sister Dolorine. "Some day, Sister Praxedes, you will be superior of that house." "Oh, no!" replied Sister Praxedes. "I belong in the adobe houses of the Southwest; my work is there."

The Sisters at the Heights and St. Mary's soon recognized the executive ability of the new superior. The financial conditions of these institutions were still a cause

of anxiety to the higher superiors at the Motherhouse and
to the communities in the city and the country house. With
her usual optimism Mother Praxedes put her hand and
mind to the duty which was now hers. The creditors in
Denver were becoming even more urgent in seeking a settlement of long-standing accounts. The sisters, utterly without resources on account of the condition of the times, began
to feel that they might be obliged to consent that the trust
company of Milwaukee foreclose a mortgage on which it
was not possible to make further payments.

On entering upon her duties as superior at the Heights,
Mother Praxedes was aware that the enthusiasm which she
had felt at that first view of the building was now redoubled.
Even though there were financial problems, she was convinced that there must be a way of solving them and she
set herself to the task of finding that way. Upon investigation the prospects of the responsibility placed upon her did
not lighten; the indebtedness assumed proportions far
beyond what she had expected.

A loan of $100,000 from the Northwestern Mutual Life
Insurance Company of Milwaukee had been secured, in
January, 1891, on the property at St. Mary's. In November
of that same year, another $100,000 had been borrowed
from the Penn Life Insurance Company by means of a
mortgage on the property at the Heights. In addition to
this the community at the Heights was responsible for the
interest on another $125,000 on St. Mary's; also for the
insurance of $200,000 on the property at St. Mary's and
the Heights. In order to give further assistance, Loretto
Academy on Pine Street in St. Louis had been mortgaged;
so also the property owned by the Sisters of Loretto in
Colorado Springs. The sums accruing from these loans
had been used in the construction of the new building. The
agreement was that eventually Loretto Heights would re-
fund these amounts, but the individual houses on which
liens had been placed, would be responsible for the interest.

In order to lighten the heavy burden resting upon St.
Mary's and the Heights, the General Council had assigned

a certain quota of money to be paid yearly by the property-
holding houses of the Society, as a fund for paying the
interest on the amounts borrowed by the Heights. Such
was the indebtedness which Mother Praxedes discovered
when she began to investigate the work upon which she was
to enter—a gloomy enough prospect.

Meanwhile the Mother Superior and her council were
deeply concerned over the heavy debt which had been con-
tracted just before the depression spread over the country.
As a final effort in seeking financial aid, Mother Catherine
Connor, the highest superior, was authorized by the General
Council and the Ecclesiastical Superior, the Reverend C. J.
O'Connell, to interview Mother Catherine Drexel in Phila-
delphia, in the hope of securing the much-needed relief for
the Denver property. Having effected nothing from this
interview and being confronted with the responsibility of
the debt which was weighing now upon the sisterhood, the
General Council and the Reverend C. J. O'Connell,
moderator of their board, on September 21, 1894, came to
this decision: "After struggling hard since February,
1892, to secure the Heights property, and having exhausted
upon it all funds and resources both at Loretto and many
of its branch houses, the property should be sold as soon
as possible."

Mother Catherine was instructed to negotiate with
other religious orders in regard to the possibility of their
purchasing the recently erected building at Loretto
Heights. On November 22 of that same year, 1894, a speedy
sale of St. Mary's was mentioned but nothing definite re-
sulted. This recommendation, namely, the sale of the
property on California Street, St. Mary's, was the last
official act of the Reverend C. J. O'Connell as Ecclesiastical
Superior of the Sisters of Loretto.

It was at this juncture that the enterprising spirit of
Mother Praxedes manifested itself. By this time she realized the critical condition of affairs and the financial ruin
which was now impending. In this emergency she wrote
to the Mother Superior and the General Council and laid
before them the plans over which she had been praying

with all earnestness. Knowing her resourcefulness and the
soundness of her judgment, Mother Catherine and her
Council did not hesitate to grant her permission to carry
out her proposal.

With Mother Praxedes, a woman magnanimous and
courageous, to decide was to act. One day shortly after
receiving the permission to try out what she had been
meditating upon in regard to the loan, she met Sister
Lavialle Daly in the main corridor of the Heights and said
hastily: "Sister, get your veil and shawl and come with
me at once." Sister hastened to obey, and seizing a small
'reticule' she made no delay in meeting Mother at the front
door. The two set out for Denver, Sister Lavialle not
knowing whither they were bound or why. As they neared
the Union depot, Sister Lavialle ventured the query:
"Where are we going, Mother?" "To Milwaukee," was
the short reply. Amazed, Sister said: "Why, Mother, I
have scarcely more than a handkerchief with me." Mother
answered: "It's the same case here, but we'll manage some-
how."

As soon as they arrived in Milwaukee, Mother Praxedes
and Sister Lavialle directed their steps to the headquarters
of the Northwestern Mutual Life Insurance Company.
When Mother asked to see the member of the Company who
had been carrying on the correspondence with the superiors
at Loretto, she was told that this was not possible since
the board of directors was having an important meeting.
After quick thought and prompt decision, feeling that the
directors were even then conferring with regard to the
foreclosure of the mortgage on the property in Denver,
she asked: "May I go into the board meeting?" The office
attendant looked his surprise at this unusual request; but
asking the two sisters to follow him, he knocked at the door
of the room where the meeting was in session. The directors,
though quite engrossed with the matter under discussion,
arose courteously and received Mother Praxedes and her
companion.

Mother Praxedes had made a correct surmise. The
matter being considered at that very meeting was the loan,

long in default, of the Sisters of Loretto in Colorado. The chairman explained to the religious that it was not possible for the company to defer foreclosure; payment was imperative. The Superior from Loretto Heights asked permission to address the board. Feeling that this was her last, her only chance to save the building for which the sisterhood had struggled now for so many years, scarcely conscious of what she said, she spoke as one inspired. When relating the circumstances at a later date, Mother Praxedes said she knew it was God who put the words into her mouth.

Mother assured the insurance company that they were taking no risk in granting the sisters time; the sisters were not asking for money, simply for time—every cent would be paid if an extension of time were granted. She explained that the houses in Denver and Loretto Heights did not stand alone as isolated units; the order of the Sisters of Loretto at the Foot of the Cross had central government, and all the property owned by the Society surely furnished sufficient assets to assure the company that their loan was a safe one.

The chairman urged his associates to bring forward any points which needed clarifying. Mother Praxedes was asked a number of questions. To all of these she gave ready, intelligent replies. Finally she was asked whether the sisters would be willing to pledge all the property which they owned. She answered that she thought she was safe in saying that they would. This reply was considered, but after some further deliberation, the chairman announced that it would be necessary for the company to foreclose and take over the building. To this Mother Praxedes rejoined: "Gentlemen, if you take the house, you will have to take the sisters also!" Hearing this, the whole assembly broke into hearty peals of laughter, and the meeting adjourned.

When the ordeal was over and Mother Praxedes rose to depart, her face glowing with the excitement caused by the siege through which she had passed, the chairman of the meeting, who seemed to understand just what was at stake, whispered kindly to her: "Cheer up; you have won the day. We are going to reconsider the matter and grant you the necessary time.''

The two religious made the return trip in a much happier frame of mind. Mother Praxedes had succeeded in preventing the foreclosure of the mortgage—the danger was averted.

Chapter IX

RETROSPECTIVE

Surely and steadily was history being made from the time that the Sisters of Loretto located in the "Queen City of the Plains"; and during the three decades which followed that date, Denver's population had increased to 85,000. One can gather from the *R. E. Gazette* interesting facts regarding the growth of the city up to 1894, namely, that it was the largest city between St. Louis and San Francisco; its natural roads were the finest in the United States; a State Capitol worth $1,000,000 and a Post Office worth the same amount were being erected. With an elevation of over 5,000 feet, Denver was known as one of the most healthful cities in the Union. It had a new and extensive military post, a cable road, and a little later a horse car, too, which traveled from the end of the Broadway line to Fort Logan, the military post, and up the Loretto hill to the academy proper, Loretto Heights.

Besides the above advantages, Denver claimed to have the finest water in the world and a perfect system of sewerage; an excellent street car system; electric lights and an electric railway; thirteen railroads entering the city; the finest opera house in the United States; eight banks and six flour mills; an artesian water supply of one hundred wells; a general system of steam heating; no coal dust; a branch of the United States mint; the largest smelting works in the world; five daily newspapers and several weeklies; and finally, the sunniest climate on the face of the earth.

When one recalls that much of the progress, which the people of Denver claimed for their city in 1894, had taken place within the small compass of thirty years, one must realize that the growth during those years was remarkable. The early part of October, 1859, saw the erection of Denver's first house, the Russell-Smith cabin, at what is now Eleventh and Wewatta. An Indian squaw, the wife of Smith, was Denver's "first lady." The development which took place during those thirty years was a presage of the growth which was to follow. The city has continued to advance at a rate surpassing the most extravagant hopes of those early settlers, who laid the foundation of what was to become the finest city in the West.

In the new Loretto Heights Academy, located southwest of Denver, the fall term of school in 1894 had just begun. When the classes were resumed, the pupils were met by another directress, Sister Mary Xavier Cunningham, who for several years had been principal of the school of our Lady of Light in Santa Fe, also of Loretto Academy at Florissant, and Cedar Grove Academy, Louisville. With such an experienced woman directing the school, Mother Praxedes was encouraged in her first year to assume the burden of superior.

One of the old files of that year contains an interesting account of an historical contest on national and local events. Sister Mary Xavier was noted for her ability to arouse enthusiasm among the students by activities of that nature. Katie Gilgallon, a pupil in the second year of high school, was the proud winner of a beautiful hand-painted scarf, the prize which Mother Praxedes donated and took special pleasure in awarding. Some of the younger relatives of Miss Gilgallon attend school at St. Mary's Academy up to the present jubilee year of the Heights, 1942.

The school year went on happily and profitably to an entertaining close in June. The third graduating exercises were comparable to those of the preceding years. Owing to the strained money conditions the students in the upper grades still remained few in number. The only girl to be crowned with the laurel wreath that year was Miss Georgia Weinberg.

Under ordinary circumstances Georgia would have been saddened at the thought of leaving the sisters, but there was no sadness this year. Shortly after the close of school, at a fashionable wedding attended by the elite of

Denver, Georgia became Mrs. Elias Cohn. Since the time of her graduation, Mrs. Cohn has remained a loyal alumna and a true friend to the Sisters of Loretto. She has enjoyed telling her two daughters of the happy days she spent at her alma mater, Loretto Heights.

Mother Praxedes, although busily engaged with her problems as superior, took an active interest in the school and its progress. She was full of happy anticipation at the approach of the fall term for she had a pleasant surprise in store for the older girls, especially for the graduates of the year, Amelia Gallegos, Ella Mullen, and Stella Nelson. The surprise, which proved to be a great pleasure to the three seniors, was the return of Sister Pancratia from Springfield, Missouri, to assume the duties of directress. The health of Sister Pancratia, so accustomed to the climate of Colorado, having become impaired, the doctors had advised her return to the invigorating air of Denver.

Although Mother Praxedes regretted the departure of the alert and energetic Sister Mary Xavier, who had just completed a successful year as directress, she was happy to make the change in order that Sister Pancratia might have the opportunity of regaining her usual health. As her superiors had hoped, the roses soon returned to the cheeks of Sister Pancratia, who had been for twenty-five years the favorite of the Denver pioneers and the "white angel" of the Indians.

Living at Loretto Heights in those days were three other sisters, busy in the work of the school: Sister Jovita Mills, Sister Lavialle Daly, and Sister Aurelia Archambault. After St. Ann's Academy at St. Paul, Kansas, was destroyed by fire, September, 1895, Mother Praxedes was instrumental in bringing Sister Aurelia, the efficient music teacher at that school, to Loretto Heights.

In all matters pertaining to the music department, Sister Lavialle and Sister Aurelia stood as one. Each sister, however, was quite free in expressing her opinion in regard to the work the other accomplished with individual pupils. Perhaps each teacher had undue interest or over-concern. The little foible or eccentricity, whatever it was, was a part of each sister, but in spite of it, the happy companionship of these sisters continued through several decades.

It was interesting to observe as recently as 1938 a trio of sisters, then the seniors of the community, the same three who had worked side by side in the early days, still vitally concerned in everything pertaining to the welfare of the school. One Sunday afternoon, surrounded by a group of junior sisters, these three were listening to a radio program which happened to be the "Catholic Hour." What a treat to come upon such a gathering! Suddenly Monsignor Sheen's voice reached a dramatic close, and the "Catholic Hour" was over. Several seconds passed before anyone broke the silence. Then comments flowed freely. From the indistinct murmur of conversation came the voice of Sister Lavialle:

"Didn't God manifest His great goodness when He inspired man to invent the radio! How marvelous to have the pleasure of listening here in Colorado to a program given in New York!"

"Oh, yes, indeed! Yes," assented Sister Jovita as she glanced apprehensively in the direction of Sister Aurelia, who always felt in duty bound to dissent from the opinion of the gentle Sister Lavialle.

"Well, yes, Sister Lavialle," Sister Aurelia unexpectedly replied, "mere man worked long and tediously on that invention. At the beginning of the century, in 1901, that remarkable scientist, Marconi, signalled the letter 'S' across the Atlantic from England to Newfoundland. You know that was the very first message sent, and since that time those interested in the field have worked tirelessly to perfect the invention so that conversation over the air waves may be understood and enjoyed without the sputtering and—and—static, I think it is called. Of course God pushed on all those who were experimenting with the air waves."

As Sister Aurelia finished her speech, she folded her arms a bit complacently within her voluminous sleeves. Then encouraged by her introductory remarks, she continued:

"Sister Lavialle, when Monsignor Sheen was urging us in his talk just now to pray for the intentions of the Holy Father, didn't he remind you of Cardinal Satolli who visited the Heights back in the nineties? Do you remember, Sister Lavialle? He, too, was always asking us to pray for the Holy Father."

"Yes, Sister Aurelia, I remember, and I'm sure that Sister Jovita remembers. It was the sixth of March, 1896. Wasn't that the date, Sister Jovita?"

"Eh! What did you say?" questioned Sister Jovita. "Ninety-three? Yes, I'm ninety-three; but let me see. To get my dates I always go back to the time that Mother Pancratia left for Montgomery, you know she was changed to Springfield later. She left the first part of March in '92. Then there's another event in March, an important one which took place in the March of 1864, the Battle of the Wilderness, fought by General Grant. You know, whenever I think of that battle, I always think of our sisters' coming to Denver; both events happened in 1864. And if ever there was a wilderness, it was Denver at that time.

"Well, now, listen to me wandering off the subject like this. You know, of course, that I'm ninety-three, and you young ladies of seventy-eight and eighty must forgive me if my mind is not so steady as yours. Now what was it you asked me a second ago?"

"It was about Cardinal Satolli's visit here at the Heights," Sister Lavialle answered. "It was the year when our superior, Mother Praxedes, and our directress, Sister Pancratia, were doing so much for the school. Didn't the Cardinal visit us on March 6, 1896?"

"That's right, Sister Lavialle," agreed Sister Jovita. "Do you remember we thought that all the saints on the March calendar had a hand in bringing us a visitor of so great dignity."

"Then you were right, Sister Lavialle; it was March 6 in 1896"; and Sister Aurelia conceded a score for the peace-loving Sister Lavialle.

Here they were, these three gracious senior sisters, who had been participators in early western history and makers of it, all eager and ready with their reliable reminiscences. The younger sisters of the group, realizing that there was an opportunity of hearing some worth-while history of the "good old days," settled themselves around the trio to listen in and learn interesting happenings of the past, so full of human interest.

Stories of the early struggles and events of a foundation, handed down as traditions from generation to generation always elicit an enthusiastic response in the pure young faces sheltered beneath the religious veil, and also in the fair faces of students crowned with the latest coiffures. Why this interest? They are learning the past history of their institution and of the Sisters of Loretto at the Foot of the Cross. Loyal devotion gives a charming atmosphere to this setting of local color: three revered sisters, resting now, after "the labor and heat of the day," on the brink of eternity, surrounded by fervent, young religious, eager to learn the traditions of the Order to which they have recently dedicated their lives.

"Sister Jovita," continued Sister Lavialle, "there is a famous saying of General Grant's that you used to love to quote in associating his Battle of the Wilderness with the coming of the Sisters of Loretto to Denver. Do you remember it?"

"Eh?" After a moment's thought, Sister Jovita recalled General Grant's well-known declaration: "Yes," she said, "I remember; it was this: 'I intend to fight it out along this line if it takes all summer!' You know our pioneer sisters had that same spirit. They overcame their difficulties not only that summer; but they kept on conquering new ones as they arose, summer after summer; yes, and for many hard winters, too. The zeal of Father Nerinckx had been imbibed by the sisters whom he trained;

they in turn transmitted the meaning of self-sacrifice to their successors, and so it was handed down. The sisters who came to Colorado in the early years surely had the spirit of our holy founder, Father Nerinckx. And those other sisters who came to these parts not long after the first sisters in the state, I mean these young sisters here— and Sister Jovita smiled at Sister Lavialle and Sister Aurelia—they also met and overcame the hardships of the first years of this foundation.''

"And you," interrupted Sister Lavialle, "you have conquered trials and hardships more completely than any of us; you are more pleasing to God than we! Sisters, don't you agree?"

"Are you talking about me?" interposed Sister Jovita. "I more pleasing to God! Oh, no! I'm just a dumb-bell!" And Sister Jovita chuckled mischievously as she always did when she knew that she had said something not exactly according to Hoyle. Sister Jovita continued: "Now don't be shocked because I said 'dumb-bell.' I heard one of the college girls use that word. You know I have to keep up with things, and people, and words! Besides, it's true; I am a dumb-bell. I'm sort of broken and gnarled and almost worn out. But I've grown that way in working for Him. I think He likes to have me look old and wrinkled. If He is pleased, I should be satisfied." And again Sister Jovita chuckled.

"Well, Sister Jovita," commented Sister Lavialle, "if we are as pleasing to God as you are, we should be happy indeed. But let's get back to the great Cardinal Satolli. I think General Grant detoured us for quite a time in his 'Wilderness.' Let us have the story of Cardinal Satolli's visit to the Heights. Sister Aurelia knows how to relate it well; you shall enjoy something at once entertaining and edifying. Come on, Sister Aurelia, the story!"

This invitation pleased Sister Aurelia for she liked nothing better than to talk of distinguished visitors. Beaming with satisfaction, she smiled appreciatively upon the eager group.

"What was the occasion of the Cardinal's coming, Sister Aurelia? Was it social, business, or just one of those things?" asked one of the young sisters.

"I think there was some business attached to it," Sister Aurelia replied. "You know, of course, that the Cardinal was the Apostolic Delegate in Washington in '96, and that ten years later he was appointed Cardinal Protector of the Sisters of Loretto. This appointment came to him on December 30, 1907.

"Whenever bishops or other ecclesiastics visited us, we were never disturbed; we were rather used to their coming. But when the great Cardinal Satolli was to visit us on that eventful March 6, I tell you Mother Praxedes and Sister Pancratia made great preparations. They surely knew how to entertain dignitaries, and they also knew how to make the rest of us step around polishing this and shining that. I remember the throne adorned with purple which we arranged in the chapel. The chapel at that time was where the library now is. In the colorful decorations in the tile hall, the papal colors, gold and white, predominated. My! My! That was an exciting time," and Sister Aurelia drew in a long breath; she realized that she had an amusing story to relate.

Chapter X

THE COMING OF THE CARDINAL

Sister Aurelia, pleased both with her subject and her attentive audience needed no further urging to begin her narrative:

"As I said before, Mother Praxedes and Sister Pancratia had everything organized to a nicety for the coming of Cardinal Satolli. In preparing for the reception of the distinguished guest, each sister was assigned her particular duty, and, when all the arrangements had been completed, every one felt that she had contributed her share to make the occasion a success. As far as we music teachers were concerned, we were more than busy; for, besides preparing the music for the Pontifical Mass, we were instructed to have some numbers ready for the afternoon program in honor of His Eminence.

"A number of priests accompanied the Cardinal, as is the custom, you know, whenever the representative of the Holy Father visits a religious house. The purpose of this formality is, I suppose, to show the proper respect to personages of high authority. The singing of the Mass went off well; the members of the choir, Sisters and students, were pleased with themselves.

"Oh, yes, I mustn't forget to tell you that Sister Pancratia, upon whom Mother Praxedes was depending for many important details, such as seeing that the proper food for breakfast was served on the proper kind of dishes and all that sort of thing, invited Sister Mary Eustachia and Sister Mary Linus, who lived in the city at St. Mary's Academy, to help with the serving. Sister Pancratia, on consulting the Baur Confectionery concerning a suitable menu for a Lenten breakfast, was told that fried oysters would be the appropriate fare for such guests.

Mother Mary Linus Maier

*First Riding Club—Burros were named for Shakespearean characters:
Romeo, Juliet, Hamlet, Macbeth, Shylock*

Modern Riding Club

"Friends in Denver had lent beautiful hand-painted dishes, all gold, for the table service. The food and all the appointments were approved by the sisters. Elegant ideas were carried out in elegant taste. Mass was now over, and, everything being in perfect readiness, it was time for the Cardinal's breakfast. Sister Arsenia was given the honor of bringing His Eminence to the breakfast room. Full of the mission entrusted to her, Sister Arsenia was about to greet the Cardinal when he, addressing her in broken English, said:

" 'Sister, will you please bring to me in the sacristy here a cup of black coffee?'

" 'Yes, your Eminence,' gasped Sister Arsenia, also in broken English; and running rather than walking, the dainty little sister soon returned with a cup of steaming coffee.

" 'Please, Sister, may I now have one slice of bread and no butter, please?'

" 'Here, Your Eminence?' Sister Arsenia was thinking of the beautifully set table in the guests' dining room and the savory fried oysters adorning the center of a gold dish. Embarrassed, Sister glanced up only to see the Cardinal smiling down on her. Now he was speaking:

" 'Yes, Sister, bring it here.'

"Sister bowed low and then tripped swiftly down to the culinary department to announce to a puzzled group that the Cardinal wished a slice of bread. Having arranged the lonely piece of bread upon a small plate, she bore it swiftly to the sacristy. Pleased with the prompt service, the Cardinal thanked Sister, adding:

" 'Sister, please tell your good superior that I shall be ready to interview the sisters of the community in ten minutes.'

" 'But Your Eminence, our superior is expecting you to take breakfast now. They are awaiting you in the breakfast room this very minute. Are not you, Father Phillips, and the other guests all coming down to breakfast?'

" 'Sister, I have had my breakfast. You were so kind

in bringing it to me just now—coffee and bread. This is the breakfast for Lent, is it not?'

" 'But Your Eminence, you are a guest. This is not a fast day. This is Lent, but it is Monday, and Mondays are not fast days. Oh, what am I saying? Am I all wrong? Please forgive me, Cardinal Satolli. You should know whether to fast or not. Of course all days of Lent are fast days, Mondays included! Oh, what shall I say to my superior?'

" 'Tell her, Sister, that I the sisters shall see in a few minutes. And will you do something else for me? It will much pleasure give to me—tell Father Phillips to take with him the priests down to your wonderful breakfast. Tell them to eat and make up for Cardinal Satolli who has you so much disappointed. And, Sister, I shall here remain for dinner, and if Father Phillips does not eat everything, perhaps for me there shall be something left. What do you say?'

" 'I say that I shall tell Father Phillips and my superior what you told me to say, Your Eminence.'

" 'Thank you. You are a good sister.' "

"Oh, Sister Aurelia, how did the other sisters feel? They must have been terribly embarrassed. The poor things," lamented Sister Mary.

"Well, of course, they did feel quite disappointed, but they were glad that the other guests had a good meal. It's an ill wind, you know.

"It did not take Sister Arsenia long to deliver the Cardinal's message to Mother Praxedes. The priests had a good breakfast, and before you could say 'Jack Robinson' every sister was in place awaiting the interview.

"None of the sisters was much disturbed. Some of them may have been a bit nervous; but the Cardinal had such a calm, kind manner that they were soon at their ease. Yet his keen, piercing eyes went right through you; instinctively you knew that he was reading you like a book. The only questions he asked me, as I remember now, were whether I received enough to eat and whether I was happy. He asked the other sisters just about the same things, so you can readily see that it did not take him long to finish his audiences.

"The next two important events were the dinner and the afternoon program. Dinner was served at noon in those days. If the breakfast was in such style, you can imagine how they had planned for the dinner. The dinner was in progress and everything was going off fine. Sister Eustachia, Sister Mary Linus, and the ever-efficient Sister Arsenia were serving. I do not remember what the menu was, but I do know that everything was elegant. The sisters were secretly congratulating themselves that there had not been a single mishap, when, just as Sister Arsenia was placing the dessert before the Cardinal, in some unaccountable way, her foot became entangled in the rug, and gold dishes, dessert, and sister herself were all mixed up before you knew what was happening.

"Not only were the gold dishes broken, but the ice also was broken! Up to this time all had been dignified and ceremonious. With the fall of Sister and the food, the formality, too, fell away. The Cardinal, very simple and very human, as you must have noticed from the story of the cup of black coffee and the slice of bread, placed Mother Praxedes and the sisters at ease with his ready wit and enjoyment of the scene. You have always observed, haven't you, that really important people dislike too much fuss and ceremony!

"The Cardinal surely enjoyed the way Sister Arsenia bore up under her mishap. The friendliness which arose over the broken dishes at the close of the elegant banquet continued during the Cardinal's lifetime. That friendliness developed into friendship and I am sure that the shattered china played no small part in bringing it about. Cardinal Satolli remained interested in the affairs of the Sisters of Loretto. He showed special kindness to Mother Praxedes and her companions during their sojourns in Rome, and, while Cardinal Protector of the Lorettines, befriended the Sisters in many ways."

Sister Aurelia settled herself back in her chair after her long, detailed account of that important visit. She knew that she had told a good story.

But the sisters were aware that she had simply referred to the reception in the afternoon. So, urging her to finish her narrative, Sister Jovita and Sister Lavialle prepared themselves to hear again that part of the Cardinal's reception which had been of most interest to them.

Sister Aurelia assured her listeners that there was not much more to tell since there were just a few special happenings which she remembered in regard to that afternoon's entertainment:

"Of course we had been preparing the musical numbers on the program for several days," she went on. "Do you remember, Sister Lavialle, that I sang Shubert's *Ave Maria,* and you accompanied me on the harp?" Sister Lavialle nodded her head in acknowledgment of the compliment. "The orchestra played several selections, which the Cardinal and his suite seemed to enjoy. The special feature of the entertainment, however, was an address read in Latin by Miss Ella Mullen, now Mrs. Weckbaugh of Denver. I wonder, Sister Lavialle, whether you still have that address? I think our junior sisters here would really enjoy hearing it, especially since it was one of our alumnae who represented the school that afternoon."

"Yes, Sister Aurelia," replied Sister Lavialle. "I was hoping you would give me an opportunity of at least showing that address to the sisters. I have it among my treasures. It has always been precious to me. Every now and then I reread it for it reminds me of the time when Latin had an honored place on the high school curriculum. Now one hears on all sides that Latin is too difficult for the ordinary girl. What nonsense!

"I happen to have that very address here in the *Loretto Annals* which I was reading before the 'Catholic Hour.' My eyesight is not so good now, so I am going to ask you, Sister Mary, to read it to the sisters." Tenderly, with a touch of reverence, Sister Lavialle brought forth the four-page brochure from her book and handed it to Sister Mary. With every mark of respect, the latter received the treasure.

"If you need any help," Sister Lavialle encouraged, "just call on Sister Aurelia; she really likes to talk. She will explain whatever you wish to know." Feeling quite honored to be asked to read the address, Sister Mary began, perhaps a little nervously, to read:

Denver

Die sexta Marti

MDCCCXCVI

* * *

Illustrissimo et Eminentissimo Domino

FRANCISCO CARDINALI SATOLLI

Delegato Apostolico

* * *

SALUTEM.

EMINENTISSIME DOMINE

Exultet jam angelica turba Coelorum! Paschali hacce voce, quadragesimali hoc tempore, Tuum celebramus inter nos adventum.

Non solum ad montes ascendis sublimes, sed etiam gaudentur ad istos Lauretanos colles pervolas, et simili amplexu diligis et pastores et oves.

Sicut stella in hisce regionibus apparuisti et vocem jam audivimus: "Gloria in Excelsis Deo, et pax hominibus bonae voluntatis!" Justitia et pax osculatae sunt. Non est jam in civitate ruina maceriae, sed Te auspice, aedificium rursus elevatur ad fastigium, et, Te medico, satis olei in vulnera nostra diffusum est.

Oves Lauretani gregis, nostrum est officium et nostra vocatio ad pedes Crucifixi, preces et lacrymas fundere, Cor amare aeterni Amantis; puellas fide, moribus et cultura instruere. Gloria haec est nostra, si humiles decet gloriari, auctoriatatem revereri, bene consciae quod libertas diruit ubi non est auctoritas, et quod sine Petra labitur domus.

Purpura indutum et Ecclesiae cardinalem effectum Te rogamus, amice Leonis, ut ad Leonis Magni pedes ovium istarum deferas vota et amplissimam pro nobis implores benedictionem, ita ut ad montium cacumina isti Lauretani colles—prima huius Americae Septentrionalis institutio— crescant atque florescant.

In Deo semper spem firmam tenentes, Tuum etiam expectamus auxilium, ut, Te protectore, consequi possimus Nostrae Societatis firmitatem et successum.

Sorores et alumnae puellae pro Tua Eminentia semper orando impetrabimus ut ad multos annos pervenias et talenta quae a Domino recepisti, Tibi promerantur ampliores adhuc coronas.

"Well, Sister Lavialle, that surely sounds scholarly," Sister Mary remarked as she turned the paper over in her hands. "Oh, you darling!" she exclaimed; "I was beginning to think that you would be asking me for an extempore version of the address, but here is the translation, too. Do you wish me to read it, Sisters, or have you already gathered the meaning from the Latin text?"

"Now, what are you suggesting, Sister Mary?" Sister Lavialle asked. "Perhaps some did follow the meaning as you read, but for the benefit of the others who are versed only in *Sanskrit, Greek,* and *Gaelic,* please read the translation."

"I was hoping you would ask me to read the English. Here it is, and not lengthy, either":

Denver, March 6, 1896

MOST ILLUSTRIOUS AND EMINENT LORD

Let the angelic hosts of heaven now rejoice! In this paschal language do we celebrate your coming among us during this Lenten season.

You not only ascend these lofty mountains but you also hasten gladly to these Loretto Heights; and you include equally in your affection both the Sisters and their pupils.

As a star you have appeared in these regions, and already have we heard the voice: 'Glory to God in the highest, and on earth peace to men of good will.' Justice and peace have kissed. There is now no decay in the walls of the city, and under your protection the edifice is again elevated to its former splendor, and, as a physician, you have poured in sufficient oil to heal our wounds.

As members of the Loretto Society, our duty and our vocation is to pour out tears and prayers at the foot of the crucifix, to love the heart of the Eternal Lover, and to instruct our students in faith, morals, and culture. This is our glory—if it becomes the lowly to glory—to reverence authority, being well convinced that without authority liberty is destroyed, and that a house falls unless founded on the rock of Peter.

We pray you, friend of Leo, you who have been invested with the purple and made a Cardinal of the Church, that you bear the desires of this Society to the Great Leo and implore for us a still greater blessing in order that these Loretto hills may increase to mountain heights, and that this first institution of North America may advance and prosper.

With firm trust in God, we likewise expect your aid that under your protection we may continue the building up and success of our Society.

The Sisters and the pupils will always pray for Your Eminence. We shall beg God that He grant you length of years and that the talents which you have received from Him may merit for you still greater rewards.

Sister Mary ceased reading. For a short time none broke the silence. Then with one accord all agreed that they had been favored in having the privilege of listening to, in fact, of living again, the events of that memorable visit of the Cardinal to Loretto Heights.

Chapter XI

MOTHER PRAXEDES AS SUPERIOR GENERAL
SAVES LORETTO HEIGHTS

Though timely was the visit of Mother Praxedes to the Northwestern Mutual Life Insurance Company of Milwaukee, it had not solved the financial cares of the Sisters of Loretto in Denver and at the Heights. She had succeeded in accomplishing the purpose of her trip—she had secured an extension of time which would serve as a breathing space, as it were, during which the sisters might exert themselves to plan further for means of paying off some of their most pressing obligations. However, the difficulties were not yet settled.

"Hard times" still continued in the city of Denver and in the western states. This had its effect on the two Denver schools for the student enrollment was much lower than in the balmy days before the depression. Friends of the sisters, suffering also from the panic, were unable to give any material aid. The only plan which seemed at all feasible was for the Motherhouse to impose a certain tax on the various houses of the Society. This, of course, was an impediment to the development of the work which they were expected to accomplish.

In order to help the struggling sisterhood in this financial dilemma, His Eminence, Francis Cardinal Satolli, Apostolic Delegate to the United States, appointed the Most Reverend Thomas S. Byrne, Bishop of Nashville, Ecclesiastical Superior of the Sisters of Loretto, with power to investigate conditions in the various houses of the Society and suggest remedies which, in his judgment, would meet the exigencies then existing.

Mother Catherine Connor had been appointed in 1893 to complete Mother Dafrosa's unexpired term as Mother Superior of the Order; and in 1894 she was elected to that office by the votes of the sisters. Mother Catherine, a model religious, was a woman of experience in financial matters since she had twice served as treasurer in the General Council. Yet, capable though she was, it was decided that another sister might be more competent in coping with the numerous problems and bringing security out of the monetary involvement.

In order to have accurate information, Bishop Byrne made a visitation of many of the larger communities. When he visited Loretto Heights Academy, he perceived that Mother Praxedes was a capable administrator, that she had a thorough understanding of the financial conditions of the two houses in Denver and of the Order in general, and that, besides possessing fine business ability, she had an affable, pleasing personality. Shortly after his visit, Bishop Byrne summoned Mother Praxedes to the Motherhouse and entrusted to her the office of Superior General on March 27, 1896, the feast of the Seven Dolors.

The duties imposed upon Mother Praxedes were manifold and onerous, but her natural cheerfulness and great trust in Divine Providence sustained her during the first trying months when she was endeavoring to acquaint herself with her responsibilities. The experience which she had gained as superior of Loretto Heights from June, 1894, to March, 1896, was now valuable. The various demands made upon her time and attention kept her so fully occupied that she had no time to think of self. As soon as possible she turned her thoughts and prayers to the pressing matter which claimed her consideration—that of refinancing for the material welfare of the Order.

Mother Praxedes accompanied by her secretary, Sister Antonella Hardy, left Loretto, December 10, 1896, and proceeded to St. Louis to negotiate the loan of $300,000 which it was imperative to make. In those days $300,000 was considered as large as $800,000 today. In order to secure this she knew that it would be necessary for her to have an exact record of all the property owned by the houses of the Order in the different states. Accordingly, January 19, 1897, from her central office at Loretto Academy, 2345 Pine Street,

St. Louis, Mother Praxedes sent to the sister superior in each of the property-holding houses of the Society a letter containing the request that each house would immediately furnish the Motherhouse adequate and reliable information regarding its history, physical set-up and equipment, cost and appraised value.

To this request, Mother Praxedes added an explanation of the intended refinancing as her reason for asking the information, and an earnest appeal to the communities for their united prayers for the success of the project.

While Mr. Theophile Papin of the firm of Messrs. Papin and Tontrup was endeavoring to secure a loan from some English capitalists, Mother Praxedes was making efforts wherever she thought there was a possibility of borrowing money in large sums. Suddenly she was called to Denver to confer with Mr. Kingsley of the Penn Mutual Life Insurance Company, who believed that the firm he represented was now prepared to enter into the deal. On April 10, 1897, Mother Praxedes asked Mr. Kingsley to secure a loan from his company for $260,000 at 5% for a term of five years.

Negotiations along this line went forward. Everything had been arranged, even the application blanks had been filled out, when Mr. Kingsley received a telegram from his superior officers stating that it was not possible for the firm to make the loan. The company, however, assured Mother Praxedes that, as long as the interest on the existing debt was paid when due, she would not be urged to pay the principal until she would succeed in obtaining a loan elsewhere.

Not too much disturbed at the unexpected conclusion of her negotiations with the Penn Mutual Life Insurance Company, Mother Praxedes decided to take the train once more to Milwaukee and again try her luck with the Northwestern Mutual Life Insurance Company, the same firm which she had visited shortly after she had gone to the Heights as superior. This time, more bold on account of her necessity, she asked for a loan at a lower rate of interest, but was informed that this could not be done without bondsmen, insurance, and security to double the amount of the sum borrowed. After two days spent fruitlessly in Milwaukee, Mother Praxedes returned to St. Louis to seek aid in other quarters. She investigated the possibilities of a loan from Mexico, but the change in Mexican currency and other requirements made the loan there inadvisable.

Finally, when it did not seem possible that the money needed could be borrowed from any of the financial corporations in this country, Mother Praxedes turned to a firm in Amsterdam. The contract was about to be closed when Mr. Festus Wade of the Anderson-Wade Realty Company of St. Louis, learning of the proposed European deal, chivalrously declared: "We will never let an American woman be forced to go from our country to make a loan." Mr. Festus Wade was as good as his word. It was his hand, kind, firm, and strong, which guided Mother Praxedes and the Sisters of Loretto to the St. Louis Trust Company, yes, into the very presence of its chief executive, Judge Madill.

The story is told that on the way to the office of Judge Madill, Mother Praxedes and her sister companion passed a certain jewelry store which she, as Susie Carty, had often patronized in the days now long past. Miss Carty was a lover of good jewelry, and the striking thing was that every piece she bought had a cross beautifully engraved upon it. Now as Mother Praxedes Carty, the superior general of several hundred religious women, while passing the same jewelry shop, she remembered the crosses on her trinkets of years ago and she was prompted to breathe this prayer: "My God, if you are going to give me a cross today, do give me the grace and the strength to bear it as gracefully as did Susie Carty when she wore the jewelled crosses on her rings and pins."

Would another refusal of a loan be awaiting her when she reached that office? If so she asked the grace to bear the cross. She was ready for whatever the good God would send. Thus fortified she and her companion entered the office of the firm of Anderson-Wade Realty Company.

Judge Madill sat with closed eyes listening to Mother Praxedes as she stated her case. He followed her as she gave an estimate of the real estate owned by the houses of her Order. She referred to the integrity of the sisters, the esteem in which they were held. She mentioned everything which she thought would prove favorable to the cause she was pleading. She spoke with earnest eloquence.

Again Mother Praxedes had won! Bonds to be effective July 1, 1898, for a loan of $300,000 were prepared. Each of the three hundred bonds was signed by Mother Praxedes Carty, president of the Loretto Literary and Benevolent Institution, and Sister Mary Simeon, treasurer; also by George A. Madill, president of the St. Louis Union Trust Company.

It is of interest to know that Mother Praxedes learned later that this company had such confidence in the ability of the members of the Loretto Society to carry out their obligations, that instead of floating the bonds, as is usual in real estate loans, the firm reserved them in its own vault as security.

Meanwhile business conditions throughout the country were improving. In an incredibly short time the mortgages on the property belonging to the various houses of the community were lifted since payments were promptly met. In this way, through the long strenuous efforts of an efficient and resourceful superior, Mother Praxedes Carty, Loretto Heights was saved from the financial ruin which had threatened, and it still remains the "pride of the Rockies."

Mother Praxedes Carty

Main Entrance, Administration Building

Chapter XII

EVENTS OF THE PASSING YEARS

When Mother Praxedes was appointed in 1896 to the highest office in the Loretto Society, Mother Francisca Lamy, who had been for some time the superior of the convent of Our Lady of Light in Santa Fe, was sent to take over the duties of the superior at the Heights until the end of the scholastic year. Mother Francisca was the niece of the Most Reverend John Baptist Lamy, Archbishop of Santa Fe, who as Bishop Latour is the central figure of Willa Cather's famous novel, *Death Comes for the Archbishop*. Scarcely had Mother Francisca become acquainted with her new responsibilities at the Heights when Mother Praxedes summoned her to the Motherhouse to become the first assistant or vicaress in the general council.

Although Mother Francisca had been at Loretto Heights only a short time, from March until June, yet in those few months the community perceived that she was a religious remarkable for her solid piety, her sound judgment, and high intellectual attainments. The sisters at the Heights, while regretting deeply the departure of their recently appointed superior, realized that their loss was the gain of the whole Order.

In August of that year, 1896, Mother Evangelista Bindewald was transferred from the Motherhouse, where she had been an efficient and much-loved mistress of novices, to take charge of the community at the Heights. From that date until the summer of 1898, Mother Evangelista fulfilled the duties of the superiorship faithfully and well.

Seven years had now passed since that first graduation in June. Sister Pancratia, as directress, was wholly devoted to the advancement of each pupil who entered the school. If she had any predilection it was for the very young children; these made a special appeal to the gentle woman in whose charge they were. Those who were well acquainted with Sister Pancratia feel that the stained glass window in the chapel which represents Christ blessing little children was most appropriately dedicated to the memory of this religious, who labored so long and so devotedly in the training and education of the pupils in the school which she had founded.

The commencement exercises remained the distinctively academic function of the year. The programs were planned in such a way that the seniors of each class might carry away happy memories of the close of their school days at Loretto. The five graduates of '96, May Mullen, Minnanne McDonald, Kizzie Mann, Katie Gilgallon, and Christine Schintz have always considered themselves fortunate, as they looked backward, in being the last class to be graduated under the administration of Mother Praxedes. Even as students, all had recognized that Mother Praxedes was an extraordinary woman; later in life they understood that she was greater than they ever realized. The years have passed swiftly since that graduation day in '96; each of the graduates, who was crowned with laurel on completing her school course, has found her place in the world and filled it with honor. May Mullen is well known in Denver circles as Mrs. John Dower; Minnanne McDonald became Mrs. J. A. DeBouzek; and Kizzie Mann, Mrs. E. J. Howard.

Mother Mary Louis O'Connor succeeded Mother Evangelista as superior in 1898. This gentle, refined woman managed the affairs of the community until she was transferred in the vacation of 1903 to the new Loretto Academy in Kansas City, which was being opened that fall.

Sister Pancratia, who had directed the school from the time she had returned to the Heights in 1895, was appointed superior to succeed Mother Mary Louis. This office she filled to the satisfaction of all from 1903 to 1910. During this period Sister Mary Edith Loughran was the directress of the school.

As each year came to its scholastic close, the June graduate was crowned with her laurel wreath. Forming the class of '97 were Emma Vezina, Mamie Carroll (Sister M. Alma,

S. L.); Ethel Jordon (Mrs. Ethel Colon); and Blanche
O'Neil. In '98 were graduated Mamie Horrigan, Locky Fort
(Mrs. Etter); Clara L'Abbe (Mrs. Ed. T. Paine); Pauline
Peyton (Mrs. Ed. Forney); Mamie Ryan (Mrs. Joseph
O'Grady); and Sara Salmon. In 1899, Katherine Mullen,
who later became Mrs. John O'Connor; Nellie Gilgallon, later
Mrs. P. H. Cullen; and Honor Breen. Nelle Finnerty (Mrs.
F. P. Lynch); Eileen Sullivan (Mrs. George Connolly); and
Rosamond Pryor (Mrs. John G. Hoye) were the seniors of
1900. Louise Seeberger (Mrs. F. L. Tobin) was the only
graduate of 1901. Lucille Moore (Mrs. Bert Shields); Marie
Berry (Mrs. C. B. Hoffer); and Margaret Fallon finished
in 1902.

It is interesting to recall that the Reverend William
O'Ryan, pastor of St. Leo's Church and friend of the Sisters
of Loretto through many succeeding years, delivered an eloquent address at the closing exercises in '99. Father O'Ryan,
basing much of his discourse on the themes the young ladies
had developed in their essays, made many happy allusions
to the bright, young girls who were bidding the school farewell. He urged the graduates to be true to the noble, woman-
ly ideals which had been inculcated as part of their training
during their years at Loretto Heights. The need of higher
education for women was especially emphasized.

Perhaps the reverend orator stressed this need of
higher education because "woman suffrage" had been
adopted in Colorado in 1893, just a few years before, by
a majority of 4,500 votes. The privilege of voting brings
the added duty of making an intelligent use of the ballot.

The valedictorian of the class of '99, Miss Katherine
Mullen, paid a touching tribute to her school, her classmates,
and her teachers. The theme of her farewell address,
"Shadows on the Mountains," was appropriate for the
occasion and well expressed. The valedictory, in minor
key, as the opening stanzas show, elicited much applause
from an appreciative audience:

> There's a shadow on the mountain,
> And a sigh floats through the air,

Like the voice of anguish resting
O'er the fair scene mirrored there.
Such a shadow on the mountain
Brings a burden to my heart—
Can you not understand it,
Have you never felt it smart?

After voicing for herself and for her companions the nameless questionings that come at the turning aside from school to enter into the world's harder discipline, she begged from her teachers a remembrance at the holy hour of prayer:

"When in the twilight's evening glow you wend your way to the quiet chapel, where we, too, so often in the cloudless days of youth have gone with willing steps and loving hearts to breathe our fervent and humble petitions; when kneeling in the mellow glow of the ever watchful sanctuary lamp, breathe a prayer for your absent but grateful children."

The academy was fortunate in having at that time Sister Mary Raphael McArdle on its faculty. Sister, a distinguished English scholar, was most successful in imparting to her students something of the enthusiasm and appreciation which she felt for good literature. As a means of fostering an interest in reading, Sister Raphael organized and directed, as an extra-curricular activity, the *Reading Circle Review,* a kind of literary magazine.

The first number of volume one, dated February 27, 1896, contains an account of the initial meeting of the Circle on January 27 of that year. Essays and studies on Sir Thomas More, Milton, St. Catherine of Alexandria, St. Cecilia, and Dante have been preserved, in a book still extant; these are done in beautiful, meticulous penmanship, which reminds one of the finely illuminated manuscripts of the Irish monks.

Now in the speed and hurry of present day living and even of present day learning, many of the finer accomplishments, including good handwriting, have been crowded out of the curriculum. Legible penmanship in these days is almost a lost art; so true is this that it has become a necessary and quite universal requirement that students hand in all themes and term papers in typewritten form.

Besides the essays already mentioned, one notices in this book that a contemporary statesman and lecturer, William Jennings Bryan, was the subject of some of the discussions and themes assigned to the girls of the club. Mr. Bryan was just beginning to attract attention by the promulgation of his views on the political situation of the day. His advocacy of free coinage of silver made him a popular candidate, a few years later, for the presidency, especially among the people living in the silver states of the West.

Another local event of importance, which took place each year from '96 to the turn of the century, was the coming of the Catholic soldiers from Fort Logan to attend midnight Mass on Christmas eve. The soldiers marched into the chapel, two and two, as their band played the *Adeste Fideles*. Those soldier boys, so far from their loved ones at the Christmas season, must have appreciated the privilege of attending midnight Mass and the courtesy, too, of the sisters, who took pleasure in serving them hot coffee after Mass. Sister Corona Griesbach, who lived at the Heights during those years, related with vivid remembrance the Christmas spirit and hospitality in days now quite remote.

With the passing of the years, events worthy of being chronicled, if this were a general history, were taking place at home and abroad. Though these happenings were often adverse, Colorado made every effort not only to survive the stress and strain but to advance by developing the natural resources of the state.

The tourist or casual visitor of today recognizes immediately that Coloradans take a particular pride in their state. One must admit that there are solid reasons for this appreciation since the state, ranking among the largest in the Union, is noted for its mineral resources and for the remarkable scenic beauty of its national parks winding their wide expanses amid the breath-taking grandeur of the up-

lifted masses of the Rockies. In addition to these advantages, Colorado has an invigorating, health-giving climate
which has lured many to a permanent residence in the state.

Even in a cursory survey, one finds that Loretto Heights
was interrelated with much that is now considered historic
in Colorado. On April 15, 1892, the Colorado blue spruce
and the blue columbine were adopted as the state tree and
flower. When two months later Loretto Heights had its
first exhibition, a feature of that commencement week was
the planting of the blue spruce and the blue columbine on
that part of the grounds which today constitute the sunken
gardens which surround the grotto of our Lady of Lourdes.
Some of the pines planted at that time are now the most
admired trees on the campus, the marvel of all lovers of
the beautiful in nature.

In the summer of 1894, roses were blooming for the
first time in the flower garden of the academy. Sister Columba Gallavan watched the unfolding of the first rose, and,
plucking it at just the right time, she packed it with care
and sent it to Sister Pancratia in far-away Montgomery.
Sister Pancratia, deeply affected by the message the rose
brought, placed it before the Tabernacle where it remained
for two days. Later she sent it to her close friend, Sister
Mary Linus, who, after cherishing it for thirty-eight
years, finally made the sacrifice and placed it among the
historic mementoes in the archives at the Motherhouse.

The sisters now living at Loretto Heights cannot remember a time when they did not enjoy the privilege of
having their own post office. Perhaps they have never given
a thought to the advantages which this federal service brings
to the large family at the Heights so dependent upon the
prompt arrival of the morning and afternoon mails.

Just thirty-seven years, eight months, and ten days
after the city of Denver was given its first commissioned
postmaster, Henry Allen, records show that on September
28, 1896, Sister Bartholomew, officially known as Catherine
Nooning, was appointed the first commissioned postmaster
of Loretto Heights. Her appointment came scarcely four

years after that first dramatic entrance into residence at the new academy on the memorable afternoon and evening of November 2, 1891. This post office was called Loretto, Colorado. Whoever knew Sister Bartholomew can readily understand with what enthusiasm she entered upon the duties of this office which she held until her death on January 29, 1915.

Sister Bartholomew was in all truth one of the pioneer sisters at Loretto Heights. She was a woman of endurance and initiative. Whenever there was something to be done, she was always one of the first to put her hand to the task. She was one of that group of sisters who helped Mother Pancratia to select the site for Loretto Heights. She was the first who saw the sun break through the clouds on that day, snowy as it was; she was the first sister to harness old "Daisy"; the first to climb into the one-seated rig; the first to take up the lines and guide the horse to Littleton to pick up the mail. This last achievement became Sister Bartholomew's daily task for five years, in rain or shine, in snow or sleet, in wind or calm; always with her was her *fidus Achates*, Sister Columba Gallavan. Naturally when the post office was established, it was Sister Bartholomew who first carried on the official business.

Post offices have a journalistic atmosphere. They are the media through which passes the written or printed word to an immense clientele. Letters, magazines, newspapers, books, in fact, any written or printed matter is a record of someone's thoughts, someone's ideas, destined for others to read. The post office is the distributing center, with a chief officer, who directs the matter confided to the office, into its various channels.

After the death of Sister Bartholomew, Sister Valena, officially known as Mildred C. Eppler, served as acting postmaster from January 29 to July 10, 1915, when she received from Washington her appointment to the office. In the fall of 1927, Sister Valena was transferred to Loretto Academy, El Paso, Texas, and Sister Constantia (officially, Constantia Schaub) was appointed acting postmaster, October 11, 1927. On January 14, 1928, she received from the

Post Office Department, Washington, D. C., her appointment as postmaster; this position she held until her death, October 5, 1933.

Sister Bathildes, the deputy, succeeded to the duties of the postmaster after the death of Sister Constantia, and on November 10, 1933, she was authorized to take over the office as acting postmaster. On February 14, 1934, Sister Bathildes, official name, Magdalene Skees, received from Washington her permanent appointment to the office. This came almost as a valentine from Uncle Sam; perhaps Sister considers it such; but valentine or not, Sister is still holding, with entire satisfaction to her patrons, the position of trust to which she was appointed on St. Valentine's day.

Chapter XIII

THE SUCCEEDING EIGHT YEARS

While Colorado was contributing its full share in making not only local but even national history, the faculty at Loretto Heights Academy was quietly dreaming dreams and pursuing plans for a greater and better school which would meet the changing standards and requirements of the educational world. Capable teachers, teachers with spiritual ideals, scholastic ability, and personality, make a school. Part of the duty which devolved on the various superiors and directresses was to foresee the needs of the institution and provide the best available instructors for each department.

Sometimes one is tempted to think that it is only now in this age of so-called progress in which the teacher's best efforts are divided between the class room and the university, in the endeavor to amass credits and secure the necessary degrees, that the best teachers are functioning. An intelligent investigation of the work done in the schools in past years will often disabuse one of this mistaken notion. The record of standards attained in former years proves that "there were great men before Agamemnon."

When Mother Praxedes became Mother Superior of the Society, she, with her Council, by arranging to concentrate the indebtedness of the whole Society and negotiate a loan to cover the amount, had done a great deal to bring financial security to the various branch houses and in particular to Loretto Heights. But successful drama requires more than a leading character. The silent actors, the supporting cast, even the stage crew contribute toward making the whole play a success. It is the same in a religious community. Some members play a major lead, others have minor assignments; but who can say which is the important, which the lesser role? The contributions of those who never appear in any important act form the bulwark of every religious community.

A community of teaching sisters must have many members who are not employed in the classroom. During the nineties and even later, there were sisters at the Heights who labored hard and bore up cheerfully under the sacrifices which of necessity were theirs. The years hurry on like a stream of fast-flowing water whose tide never returns; in their passing they carry into obscurity names which should not be forgotten. The sisters of the Heights community who supervised dormitories, wardrobes, kitchen, refectories, laundry, and poultry yard were capable women who performed these duties for years and added their goodly contribution to the success of the menage. These sisters, while being chiefly responsible for the material comfort and welfare of the students, taught them many a lesson in household management, cleanliness, order, and faithfulness to duty. The names of Sister Flora McCauley, Sister Antoinette Logsdon, Sister Jovita Mills, Sister Dominic Early, Sister Mary Luke Barrett, and Sister Floscella Keating must not be passed over in these pages; the names of these sisters are hallowed among the girls for whom they labored—heroines all, makers of history, who are still concerned, it is hopefully believed, even in their everlasting home, for the success of Loretto Heights.

Another name belonging to those early days and deserving mention in this history of Loretto Heights is that of Sister Mary Agnes Flynn, who contributed generously to the welfare of the community by her care of the charges assigned her—the chapel, the chaplain's dining room and living quarters; and in later years by her service in the sisters' sewing room. At the present time, Sister Mary Agnes, though retired, still gives her full share to the community by her daily observance of all the chapel exercises.

Sister Mary Helena Cambron who came to Loretto Heights on the first Friday of September, 1897, from the Motherhouse, belongs to this galaxy of names. What a record she has made during all the years which have elapsed since then! Guiding, counselling, chiding, teaching the girls among whom she has carried on her duties, but working and praying all the while; and she is still carrying on, in much the same way, laboring with her hands but with her heart wholly in heaven. Why should not the old girls at their return to alma mater remember her as they do?

Loretto Heights Academy was not a country day school, it was a country boarding school. The sisters living there in the early days still remember the many opportunities which came their way of acquiring varied experiences: going on walking excursions with the girls, overseeing playground activities, arranging and even inventing evening games, presiding over reading circles, keeping order in the dormitories, teaching darning and sewing—these were just a few of the extra-curricular activities which they counted among their duties.

As the school became gradually better known, the enrollment increased. Accurate information of the attendance goes back to the year 1901 when Sister Ludmilla was bookkeeper; her ledgers and day books, still on file, are reliable records of the first decades of this century. The reader who enjoys such data will find the following figures interesting. The table shows the number of boarders in residence in each of the eight years, also the number taking music and art.

Year	Boarders	Music	Art	Specialties
1901, June	76	60	8	
1902, June	126	100	12	
1903, June	134	97	15	
1904, June	116	97	22	
1905, June	100	80	20	
1906, June	123	96	20	
1907, June	102	75	20	Vocal 25; Com'l 15
1908, June	127	90	12	Vocal 50; German 8
				Elocution 10

During these years the enrollment fluctuated, the greatest increase being in 1902; in 1903 the apex of those years was reached. The music department, in comparison with the entire enrollment, was large; the number of students taking art was relatively large. Music, art, vocal, elocution, and commercial subjects were not included in the regular course of study, hence they entailed extra fees.

This tabulation shows that, even though Colorado was still considered a part of the "wild and woolly West," parents and guardians were eager that their daughters and wards should have not only a solid religious training and secular education but also the refining and cultural subjects.

As school drew to a close in 1904, a program of closing exercises, more ambitious than any hitherto presented, extended over several days. The elocution contest was open to the public on Sunday morning, June 5. Nine young ladies competed for the gold medal award, which the judges conferred on Miss Louise Cochran of Denver. In the afternoon of the same day the younger children presented a cantata which was much enjoyed, especially by the parents of the little ones.

On Wednesday evening at seven o'clock the juniors gave a literary and musical recital; the seniors appeared in a similar program on Friday evening, June 10. While the excellent work of the art students was on display in the attractive studio during the whole of commencement week, on June 12, the youthful artists took special pleasure in greeting their friends at the open house and calling attention to the pieces on display which, in their opinion, were worthy of notice.

Monday, June 13, was given over to the alumnae homecoming. The graduates of the school were by this time sufficient in number to warrant an alumnae association, which had for its immediate purpose the formation of a bond among the old girls and with their school. This would seem to be an important date in the history of the Alumnae of Loretto Heights. At four-thirty in the afternoon a columbine luncheon was served in one of the dining rooms of the academy. An immense bouquet of columbines was the floral center piece; all the decorations were in harmony with the state flower, even to the hand-painted place cards which were adorned with the graceful columbine. The state flower retains its popularity as a decoration at luncheons and other social gatherings. Not so long ago, in fact in May, 1941, the *Rocky Mountain News* in the society column announced a special entertainment which was centered around the columbine.

The Reverend Richard Brady, chaplain of the academy, and the Reverend H. R. McCabe of Idaho Springs were guests of the alumnae during that afternoon. In the course of the luncheon the following toasts were given: "Our Chaplain," Miss Nellie Finnerty; "Our Alumnae," Mrs. P. Cullen; "Our Alma Mater," Mrs. E. J. Howard; "Our teachers," Miss K. Gilgallon; "The Silent Partners of the Alumnae," Mrs. E. Weckbaugh; "Our Bachelor Girls," Miss Eileen Sullivan; "Our Matrons," Miss K. Mullen; "Our School Days," Miss May Mullen; "The Alumnae of the Future," Miss Honor K. Breen.

On Tuesday morning, June 14, a high Mass of thanksgiving was sung by the Reverend H. R. McCabe. The convent choir sang *Gerald's Mass*. In the afternoon of that same day at two-thirty the graduating exercises took place. Miss Ethelle Manning Corson of Denver, Colorado (Mrs. William H. Hermes of San Diego, California); Miss Mable Gordon Grimes of Pueblo (Mrs. J. J. Murphy of Oakland, California); and Miss Marie Cecilia Foley of Denver (Sister Kathleen Marie, Loretto, Kentucky) received graduating honors.

The Most Reverend N. C. Matz, D.D., after conferring the diplomas, delivered an eloquent address on the advantages of Christian education. He urged upon the graduates the necessity of lofty ideals and a high standard of conduct in order to counteract the materialistic tendencies of the age. In a word he exhorted them to follow in their daily lives the example of the queen of women, Mary Immaculate.

The words which Bishop Matz uttered many years ago at that commencement address, June 14, 1904, bear a close resemblance to the exhortation which the Most Reverend Urban J. Vehr might speak today in addressing the college graduates of Loretto Heights. Every age has its materialistic tendencies; our bishops and priests, recognizing the evils, are zealous in urging the members of their flocks to prepare themselves to withstand the trend of the times by a thorough knowledge of Catholic faith and morals.

One of the members of the class of 1904, Miss Marie Foley, understood even from her graduation that the relationship with her school did not close when she received her diploma. Marie identified herself with Loretto Heights after she left school by her activity in the alumnae association. The other members, recognizing her efficient leadership, chose her more than once as their president and representative at the conventions of the International Federation of Catholic Alumnae. Closely associated with Marie in all that pertained to the welfare of their school were her lifelong friends, the Misses Fallon, Margaret and Anna.

After holding for several years a responsible business position in Denver, Miss Foley, on the death of her mother, entered the community of her former teachers, the Sisters of Loretto at the Foot of the Cross, receiving the name in religion of Sister Kathleen Marie. Some time after the unexpected death of Mother Ann Marita, the secretary general, the members of the General Council appointed Sister Kathleen Marie to fill the unexpired term. At the time of the next general election of council officers, Sister Kathleen Marie was elected by the delegates of the general chapter to the office of assistant and secretary in the General Council.

Three girls who are remembered for their many good qualities—Mamie Mackin of Omaha; Elisa Salazar (Mrs. A. Moloney of St. Louis); and Mayo Bransom (Mrs. Fayette Stevens)—were graduated in June, 1905. The Sisters at the Heights love to recall the spirit of loyalty which existed and has continued to exist among these former students. This devotedness has been manifested not only to the faculty of their beloved school but to every Sister of Loretto, whether personally known to them or not.

In June, 1906, Lenore Durkee and Marian Harwood were the only two to be graduated. Miss Durkee became later Mrs. Percy Pickenpaugh. Miss Marian Harwood kept in touch with the alumnae for several years, even as late as 1916.

In 1907 four girls were graduated, Grace Judge (Mrs. G. Eckert of Ashtabula, Ohio); Estelle Desserich (Mrs. G. H. Plunkett of Denver); Marie Enneking (Mrs. Robert Ilg of Chicago); and Anna Dick. The class of 1908 had six members: Marie Murphy, Vina Fern Byron, Rebecca Henriques, Dora McCoy, Salina Casey, and Irene Hartford. Marie Murphy later entered the novitiate of the Sisters of Loretto; with the religious habit she received the name Sister Marie Clyde. For many years after finishing her novitiate in Kentucky, she taught at Nerinx Hall, Webster Groves, Missouri, and later in the English department at Webster College. Since September, 1935, Sister Marie Clyde has been one of the efficient professors in the English department at Loretto Heights College. As a matter of history it is interesting to know that Mr. Jeremiah Murphy, Sister Marie Clyde's uncle, owned in the early days the land upon which the college now stands.

Rebecca Henriques of the class of '08 became Mrs. Weiman of Fort Sumpter, New Mexico; Dora McCoy, Mrs. Charles Maddox of Waverly, Illinois; Irene Hartford, Mrs. Ben Williams of Denver; Salina Casey, Mrs. Joseph Wirka of Madison, Wisconsin; Vina Fern Byron is deceased.

During these years the academy continued to prosper. The work of the faculty was more inclusive than simply teaching the assigned subjects. Their duty, as the sisters understood it, was to educate both mind and heart; the development of character was of prime importance. The students of all grades were taught self-control and respect for authority, without which there is no education. Each girl was advised to study her own nature, to know its weakness and its power, that she might strengthen the one and make good use of the other. Whatever the child's propensities, the sisters believed that acts repeated with patience, time after time, finally uproot what is undesirable and implant the beginnings of better traits, which in due season will develop into the ideal character. The well-planned schedule of the student's daily routine of work and play and little homely tasks helped to attain the object sought: a conscience unswervingly upright, a will always seeking the good, a heart sympathetic and devoted, and a bearing never undignified.

While inculcating standards and ideals such as these, the superior and sisters at the Heights were practical in planning improvements which would add to the efficiency of the institution and the comfort of both faculty and students. From the record of proceedings of the Board of Trustees of Loretto Heights, one learns that on April 8, 1908, a meeting of this board was called for the purpose of discussing the installation of machinery for a cold storage and ice plant. The members being agreed on the necessity of this installation, bids were obtained, and on April 18, ten days after the meeting, the contract was given to Mr. George L. Vail of Denver. This cold storage and ice plant, approximating a cost of $3,000, has been a boon through all these years to the culinary department and the dining rooms of the school.

In September of the same year, Mother Pancratia called another meeting of this board, in order to submit plans for a lighting system for the lawns and playgrounds of the school. The terms submitted by Mr. W. C. Sterne of the Arapahoe Electric Light and Power Company of Littleton, Colorado, were accepted. According to the contract, the company agreed to erect seven poles, lamps, wires, and meters at a cost of about $500. Later, in 1925, during Mother Eustachia Elder's first year as superior, this lighting system was further perfected by the installation of two powerful flood lights which illuminated the tower and the front of the administration building.

It was about this time that the veil worn by the Sisters of Loretto underwent a change. The present headdress, which was adopted on January 1, 1909, needs no description; an idea of the former veil may be gleaned from some of the pictures shown in this volume. It meant a sacrifice for some of the older sisters to make the change for they loved the red hearts, which adorned the front of the veil and symbolized the sufferings of Jesus and the sorrows of Mary.

Although this change in the veil took place some years ago, many a sister has preserved among her treasured keepsakes a pair of these beautifully embroidered hearts, mementoes of those other days when in youth she offered herself generously to a life of loving self-denial and service.

Sister Eudocia Chacon, one of the pioneer sisters long associated with Loretto Heights, took great interest in jotting down in her diary the everyday happenings in her community life, especially the dates on which various members of the Order died. In the pages of this book was found the entry: "Sister Ann Van Aschen, the five hundred twenty-second sister to die in the Society at the Mother-house, December 8, 1908, and the last to be buried in the black veil and hearts." A few pages after this is another notation: "Sister Mary Ann Costello was the five hundred twenty-third sister to die in the Society at Bethlehem, Kentucky, January 20, 1909, and the first to be buried in the new veil."

From the time that the sisters and students had taken up their residence in the academy building, the large room used in '42 as the college library, served until 1912 as the chapel. During the first years it was sufficiently large, but when the enrollment of students increased and also the number of sisters in the community, it was necessary to consider the erection of a separate chapel building. No little thought was given to this matter, the most important building project since the erection of the school. After much deliberation, it was finally decided to construct a building, the upper floor of which would be the chapel and the lower, the auditorium.

The Board of Trustees of Loretto Heights met on August 16, 1909, and authorized the drawing up of plans for the chapel and auditorium. About three months later, November 10, at a special meeting of this board, Mr. F. E. Edbrooke, the architect, submitted plans and specifications; these were carefully considered by the various members and accepted. Four months later, March 10, 1910, the contract between the Des Jardins-Bundy Building and Manufacturing Company and the Loretto Literary and Benevolent

Institution of Colorado for the erection of the chapel and auditorium was submitted to the board. The sisters who were the trustees of the board agreed to the contract and directed the president and secretary to sign the document authorizing the erection of a building costing about $40,000.

The chapel, which was finished in June, 1911, is considered an architectural gem. This was the last great undertaking which Mother Pancratia saw completed for the Heights. Into the plans of the chapel she put her best efforts. Mother Pancratia was most devoted to God and to everything that pertained to His external worship. She could in all truth utter the words of the Psalmist: "I have loved, O Lord, the beauty of Thy House and the place where Thy glory dwelleth."

Shortly after the chapel was opened for worship, the Stations of the Cross were erected in time for the August retreat, 1911, by the chaplain, the Reverend Richard Brady. The following letter asking permission to erect the stations is a reprint of the original:

Loretto Heights Academy
Loretto, Colorado, August 2, 1911

Right Reverend dear Bishop:

I, the undersigned Chaplain of Loretto Heights Academy, with the consent of the Superior, Mother Mary Edith, hereby humbly request the permission to erect the Stations of the Way of the Cross in the Chapel of Our Lady of Loretto adjoining this academy.

Respectfully,
Richard Brady, Chaplain
Mother Mary Edith, Superior

Right Reverend N. C. Matz, D.D.
Bishop of Denver

Successive superiors at the Heights have contributed to the beauty of the chapel of Our Lady of Loretto. Mother Clarasine Walsh had the chapel beautifully frescoed and the sanctuary redecorated. Mother Mary Linus, who succeeded Mother Clarasine as superior, installed the magnificent pipe organ. Mother Eustachia, the next superior, in the fall of 1926 ordered seventeen more stained glass windows from the same firm in Munich from which the original six windows had been purchased. The nine windows on the left of the worshiper as one faces the main altar depict Our Lady in some of the eventful scenes of her life such as the annunciation, the visitation, the birth of Our Lord, the flight into Egypt, the presentation in the temple, and the finding of Jesus in the temple. Other windows represent Our Lord in his private and public life: on the right, or epistle side, scenes are depicted from the sorrowful and glorious life of Our Lord. The last two windows show the crowning joys of the Blessed Virgin, her assumption and coronation. Mother Consuelo Baumer was responsible for the life-like crucifix which now stands in the sanctuary.

Others who had windows donated in their honor or to their memory were Right Reverend J. P. Machebeuf, Mother Praxedes Carty, Mother Pancratia Bonfils, the deceased Sisters of the Loretto Heights community by Daniels and Fishers, Knights of Columbus, Mr. and Mrs. G. A. Enneking, Mr. Robert E. Morrison, Mrs. T. W. Engles, Mr. and Mrs. John A. Keefe, Mr. and Mrs. John K. Mullen, Mr. and Mrs. Charles D. McPhee, Wm. and Martha Elder, Mr. and Mrs. M. J. O'Fallon, the College '24, '25, '26, the Academy '26, and the Alumnae of Loretto Heights.

The Rose Window of the Mater Dolorosa in the organ loft and the first six of the beautiful stained glass windows were set in place in June, 1911. They and the other seventeen windows later placed were the work of the world renowned firm of "Myer" of Munich. The gorgeous colors of these windows are perfect, the tints rich and harmonious, the blending of light and shades exquisite, and the beauty and dignity in the figures are such that one never grows tired of admiring them. The Stations of the Cross from the same firm are artistic and devotional.

On either side of the main altar are statues of full-length angels, graceful in design and delicate in coloring, each of them supporting a sanctuary lamp. One of these statues was donated by the academy students in honor of the centenary celebration of the Loretto Society in 1912;

the other was given by the alumnae of the school. During Mother Clarasine's superiorship, a holy water font held by a kneeling angel was donated by Sister Willian Joseph in honor of her parents, Mr. and Mrs. J. A. Garcia.

In this new chapel, radiant with illuminations, the first Mass was sung in early June of 1911. Into it the white-veiled young worshipers filed. The sisters knelt with bowed heads, their souls filled with sentiments of mingled joy and devotion during the Holy Sacrifice. After the Mass, Bishop Matz ascended the marble steps of the sanctuary to give the Apostolic blessing.

Mother Mary Edith, who had been directress of the academy for several years, was appointed superior when Mother Pancratia was transferred to St. Mary's Academy in Denver, in the summer of 1910. This admirable religious and highly intellectual educator was superior at Loretto Heights from 1910 to 1913. The new chapel was built dur-ing her administration, as was also the auditorium. Mother Mary Edith took special pride in pointing out the com-fortable seats in the Little Theatre situated under the chapel. In those days, these seats were quite a luxury. At the close of the school year in 1913, Mother Mary Edith was transferred to Loretto Academy in Kansas City, where she was superior until 1919.

Sister Dolorine Morrison was in charge of the school at the Heights from the summer of 1910 until October, 1911, when she went to St. Mary's to direct the newly opened academy on Fourteenth and Pennsylvania Streets. Sister Eulalia McFarland replaced Sister Dolorine as directress at the Heights; but, after a few months, Sister Miriam Judd was placed in charge of the school and fulfilled the duties of that office until she was sent to the Catholic University the next fall. Sister Faber Wheat was directress from September, 1912, until the summer of 1913.

At the close of the scholastic year, 1909, four girls were graduated: Ella Menke, Ethel Enright, Grace Warshauer, and Lottie Fowles. In June, 1910, three students finished: Margaret Connolly, Genevieve Morrison, and Ida Heibler.

The following year, Alma Redmond, Casilda Salazar, Gladys Menke, Mary Cassell, Nora Schang, and Violet Rapson formed the class. And in June, 1912, the centenary year of the Loretto Sisters, the largest class thus far in the life of the school was graduated: Emma Archuletta, Ruth Carroll, Dorothy Adams, Nellie Bowles, Eulalia Loomis, Angeline Durocher, Catherine Brady, Elizabeth Prince, Agnes Neuer, Hazel Menke, and Ismena Roper.

The class of 1912 marked the coming of age of Loretto Heights, that is, this class was the twenty-first senior class, counting from that first commencement in 1892. The school was firmly established; it was old enough to have traditions; it had weathered the first difficult years and was now in a fair way to succeed and prosper.

Chapter XIV

THE LORETTO ORDER CELEBRATES
ITS CENTENARY

The first hundred years of a religious community are all important in its history. They are formative years during which the members shape both their spirit and their work. Time is a relative term. In world history one hundred years is a brief period; in the history of a religious Order, it is a span sufficiently long for a sisterhood to establish itself and give proof that it has a place in the work of the Church. The Sisters of Loretto at the Foot of the Cross, as religious teachers in various grades of schools, gave evidence, in those first one hundred years of their existence, that they were accomplishing the special work that was theirs from the time of the inauspicious beginnings, in far-away Kentucky, in the early part of the nineteenth century.

It is customary for a religious Order to celebrate its hundredth year, not through a desire of calling attention to the work of the years, but rather as a thank offering to God through Whom and in Whom and by Whom the work was begun and continued.

In accordance with the general plan of the Motherhouse, all the Loretto schools commemorated with appropriate ceremonies this important event. In the larger houses and academies, the celebrations were more elaborate and extended over several days; in the parochial grade and high schools, the observance of the centennial year began with a Requiem Mass for the deceased members of the Order; this was followed by student programs—to which were invited the parents of the pupils and the friends of the sisters—commemorating in general the work of the Lorettines and emphasizing the history of the particular house or school.

The Sisters at Loretto Heights and St. Mary's Academy planned to mark their centennial by turning their attention first of all to the Lorettines who had labored and died in Colorado. It was fitting that their thoughts at the time of this anniversary should center on those sisters who had borne the hardships of the early, trying years which had tested the endurance of even the most devoted and zealous. Accordingly a Requiem High Mass, offered on Monday, April 22, 1912, for the deceased members of the Loretto Society inaugurated the centennial celebration. A few hours later, the remains of the ten Lorettines who had been buried in Mt. Calvary, Denver, were reverently removed to the plot of ground which had been set aside on the property at Loretto Heights and consecrated as the convent cemetery. Their gravestones bear the names of Sister Davina Burns, Sister Augustine Chavez, Sister Peter Joseph Benevedz, Sister Ignatius James, Sister Jerome Murphy, Sister Joachim Houlehin, Sister Olivet McLean, Sister Nerinckx O'Neil, Sister Benigna Brady, and Sister Victorine Renshaw.

Before the bodies were transferred from Mt. Calvary, seven Sisters of Loretto had been buried in the cemetery at Loretto Heights. Sister Josephina Ortiz, who died at Colorado Springs, February 12, 1896, was the first to be interred, and Sister Frances O'Leary, who died November 5, 1898, at the Heights, was the second; then later Sister Teresa Augusta Owings, who died in 1899; Sister Augusta Wall, in 1907; and Sister Eutropia Toolen, in 1910, also members of the community at Loretto Heights. The following sisters, belonging to other Lorettine communities, were interred at the Heights: Sister Mary Paschal, directress in Santa Fe, having come to Denver for medical attention, died at St. Joseph's Hospital, December 9, 1903; Sister Carmelita Hodapp, a member of the community of St. Mary's Academy, died in 1909; and Sister Claudia McCauley, who died at St. Mary's School, Colorado Springs in 1904.

The list of the Sisters of Loretto who had died in Colorado from the first foundation in 1864 to that eventful day,

April 22, 1912, when the mortal remains of all were gathered into the convent cemetery at the Heights, numbered eighteen. All these sisters, however, had not labored in the Colorado missions; some had been sent from the East in quest of health but had come too late to be benefited by the climate.

With the exception of a few sisters who were buried in Roselawn cemetery in Pueblo, all the Lorettines who have died in Colorado have been buried in this place. As the years have passed, the gate of the cemetery has opened again and again to receive into this silent abode now one, now another of the sisters who have labored for a longer or shorter period at Loretto Heights, until in the jubilee year of this institution, forty-seven graves surround the large Crucifix which occupies a conspicuous place in the cemetery. Loving, devoted hands have given such care to this consecrated place that the one-time arid plot has blossomed like the rose; flowers in their season beautify the abode of the mortal remains of friends who have completed their earthly journey and who now, though silent, speak their salutary message to the living who come to visit this quiet place and learn wisdom from the dead.

As far as available records show, Sister Olivet McLean was the first girl educated at St. Mary's, Denver, who entered the Loretto Novitiate at the Motherhouse in Kentucky. Concerning her death a newspaper clipping of that time gives this information:

Sister M. Olivet died at St. Mary's Academy of consumption yesterday, November 16, (1888). Although but a little over twenty years of age, yet her young life was spent in that noble work of love and charity for which the Sisters of Loretto, of which she was a member, are noted. The funeral will be held tomorrow, Father Carr officiating. Sister Olivet was loved by all, and her pale sweet face will be sadly missed by those who knew her.

Next to their dead, the Sisters of Loretto were mindful in their centennial year of the living. A High Mass was offered on Tuesday, April 23, for their benefactors and friends. Many of these good friends were present at the

Holy Sacrifice to share in its celebration and to offer their congratulations and felicitations to the sisters.

During the period of the centenary celebration, the work of the Sisters of Loretto received commendation both in the press and from friends. The Most Reverend Camillus Paul Maes, Bishop of Covington, Kentucky, wrote on that occasion:

A teaching order from the beginning, Loretto has remained true to this highest of missions. She has never faltered, no matter what the obstacles, and only God knows the difficulties with which she has had to contend. She is alert and progressive, apace with every advance, aiming ever at the Christian ideal of education.

It is with the strength of a century of sacrifice and faithful service, of renewed vigor and redoubled fervor, with the same spirit that animated her venerable founders, Loretto comes to her centennial to add the gleam of the first purely American star to the galaxy of the religious communities in the Church.

The *Loretto Pioneer,* the literary magazine of the students of Loretto Heights Academy, has preserved in its centenary number, a poem written for the occasion.

LORETTO HEIGHTS

A palace it seems, where the artists' dreams
    Have framed themselves in stone
On a stately hill where the winds at will
    From the snow-crowned mountains blown
Come, bringing afar from the clouds and star
    A message of joy divine,
It stands alone, that beautiful home,
    Where faith and virtue shine.

The years are few since sprang to view
    Its halls and stately towers;
But written above are the deeds of love
    That have marked the passing hours;
And lingers still on the dear old hill
    Each pupil's tenderest prayer;
For they loved the Heights where the holiest lights
    Have sought them and blessed them there.

The Rockies, sublime, that laugh at time,
    In the hazy distance gleam,
And the thoughts that start in the inmost heart—
    Every golden, girlish dream—
Have a twilight glow that none may know
    Save those who have spent youth's brief day
Near these mountains grand, in this golden land,
    Where the heart doth unconsciously pray.

'Tis the holy thought, with blessing wrought,
    This thought of Eternity,
That the Heights inspire with that glowing fire
    That marks true charity;
And science and art have done their part
    To aid God's holy plan,
To shelter and win, and save from sin,
The restless heart of man.

True knowledge is blest, for 'tis but the quest
    After everlasting light;
'Tis wisdom calls in those stately halls,
    And it speaks forth in tones of might;
'Tis the cultured mind that is most inclined
    God's wondrous power to praise,
And no matter the loss, to bless the cross
    That reveals His most blessed ways.

Ah, stately home, so well thou art known,
    Thy praises have been sung,
In many a soul, as the swift years roll,
    By many a golden tongue.
Thy shining fame has enrolled thy name
    With the brightest of all our lights,
Long may you stand, so proud and grand,
    Our own Loretto Heights.

                        L.S.

The centennial number of the *Loretto Pioneer* does credit to the editorial staff of the magazine, whose members were Emma Archuleta, Ruth Carroll, Angeline Durocher, Elizabeth Prince, Ismena Roper, Eulalia Loomis, Dorothy Adams, Agnes Neuer, Hazel Menke, and Nellie Bowles, all of the class of 1912.

Centennial day, April 25, 1912, had a double significance for Loretto Heights, for besides commemorating that memorable April 25, in the year 1812, when the first three Lorettines pledged themselves in the rude Church of St. Charles near Hardin's Creek, Kentucky, to a life of poverty, chastity, and obedience, the new chapel, which had been in use since June, 1911, was to be dedicated. Perhaps the ceremony of dedication had been postponed that it might take place on that historical date.

At six o'clock on the morning of April 25, 1912, the Most Reverend Nicholas C. Matz, Bishop of Denver, offered the community Mass in the convent chapel; that same morning, at ten o'clock, assisted by twenty priests, the Bishop dedicated the new chapel under the title of "Our Lady of Loretto."

After the dedication ceremonies, solemn High Mass, *coram pontifice,* was celebrated by the Reverend Richard Brady, chaplain of the Academy; the deacon was the Reverend H. R. McCabe; sub-deacon, the Reverend Charles J. Carr; assistant priest, the Reverend J. J. Cronin, C.M.; deacons of honor to the Most Reverend Bishop were the Reverend A. Schuler, S.J., and the Reverend J. J. Brown, S.J.; masters of ceremonies were the Reverend P. A. Phillips and the Reverend J. P. McDonough.

Other priests in the sanctuary were the Reverend T. M. Conway, M. P. Callanan, D. T. O'Dwyer, Edward Barry, S.J., Joseph Bruner, S.J., Garret J. Burke, Athanasius Hienfield, O.F.M., Agatho Strittmatter, O.S.B., Louis F. Hagus, William Donovan, Christopher Walsh, George Cone, and Patrick Riordon. The Reverend William O'Ryan preached the sermon for the occasion, an eloquent tribute to the work of the Sisters of Loretto, especially to their labors in the state of Colorado. The text chosen was "He that is mighty hath done great things to me and holy is His name." The Reverend speaker showed in a sketch of the Society, from its foundation to that date, and in a review of the lives of its most prominent members, the great things that God had worked through the Sisters of Loretto.

At noon, dinner was served to the clergy and guests in the spacious student dining room, which was artistically decorated in white and gold; the same color scheme was effectively carried out in the table appointments. The Reverend William O'Ryan, the toastmaster, introduced a number of the clergymen who gave wise and witty after-dinner talks in keeping with the celebration. The Reverend Edward Barry, S.J., the first speaker, reviewed the labors of the Sisters of Loretto in the field of education; going back to the very foundation of the Society, Father Barry showed that its members ever sought the fulfillment of God's will. The Reverend G. J. Burke, when introduced, surprised and delighted the guests by doing the unusual, namely, singing to an appreciative audience "Kathleen Mavourneen" and the "Last Rose of Summer."

These familiar songs must have made a special appeal to the Irish heart of Father O'Ryan, for, rising, he toasted the Sister of Loretto as the ideal of American womanhood. "The members of the Society," the speaker recalled, "were from the best families of the country—families that in Ireland and in England cast aside rank and wealth in order to preserve the Catholic faith, and for its sake suffered persecution and exile." Father O'Ryan emphasized the influence of such traditions on the character of a religious Society which in itself was so eminently American.

The Reverend D. T. O'Dwyer closed the dinner program by referring to the spiritual retreat which he had conducted for the pupils at Loretto a few weeks previously and expressing his hopes for that present generation of students who had the advantage of receiving their education in an institution where all the noblest ideals of life were held in veneration.

Mr. Joseph Newman, who for many years enjoyed an enviable reputation in Denver circles as an entertainer of high order, contributed to the pleasure of the guests by his ready wit, songs, and recitations. Every one who knows Colorado knows Joe Newman and the role he has filled as a much-sought contributor to good, amusing programs.

In the afternoon the students of the academy presented in the auditorium an historical pageant. Episodes, realistically portrayed, showed the sisters on their journey to Colorado, crossing the western prairies and the Rocky Mountains. Some of these scenes depicted tragedy and some showed glimmering hope; then, finally, the shimmering gold of ideal education was depicted vitalizing the hearts and souls of Colorado's young womanhood. Souvenir medals bearing on one side the image of Loretto's revered founder, the Reverend Charles Nerinckx, and on the reverse, the log cabin which was the cradle of the order, were presented to all the guests as well as a copy, beautifully bound, of the Centennial Ode, written by the gifted pen of Sister Mary Wilfred LaMotte, a Sister of Loretto, the author of *Flowers of the Cloister,* a book of poems. Sister Mary Wilfred, or Mother Wilfred, as she was known for many years, was a woman richly endowed with natural gifts; these, though outstanding, were all eclipsed by her pre-eminent virtues as a simple, humble religious.

LORETTO

1812——Centenary Ode——1912

Above the same arched firmament, so blue,
  Two distant shores the rolling sea embraces;
The same North star, in guidance always true,
  Whatever craft the watery highway traces,
A century has spanned that billowed deep,
  A century its chain of years hath lengthened,
One hundred times hath earth known bloom and sleep,
  One hundred links our claims on heaven have strengthened.

A heart heroic, saintly in its mold,
  A stranger, in an unknown way nought fearing,
Sought the stray sheep of his dear Master's fold,
  In forest depth—'mid pioneer's rough clearing.
From sacred duty sworn, at home, debarred,
  Constrained by laws, his priestly soul rejected,
He left that land, whose future was ill-starred,
  For one, where Heaven-sent tidings were expected.

More than one hundred fruitful years ago,
    Brave Nerinckx crossed that sea, in tearful yearning,
Our language even yet he did not know
    But zeal impelled with its resistless burning,
Hard was his lot in missionary field
    Lonely his life in unrequited labor,
But faith assured him of a future yield,
    When he, by Calvary, had won his Thabor.

Two single handed laborers soon found,
    Beyond their reach this vineyard of their choosing;
Tho' ripened harvests covered the vast ground
    Much of its rich fruit was their weakness losing,
Oh! If the growing lambs could be prepared
    For worthy life-work and eternal blessing,
If Christian teachers but their labors shared,
    A hope would gleam amid this dearth distressing.

Three young hearts waited for God's holy will,
    Waited, and hoped, and prayed without dejection,
They heard the spirit's voice, so small, so still,
    Already virtuous, they sought perfection.
As glimmer tremulous of light afar,
    Of mighty worlds may be the intimation,
So shown this hope, a small but potent star,
    The harbinger of Heaven's indication.

Earth threw no glamour o'er the thorny way,
    They saw but trials where their feet were treading;
They knew death's shadow would enshroud their day,
    Before the sun's rays prosperous could be shedding.
They were content; they sought not soft repose,
    Nor asked of God e'en purest consolation;
Theirs was the lofty aim the spirit knows,
    When love aspires to total consecration.

Like Bethlehem, their home was poor and bare,
    Rough forest logs their only sheltered dwelling.
Yet was this blest abode the house of prayer,
    Its atmosphere all worldly thoughts expelling,
Their garments homespun, work of unskilled hands,
    Devoid of comfort, elegance, or beauty.
Their fortunes but a stretch of untilled land,
    Their recreation but hard round of duty.

But nothing daunted, these three maidens sighed
 To see their choice heroic sealed by Heaven,
And with each other charitably vied
 To free their souls from earthly dross and leaven.
And Heaven's ear bent low; light banished gloom,
 A radiance filled their inmost souls with gladness,
Never could world its cast-off claim resume,
 Never again their hearts feel hopeless sadness.

The early springtide saw three veiled heads bow
 Low 'neath religious yoke, like blossoms tender
June roses decked the shrine and wreathed the brow,
 When two more made a joyful heart-surrender.
Warm August sun-rays o'er the altar gleamed
 When she, the sixth, in willing self-oblation
Secured the privilege of which she dreamed,
 And placed the heart beyond earth's desecration.

This was Loretto's birth. No saint's first choice,
 Could poorer be: on Providence dependent,
In what God loved; they too might well rejoice
 For he was poor, tho' of earth's King descendant.
Not always rapid, but with steps full sure,
 Loretto's march advanced towards western ocean,
God led the way with guilding hand secure,
 The Sisters followed with lives' devotion.

The forests lessened, hardy pioneers
 Blazed roads direct to settlements intended,
And as the highways grew defined and clear,
 The growing Sisterhood its work extended.
And thus in mountain-side and grassy plain,
 Loretto's standard was in meekness planted,
Though crude for years the soil, tho' small the gain,
 One soul sufficed—'twas souls alone they wanted.

But God is faithful, and the hundred-fold
 Promised to those who home and friends forsaking,
Seek heavenly treasures, neither bought nor sold.
 Permits them e'en of worldly goods partaking
To do His work; to spread His blessed name.
 Where once reigned ignorance and superstition,
To set cold hearts with love divine aflame,
 To win men's souls, while bettering their condition.

Now lapsing years to a century have grown,
    Both Founder and first members calmly resting,
In Heaven may know how well the seed was sown,
    How their successors are life's rude storm breasting.
Though stately walls the cabin home replace
    And far and near Loretto's branches bending,
The Via Crucis oft the Sisters trace,
    Still at the Cross with Mary, each attending.

They do not ask to lead unsaintly lives,
    Nor choose but flowers, while thorns are waiting.
Like bees, content in rude or crystal hives,
    Their golden honeystore no whit abating.
Apart from duties which the world may view
    Their daily lives are stamped with Mary's Dolor.
A high vocation must each soul pursue.
    Religious first, then teacher, friend, consoler.

O tiny seed! O labor's fruitful years!
    O chain, a century hath left unbroken!
Fulfillment of good Nerinckx prayers and tears.
    Work blest throughout with many a heavenly token.
The future may be trusted as the past
    While Providence your little bark is steering,
May power for good thro' earth's endurance last,
    And *souls,* Loretto's jewels, Heaven be nearing!
                    Sister Mary Wilfred, S.L.

"In this way," concludes an article in the centennial
number of the *Loretto Pioneer,* "was observed the hundredth anniversary of the founding of that Society, which
in distant Kentucky took its rise in poverty and humility.
It was a day of rejoicing for labors crowned with success
and victories won. But above all, it was a day of thanksgiving to Him whose protecting care had never failed those
faithful hearts which had trusted in Him. The day closed
with Benediction of the Blessed Sacrament and fervent
prayers that the Society would continue to grow and prosper; this it will do if true to the tradition of its founders."

Chapter XV

LORETTO BEGINS THE SECOND CENTURY

After the centenary celebrations, life in all the schools of the Society resumed its wonted pace. Activities in the scholastic affairs in the Academy at Loretto Heights returned to normal; the usual routine of daily tasks occupied both teachers and pupils for the remainder of that term since all realized that a careful performance of the duty of the hour was the best preparation for meeting the unusual occasional celebration such as a centenary year.

Though many encomiums had been heaped upon the academy, its teachers, and students, through the centennial days, the sisters were not too elated by public opinion, at best a fickle thing, for they were well aware that along the way many mistakes had been made, but from the mistakes profitable lessons, too, had been learned. With renewed courage and zeal they prepared to continue their work in education with the hope of bettering their best in previous years.

The fall months passed rapidly, and before anyone was aware the Christmas holidays were at hand. The majority of the students returned to their families for the vacation; others, who lived at great distances, remained at the Heights. This was for them a novel experience; to spend Christmas with their teachers was an event in the lives of those Loretto girls. The faculty, understanding child nature, made that a real Christmas for those away from home. Many an extra stocking was hung there alongside those of the expectant good little girls whom Santa Claus would be sure to visit.

New Year's resolutions were readily made and readily broken by the girls who vacationed at the school; cheerfully the shattered pledges were either remade or were replaced by new ones equally good. Resolutions have the nature of a tonic; being mainly restorative, they revive one's courage and assist one in going on until the goal is finally reached.

In all their training, the students were taught that the habit of determining to be good is a deciding factor in strengthening the will towards goodness. This was especially true in the nine girls, Alice Marie Davoren, Angelic Early, Helen Howard, Orpha Ritter, Frances Loomis, Frances Keefe, Helen Ross, Helen Enright, and Teresa Loisel Lange, who finished their high school course in June, 1913.

Some years after graduation, Angelic Early, now Mrs. F. J. Mushaben, took charge of her father's business, the Early Coffee Company; and Frances Keefe, at the death of her father, became the responsible manager of the Keefe Manufacturing and Investment Company. Both women have been devoted friends to the Sisters at Loretto Heights and benefactors of their alma mater.

Shortly after school closed, June 11, 1913, the Reverend Edward Clarke, for many years chaplain of the Glockner Sanitorium in Colorado Springs and brother of Bernard, James, and Philip Clarke of the Clarke Church Goods Company of Denver, became chaplain of Loretto Heights, replacing Monsignor Brady whom Bishop Matz had appointed Vicar General of the diocese and pastor of the Annunciation Church in Denver.

This change was followed in quick succession by others. Mother Mary Edith Loughran, who had been superior at the Heights for three years, received her appointment, July 16, 1913, as superior of Loretto Academy in Kansas City, Missouri; Mother Pancratia who had been superior of St. Mary's Academy, Denver, from July 16, 1910, was reappointed as superior of Loretto Heights. Sister Dolorine Morrison, directress at St. Mary's, returned to the Heights as directress of the academy. When classes were resumed in September that year, the students found that Reverend Edward Clarke, the chaplain, would guide them spiritually, Mother Pancratia would look after their material needs and comfort, and Sister Dolorine would direct them in their scholastic courses.

October of that year, 1913, held two dates to which the girls looked forward with eager anticipation, October 12 and 28. October 12 was important, not so much as an historical date which commemorated the discovery of America by Columbus, but rather because it always brought a half holiday and a patriotic program, given in the evening, to which one of the Denver Knights of Columbus contributed as guest speaker. On the second date, October 28, the older students were to have the privilege of attending at Littleton "Joe" Newman's benefit program for St. Mary's Church of which Father Clarke was the pastor. This diversion meant as much to the students in 1913 as a trip to a Chicago or New York convention would mean now, thirty years later.

On November 1 of that year, the feast of All Saints, the Most Reverend Bishop Matz brought an unusual visitor to the school, the famous Greek priest, Monsignor Salome. The reverend clergyman kept his audience highly entertained as he deftly displayed before their appreciative eyes not only oriental laces but every imaginable type of needle craft. The interested spectators followed Monsignor Salome as he demonstrated his intimate knowledge of the subject of his lecture. Bishop Matz delighted in surprising people; the student body gave the Bishop entire satisfaction when he introduced a Greek priest who could lecture so intelligently on the values and beauties of oriental laces.

From Greece to Rome is a short trip. Just twenty days later the pupils of the academy celebrated the feast of one of Rome's martyrs, Saint Cecilia, the patroness of music. Talented musicians presented a delightful program in honor of this Roman virgin and martyr.

At Thanksgiving time an event occurred which to the casual observer was not wholly in accord with the general connotation of the term thanksgiving; the event, however, had been looked forward to with eagerness by the one vitally concerned, Sister Columba Gallavan, who on November 25,

1913, paid her debt to nature by giving back her pure, gentle soul to her Maker. Sister Columba had been ill but a few days and was apparently on the road to recovery when suddenly the summons came.

Sister Columba, known in the world as Laura Gallavan, was born in Kentucky, December 22, 1857. She was educated by the Sisters of Loretto at St. Mary's School, Elizabethtown, Kentucky, where she was graduated in 1876. Having been reared in an atmosphere of piety and devotion, it was not surprising that, turning a willing ear to the Master calling her to labor in His chosen vineyard, she entered the Loretto Novitiate in Kentucky the same year she finished school. Two and one-half years later, Sister Columba pronounced her first vows and was missioned to Loretto Academy on Pine Street in St. Louis. After a short time of service, the health of the young religious seemed to be seriously impaired.

About this time, Mother Elizabeth, the superior of St. Mary's Academy in Denver, visited the Motherhouse in quest of help for that mission in Colorado. The superiors told Mother Elizabeth that the only member they could give her was Sister Columba, but it seemed to them that the grave had spoken first. Nothing daunted Mother Elizabeth answered, "Let me have her; I'll see what Colorado sunshine will do for her." In a few days Mother Elizabeth and her invalid companion were journeying westward. The marked improvement in Sister Columba's health, after she had been in Colorado for a short time, proved that Mother Elizabeth's faith in the climate of her adopted state was justified.

In the thirty-three years of her residence in Colorado, Sister Columba lived one year in Colorado Springs, one year in Pueblo, then at St. Mary's Academy, and later at Loretto Heights, teaching music in these schools and serving for three years as superior at St. Mary's. Her sojourn on earth records nothing heroic or wonderful; hers was the truly hidden life, marked only by fidelity to rule and principle. Countless were the souls who came within the range of her influence and were made better because they had known and loved her.

Sister Columba's obsequies were conducted on November 26, by the chaplain, the Reverend Edward Clarke, assisted by the Reverend William O'Ryan. Mrs. D. Mathes, sister of the deceased, and Miss Della Mathes, her niece, came from Arlington, Colorado, for the funeral. Miss Della Mathes attended school at the Heights; later she married, and her two daughters, Laura Mae and Gladys Givans, were graduated from the high school of Pancratia Hall and four years afterwards from Loretto Heights College.

In the early part of December, the exact date was December 3, 1913, snow began to fall steadily and uninterruptedly for several days and nights. This state-wide snowfall proved to be one of the heaviest in the history of Colorado. After days of incessant snowing, those on Loretto hill found themselves completely barricaded by piles of snow; in some places the drifts were fifteen feet high. At first the students thought it great fun to watch the feathery flakes falling so steadily and covering everything with an immaculate blanket; after a time, when all were enveloped in a white silence and cut off completely from communication with the outside world, they began to wonder and question.

Fortunately the buyer at the Heights was accustomed to provide food supplies far in advance of immediate needs; for several days all went well for there was no dearth of food or fuel. However when the storm continued unabated, those responsible for the maintenance of supplies began to grow anxious. Since the family was large and the weather was cold, great inroads were made upon the storeroom and the coal supply. Just when the superior and the procurator were beginning to really worry about conditions, the officer in command at Fort Logan, realizing what must be the situation of the residents in the near-by boarding school, sent three of his men, mounted on army horses, with sacks filled with all kinds of provisions for the snow-bound students and sisters. This surely was an example of "the good neighbor policy" verified in a practical way!

During the time of this sequestration caused by the snow storm, good humor and good fellowship prevailed. The sisters did their utmost to keep all going smoothly, and the girls made the best of everything. Some of the students tried to put into verse their unusual experiences during those days. Helen Buehler of the class of '14 had the honor of having her poem, *Loretto Snowbound*, published in the *Denver Register*, December 25, 1913. The poem gives the student's reaction to the snow storm and contains many allusions which will be understood by the students then in residence at the Heights.

LORETTO SNOWBOUND

(With Apologies to Whittier)

I've oft heard it said in accents wise
That next to winning a poet's prize
Is being able to read and feel
The magic and charm his works reveal.
Our friends, I think, will banish doubt
If we say, at last, we have found out
The charms in verse that do abound;
For we've learned to read and feel "Snowbound."
So, magic, along with tardy mail
Accounts for this belated tale.
November's charms our praise we'd sung,
But soon December's pall was hung
For, on Wednesday night, the famous third
The scene was changed—no sound was heard.
But morn revealed a sheet of snow
That wrapped old Earth from head to toe.
And still the flakes came fluttering down.
Many a Miss was bent on going
'To Town' that morn, but now 'twas snowing.
All day it came, all night it fell—
When morning dawned no one could tell
The road from any other part;
And sighs revealed the saddened heart.
The "Eighth" was coming fast
But still on blew that dreary blast,
All day the snowdrifts higher rose—

But look! in the west a bright spot glows.
Yet night, relenting, with howl and moan
Flung sounds about like a lost soul's groan;
And swifter, surer, forged the chain
That meant right here we must remain.
Next morn, how'er, a calm was felt,
The snow, at last, had ceased to pelt.
Then came the smile of the rising Sun,
And gazing on, he said, "Well done!"
In vain we looked for each dear spot—
They'd all departed like things forgot.
There stood the swing so stiff and still;
And silent, too, was the rippling rill.
The rustic bridge—ah! where'd it go?
Look right or left, we saw but snow.
Then thought we on our coming feast—
But naught was stirring, bird nor beast—
What would we do for extra fare?
Would bread and butter be our share?
So far, of food we had no lack,
And steam pipes sizzled at our back;
But when, at last, we went to bed,
Our thoughts were sad, it must be said.
We thought of friends that we'd not see,
Of cream and cake that had bid "awee."
But our better self seemed us to chide,
And made reply, "Let God provide."
Commending all to His loving care,
Sweet dreams soon took the place of prayer.
At break of day, all wide awake,
We bounded out with shiver and shake.
But now a holy joy was ours—
A joy such as Heaven often showers
On mortals in this land of cares;
And well we knew our fervent prayers
Had passed beyond the Heavenly gates,
Where Mary, our Mother, ever waits
To show her love is yet the same
As when our Mother she became.
In spotless garb at last arrayed,
To the chapel we walked in grand parade,
There stole to us the violin's sweet strain,
And the organ swelling the glad refrain.
Then one by one we marched along,
Till soon our joyful, happy throng
Within God's house their footsteps staid—

Four lines we formed, an "M" was made.
It seemed we n'er before had known
Such joy. All sorrow now had flown.
And we think God's Mother whispered low
Sweet words that sped across the snow;
And other sounds that none could hear,
For these were meant for Mother's ear.
Then from the "Fort," 'tis Logan by name—
Across the wires a message came;
Said Captain Schoeffel, in accents kind,
"If you're in need, now never mind
The bother, but quickly let us know—
I think that we can cross the snow.
Then up spoke Gamble, the Major,
And said, "I'll bet you any wager,
About this Fort there's not a man,
That wouldn't aid you all he can!"
Thus we learned in this age of "Woman's rights"
There still exists what we call Knights.
Then like the Wise men from the East,
Three riders came to aid our feast.
At eve, Benediction blessed our way,
Ah, with joyful hearts we spent that day.
Another lamb to the fold was led,
And on the Heavenly banquet fed.
Yet one more Grace must claim our thanks,
For Mary's Children increased their ranks.
Then the way to the banquet hall was led
By Father Clarke with martial tread,
And seated round the festive board,
We soon forgot the snowy hoard
With which Jack Frost had housed us in,
As you'd soon know if you heard the din.
The cream and cake were soon forgot
Before plum-pudding, steaming hot.
The banquet o'er, we all did go
To "trip the light fantastic toe."
When bed time came, we voted this,
Of all our days, a day of bliss.
On the stage next night we glad appeared,
And while our audience loudly cheered,
"Rebecca's Triumph" there we played
Until the clock to nine had strayed.
My reader kind, if from Denver's lights,
A pitying look to Loretto Heights
You should happen to cast, and tenderly say,

"I'm sorry for poor old L. H. A."—
Don't forget, we're not so sad and lone,
We've a little heaven all our own.

In this poem Miss Buehler alluded to the celebration
of the great feast day of the Children of Mary on the eighth
of December. The feast of the Immaculate Conception was
a day belonging in a very special manner to the members of
the sodality at Loretto Heights and as such it was celebrated. When old students of Loretto Heights Academy
are asked what day in their school life stands out in their
memory as the one they like best to recall, they invariably
reply: "Oh, our day, of course! The eighth of December!
That was surely the girls' day at the Heights. Everything
was so beautiful—the chapel, the girls looking so sweet
in their white dresses and veils, the wonderful banquet, the
plays in the auditorium. When we think of that day our
hearts run all the way back to Loretto; we relive the dear
familiar days, but especially the day dedicated to Our
Lady's honor, the feast of the Immaculate Conception."

On December 9, "Rebecca's Triumph," a three-act
comedy, was well rendered by the senior dramatic club.
Madeleine Keefe and Janet Mathews took the leads in the
character parts, "Katie Connors" and "Gyp." This play
was followed ten days later by the Christmas cantata on
December 19 which marked the beginning of the holidays.

To the world at large February is the "month of
hearts"; on the fourteenth of this month, especially, does
Dan Cupid hold sway. February 14, 1914, the students had
their usual Valentine party; two days later, February 16,
Reverend Edward Clarke, the chaplain, who was indefatigable in his efforts to attract souls to the only lasting Love,
organized the League of the Sacred Heart. On the first
Friday of March twenty members were received into the
League as a surer means of being guided to the Source
of all love and consolation.

On February 25 of that year, 1914, the students were
saddened by the departure of Miss Winifred Bonfils, a
young cousin of Mother Pancratia. Miss Bonfils, having
endeared herself to her companions during her student

days at the Heights, was greatly missed when she had to leave to take up her residence in San Francisco. Miss Winifred Bonfils was a daughter of Winifred Black, a newspaper woman, who under the pen name, "Annie Laurie," wrote at one time for *The Denver Post*. Winifred Black later married Mr. Charles A. Bonfils of Denver.

Just as the 1914 *Loretto Annual* was going to press in early May, the editors learned of the serious illness of Mrs. Mary A. Perry, mother of Judge John Perry of Denver. Mrs. Perry, a pioneer Catholic of the capital city, was one of the ladies who helped to prepare the home for the Sisters of Loretto when they first came to Denver, June 25, 1864. Associated with Mrs. Perry in receiving the sisters, was Mrs. Charles Marshall, the mother of the Reverend Charles Marshall, the well-known Episcopalian minister. Mrs. Marshall, though not a Catholic, gladly welcomed the sisters, for she knew that their coming would do much to foster Christianity and culture in the city and state.

The feast day of Mother Pancratia, May 12, was a red-letter day for the students at the Heights. It meant the proud offering of their spiritual bouquets to the superior after they had assisted at Mass and received Holy Communion for her intentions; then a holiday and a banquet in the evening.

The chaplain, the Reverend Edward Clarke, departed that afternoon for a two months vacation in the East. In his absence the former chaplain, the Reverend Richard Brady, was reappointed to the Heights as chaplain. Never of robust health, Father Brady had found his duties as pastor of the Annunciation Church in Denver and Vicar General of the diocese too arduous. When Father Clarke returned from his vacation, he took up his residence at Littleton as pastor of St. Mary's Church.

In June, 1914, St. Mary's Academy in the city of Denver celebrated its Golden Jubilee. This was an important date, too, for Loretto Heights since its foundation was so closely associated with the first Colorado school at St. Mary's. The *Loretto Annual* gives interesting historical information with regard to the Jubilee Mass which was the center of the celebration:

At this Mass articles will be used which have loving reminiscences clustering around them, for they are associated with pioneers of Catholicity in the golden West. The alb to be used on this occasion by the Right Reverend Celebrant is the one which was worn by the Right Reverend Machebeuf, D.D., when he was ordained priest, and also when he was consecrated bishop. It is an exquisite specimen of hand-made lace and is the work of the Bishop's sister, Sister Marie Philomene of the Visitation Convent of Paray-le-Monial.

The chalice which will be employed in the service is the one presented to the Very Reverend J. B. Raverdy, V.G., by the Most Reverend J. B. Lamy, D.D., at the time of Father Raverdy's ordination, four decades before. The cruets which will be used at the Mass also belonged to Father Raverdy; they were given to him as an ordination gift by the Right Reverend J. P. Machebeuf, D.D. These cruets are at present (1914) owned by Mr. Maurice Dolan of Denver, who kindly lent them to the sisters for this occasion, their golden jubilee year since coming to Denver.

From the golden jubilee celebration of St. Mary's Academy, the Heights sisters returned to the quiet of their country home and to the graduating exercises of the twenty-third class in the history of the academy. The seniors of that year, Gladys Browns, Helen Buehler, Doris Stewart, Olive Trail, and Mildred Welch, in the foreword of their annual give the setting of their alma mater and its significance to them:

Like a mammoth relief standing out against the sloping perspective of the eternal prairies are the spires, the comfortable homes, the princely villas, the gardens, and the parks of the "Queen City of the Plains." And raising its lofty convent tower above the Colorado valleys is Loretto Heights. Uplifted masses of the Rockies with cloud-piercing peaks stand as a symbol of Loretto's holy work whose heaven-fixed aim has always been to raise things from the earth, nearer to heaven, closer to God.

All the traditional events took place during the fall of the next scholastic year. Shortly after the Halloween party, the Reverend T. H. Malone gave a series of stereopticon views and a lecture on World War I, which was then in progress. These views brought home to the students an idea of some of the disasters which were being enacted while they were quietly pursuing their studies.

School days were fittingly diversified with many enjoyable outings and amusements. The annual retreat was followed by the celebration of the students' feast of the year, the Immaculate Conception of Our Lady. An entertainment in honor of the Immaculate Queen was given in the evening under the auspices of the Children of Mary. The *Loretto Annual* of 1914 gives a detailed account of the various numbers:

The program opened with the *Magnificat*. From the initial number to the conclusion the program was faultless. Deserving of special mention was the reading by little Miss Mary Pearl Queen, who, with wonderful depth of feeling, recited "My Beads." "The Madonna of Palos" was given by Miss Isabella Horan, in her usual gifted way. Miss Genevieve Doyle's rich contralto blending with the clear soprano of Miss Isabella Horan never sounded better than in the hymn, "Holy Mother, Guide Our Footsteps." Miss Agnes Berry, who is at home in comedy, surprised her audience by showing that she is familiar with the shadows of life as well, and gave in a charming manner, "Old Matthew's Picture." The tableau by the Children of Mary made a fitting conclusion for a day filled with so many spiritual blessings. Miss Ina McMahon represented the Blessed Virgin; her pure countenance and her faultless posing made one feel that she was visiting the studio of an Angelo or a Raphael.

On January 29 of the following year, 1915, Sister Bartholomew Nooning, one of the sisters who had been at Loretto Heights from the beginning, even from the selection of the site, died after a brief illness. With the passing into eternity of Sister Columba, Sister Bartholomew, and others so closely associated with Loretto Heights, the bonds uniting those sisters who had labored and suffered for the institute began to break:

One by one the links fall off
    From the circle of friendship's golden chain;
One by one new faces come,
    But of olden friends, how few remain!

Sister Bartholomew deserves more than a passing mention in these pages. With the exception of four years spent at St. Ann's Academy, St. Paul, Kansas, Sister Bartholomew labored from the opening of the school in November, 1891, until her death in 1915, at her beloved Heights. Sister Bartholomew, Miss Catherine Nooning, was born at North Hampton, Massachusetts, December 13, 1849. She received the religious habit in the Loretto Society on August 15, 1867. After finishing her novitiate she was first missioned to Cape Girardeau, Missouri; on December 31, 1875, she was transferred to Denver.

At St. Mary's and Loretto Heights Academies, Sister Bartholomew was a successful teacher of mathematics and art. Many of her paintings adorn the parlors and walls of both these institutions. During her years in religion, she was an indefatigable worker; when failing health made it necessary to give up her duties in the classroom, she was ready to labor according to her ability at other tasks. Sister Bartholomew was the first postmaster at Loretto Heights and fulfilled the duties of the office up to the time of her last illness. A staunch friend, a loyal member of her Order, a silent worker, this faithful sister's outstanding virtue was freedom from ostentation. Sisters who came in close contact with her, after her career as a teacher was over, lived with Sister Bartholomew for years without knowing that she was an artist of marked ability.

During the spring months of 1915, the usual religious, scholastic, and social events followed one another at their scheduled time. On April 18, the students were favored in having Mr. C. E. W. Griffith, the noted Shakespearian scholar and interpreter, read selections from a number of Shakespeare's plays. Mr. Griffith read also Francis Thompson's *Hound of Heaven* and Cardinal Newman's *Dream of Gerontius*.

The school calendar for the month of May was filled with events interesting and meaningful: the May Crowning, the Reading Recital, and the annual Homecoming of the Alumnae. On June 2, there was a strawberry festival, a gala occasion for the students and the school, enjoyable and lucrative; on June 7, the school gave the seniors a fare-well dinner, and June 8 was graduation day.

One of the school publications, the *Loretto Annual,* gives this information concerning the graduates of 1915:

Jeannette Spiess, thoughtful, dictatorial, argumentative— "A woman convinced against her will is of the same opinion still"; Madeleine Virginia Keefe, modest, impulsive, un-sophisticated—"The maid is meek, the maid is sweet, the maid is modest and discreet"; Lotus Lee Watts, musical, proud, and stubborn—"Pretty to walk with, witty to talk with, and pleasant, too, to think of"; Hazel Velma Hewitt, irresponsible, winning and merry—"In faith, lady, you have a merry heart"; Ina Elizabeth McMahon, good-natured, generous, and careless—"Laugh away sorrow, laugh away care"; Janet Amanda Matthews, talkative, tal-ented, and tactless—"When joy and duty clash, let duty go to smash."

In the publications of the school, during the early days of the second century of the history of the Lorettines, there is evidence that the students of Loretto Heights Academy were happy and busy with their school projects. There must have been plenty of school spirit which is ably defined by the editors of the *Loretto Annual* for 1915: " . . . School spirit is the soul, the animating principle, that makes a little school great and a great school greater. It is the strange 'unknown,' feared by freshmen and reverenced by seniors. It is the union of young blood, young patriotism, and young ideals. It is born in September when the sunset is scarlet and the air laden with the incense of pine and burning brush.

"Through crisp winter days, when the north wind whistles, and the blue mountains grow old overnight, the spirit thrives. The girl who keeps in touch with the spirit of her school will rank high in the roll call of the world."

Chapter XVI

DEATH COMES TO MOTHER PANCRATIA

Nothing in this world is the result of chance. Everything forms part of the universal plan of the great Artificer. The individual is free, however, to co-operate in the design of the Architect. In looking back over the life work of Mother Pancratia Bonfils, one readily follows the pattern which she by her obedience to her religious superiors brought to completion; yet she herself was wholly unaware of the important part she was fulfilling in God's plan for her and for the Sisters of Loretto who were to come after her, to take up the work of education in Colorado where she had laid it down.

Viewed in retrospect, however, the life of Mother Pancratia was an eventful one, filled with great plans brought to fruition, especially in and near the city of Denver where she spent the greater part of her life.

The future foundress of Loretto Heights was born September 24, 1852, in what was known as the "old Chouteau place," near St. Louis. Her father was Dr. Francis Bonfils, a prominent physician of St. Louis; her mother before her marriage was Miss Marie Whitlock. The little Mary Louise was placed in the country boarding school of the Sisters of Loretto at Florissant, a village about sixteen miles from St. Louis. Here the beauty and truth of the Catholic religion appealed to the heart and mind of the precocious child. With the consent of her parents, she entered the Catholic Church and, not long afterward, July 16, 1866, when only thirteen, began her novitiate as a Sister of Loretto at the Motherhouse in Kentucky, receiving the name of Sister Mary Pancratia. Two years later, still quite a young girl, she was sent to the far-distant mission which had been opened just four years before, in 1864, at St. Mary's in Denver, then a rude mining camp. Here in God's providence, Sister Pancratia was to spend the greater part of her life; here she was to expend herself in her work as teacher, builder, and superior.

There was nothing in Mother Pancratia which would on first acquaintance distinguish her from the other members of the community; she was modest and retiring, having the dignity and decorum which mark the true religious. Of her initiative and ability as an executive, little need be said since the academies which she erected, Loretto Heights and the new St. Mary's, are sufficient proofs of these qualities.

Of her influence as a teacher, it is not possible to speak adequately. Hundreds of women now grown old bless her memory. The positions she held for so many years, either as directress of a large boarding school or as superior, were sufficient to tax the most ingenious. Yet she was patient with the difficult student; gentle with the forward; anxious and careful with those who were suffering; loyal to her friends; generous in her attentions to all who came under her care; but she was especially devoted to the little ones, who in their innocence and helpless dependence made a peculiar appeal to her heart.

During the greater part of her religious life, Mother Pancratia filled various positions of authority. Although duties of administration make a great demand on one's time, yet it was Mother Pancratia's special delight to supervise personally many of the details which make for happy living in a boarding school. When superior of the Heights and St. Mary's, she made her rounds to the kitchen and dining rooms, to inform herself with regard to the menus of the day. If they met her approval, she was clever in letting her pleasure be known; if she thought they could be improved, she offered helpful suggestions, which were accepted in good part, for all knew that Mother Pancratia had made herself proficient in the art of cooking and serving.

In previous chapters of *Loretto in the Rockies*, frequent allusions have been made to Mother Pancratia's years of service at Loretto Heights; how active she was, how all-observant, how unsparing of herself in her efforts to bring undertakings to a successful issue. During the last annual retreat which she made in August, 1915, the sisters of the

Mother Pancratia Bonfils—1915

Mother Clarasine Walsh—1916

community and even those from other houses in the state, who were present for the retreat, noticed a difference in her; she was not so concerned about the management of the house and other details which a retreat entails. She was found more frequently in the chapel during free time, sitting with Mary, rather than serving with Martha.

In preparing for the opening of classes in the fall, Mother Pancratia manifested the same interest in providing everything which might contribute to the progress of the school and the material comfort of the faculty and pupils. Shortly after registration, to the great surprise of the sisters but not to herself, she was stricken with a mortal malady which necessitated an operation at St. Joseph's Hospital on September 17. For a short time after the operation, Mother Pancratia, seeming to rally, inspired all with the hope that she would soon be able to return to her duties. Then the crisis came and the struggle began between life and death, ending with death as victor; for at 9:45 on the morning of October 12 Mother Pancratia went to begin that eternal life for which years on earth had been a daily preparation. Her last words were: "Jesus in the blessed Sacrament, have mercy on me."

Mother Pancratia was characteristically practical and proudly American. This was manifested on her deathbed when, sensing that on account of her illness the exercises of raising the new flagpole and dedicating the flag were to be postponed, she insisted that whether she was living or dead the program as planned should be carried out on the Sunday for which it had been scheduled. In accordance with her urgent desire, the ceremonies of the flag raising took place Sunday afternoon, October 11, while she was entering into the shadows of the valley of death.

Mother Pancratia died as she had lived, full of courage and hope. The news of her apparently premature death— she was 64 years old—was a shock to her many friends, for there still seemed so much for her busy hands to do, in spite of the many years of service she had given to her community. In the words of her eulogist, the Reverend

William O'Ryan: "Almost fifty years of service she gave
to God and men as a nun; fifty years of patience and
prayer; fifty years of self-sacrifice in the great work of
guiding little children and young maidens to fine womanhood, to noble citizenship, to loyal and earnest Christian
lives."

As one recalls the life and work of Mother Pancratia
as a zealous Sister of Loretto, the lines of Owen Meredith
which aptly describe this religious in her work for souls
come to mind:

> The mission of woman on earth! to give birth
> To the mercy of heaven descending on earth.
> The mission of woman; permitted to bruise
> The head of the serpent and sweetly infuse,
> Through the sorrow and sin of earth's registered curse,
> The blessing which mitigates all; born to nurse,
> And to soothe, and to solace, to help and to heal
> The sick world that leans on her.

Expressions of sympathy came from far and near to
the Sisters of Loretto at Loretto Heights, from those who
had known and loved this gentle religious woman. The
funeral services were held in the Chapel of Our Lady of
Loretto, which she had so recently planned and had seen
completed. Monsignor Richard Brady, so long associated
with the deceased in his office as chaplain of the convent,
offered the Requiem High Mass. The pallbearers, the Reverend William O'Ryan, M. F. Callanan, William Donovan,
W. McCabe, A. Schuler, S.J., and Robert Servant, were
priests who had labored for many years in the diocese of
Denver and had been witnesses of the heroic life of the
religious whom they were to bear to the little convent
cemetery.

The Reverend William O'Ryan, devoted and trusted
friend of Mother Pancratia, delivered the funeral sermon.
Father O'Ryan took as his text the comforting verse of
Psalm 22: "Though I should walk in the midst of the
shadow of death I will fear no evil, for Thou art with me."
Father O'Ryan knew Mother Pancratia well, her joys and
sorrows, her successes and defeats. His sermon over her

mortal remains was a masterpiece of eloquence, which brought consolation to the sisters, students, and friends, who felt deeply the loss which they had suffered in the death of her who had been so intimately connected with the work of the Sisters of Loretto in Denver. The sermon in its entirety is a treasured memento both of Mother Pancratia and her eulogist, the late Monsignor O'Ryan, Denver's golden-mouthed orator. Owing to the length of the sermon, only excerpts can be given here.

After speaking of the toll death makes on one's loved ones, Father O'Ryan emphasized its consolation, its salutary reflections; for all must pass that way:

The death of the good and holy is but the Father hearing the prayer of His Son: "Father, I will that where I am they also may come that they may behold Thy glory." They have been true disciples; they have been snatched from the poor and painful ways of life to behold His glory.

Death always has its burden of sorrow. For this was it made; not by God, but by sin, to punish us. It is the sentence passed upon the first sin. It is the desert of sin. Who that looks over his own life with its many infidelities to God and His Grace, with its multitudinous falls and failures, will not say that death is a just punishment.

We grieve for this last life taken from us; but our faith and our knowledge of the loveliness of that life leave us large consolations. Fifty years ago our beloved Sister Pancratia had come to the threshold of womanhood, rich in education, in innocence, and carefully guarded virtues. She looked out on life and its various ways, and saw that some were sweet, and good and pleasant.

But in the life which she chose, Mother Pancratia sought the truest guides. Knowing that Poverty, Chastity, and Obedience guarded the lives of Jesus and Mary, she vowed her life to the practice of these virtues. She reached one unselfish hand to poverty and one lily hand to purity; she asked obedience to seal the eyes of her will since the angel of humble submission would be her light and her eyes, until God would open them in His home.

In reply to the question, "Who can fitly describe the life of a nun? To what shall we compare it?" Father O'Ryan drew this comparison:

Upon the mountain top, under the mighty boulder, springs the crystal water. No eyes of man can see it; the bald eagle stays his wheeling flight to admire it; the red deer glasses his rugged front in the tiny pool. But, the clear water will not stay there. Something whispers that far away is the boundless ocean of its true rest. And down in a hurrying stream over the crags it leaps; it slips through the grandeur of mighty canons that cry to it; "Stay with us and our glory shall be mirrored in yours, and those who admire us shall admire you." But the stream will not stay. The glamor of the ocean is on it and in its broad bosom, not under the shadow of towering cliffs, lies its happiness. And down through the splendor of rich plains it rushes, and ever as it goes for its constancy it is given increase; blessing, it is blessed. And the odorous meadows cry to it; "Stay with us, and water us and be our delight;" and the water lilies sing: "Stay with us and we will bend our beauty to you and mix and mingle with you." But the stream flows on, knowing well that the lilies should perish, and the beauty of the meadows turn to the foulness of the swamp, if it stayed. And, lo! the stream has gone to a broad river, a rushing torrent that no hand may stop, no meadow hold; only the great ocean can receive it and give it content. Such is the true Sister's holy life.

Reverently and lovingly the remains of Mother Pancratia were borne to the convent cemetery and laid to rest in the midst of her sisters in religion who had died before her, many of whom had worked by her side for years either at St. Mary's or at Loretto Heights and had preceded her in death.

Chapter XVII

SILVER JUBILEE CELEBRATION AND
OTHER EVENTS

After Mother Pancratia's death on October 12, 1915, Sister Harriet Moore, the first assistant of the community, became the acting superior and carried on the duties of the office until a local superior was appointed after the general elections of the higher superiors of the Order at the General Chapter, which took place in July, 1916. Though both the sisters and students missed Mother Pancratia at every turn, yet, since everyone performed her duties conscientiously, the school year was brought to a successful close.

In the graduating class of June, 1916, were Dorothy Besse, Agnes Berry, Josephine Casey, Vada Fennell, Anna Gill, Emma Hill, Elizabeth Keefe, Helen Lopez, Isabella Horan, and Eva Toole. This group of students gave proof of unusual talent, through their high school course, not only in their scholastic work but also in the fine arts, drama, music, and voice. It is interesting to note that Josephine Casey, one of the graduates of this class, was the niece of Katherine Casey, Sister M. Menodora, S.L., a member of the first class to finish at Loretto Heights Academy in 1892.

Mother Clarasine Walsh, who was appointed superior of the Heights in the summer of 1916, was eminently fitted for the duties of this large boarding school since she had filled the same office at Loretto Academy, Pueblo, Loretto Academy, Kansas City, Missouri, and other schools of the Order. It was not easy for any sister to be the successor of Mother Pancratia, who had been so long associated with the Heights, so well loved, and so deeply missed. Mother Clarasine, fully realizing this fact, entered into her work with her usual calm trust in Divine Providence, Who did not fail her. The sisters of the community soon perceived that Mother Clarasine was a woman of strong faith, pru-

dence, and practical common sense. The school, continuing
to prosper, reached the unprecedented number of one hundred eighty-seven boarding pupils. During the first two
years of Mother Clarasine's term of office, Sister Dolorine
Morrison was directress of the Academy, an office which
she had held from the time she had returned from St. Mary's
in 1913 and continued to hold even after she was appointed
dean of the college in 1918.

The fall of 1916 brought an important anniversary.
Twenty-five years had now passed since that memorable
November 2, 1891, when the sisters and pupils first occupied
the new school on the heights southwest of Denver. While
those twenty-five years had brought many changes in the
personnel of the faculty and many improvements on the
campus and within the building, the school had been conservative in its educational policies. The same may be
said of the faculty of today and its policies. Loretto Heights
takes reasonable pride in the fact that many of the time-
honored virtues, the old-fashioned courtesies, and gentle
manners which contribute to refined living have been preserved.

Loretto Heights Academy had been functioning, in the
fall of 1916, for twenty-five years. How many of those
who helped to "move in," on that November night in 1891,
were there to celebrate the successful rounding out of that
space of time? Mother Pancratia, who had been with the
school from the time that it began to exist in the minds of
the sisters, who had planned for its construction and had
seen it go up, stone by stone and floor by floor, had died
just the year before. Events often happen that way in this
world. Sister Columba and Sister Bartholomew, who had
labored for years side by side with Mother Pancratia, had
recently been laid away in the little convent cemetery.
Surely those first sisters were missed on that anniversary
day.

The silver jubilee commemorating the opening of
Loretto Heights Academy was observed November 1, 1916,
by a series of events which made the day worthy of remembrance. The Right Reverend Richard Brady, chaplain,

was the celebrant of the Solemn High Mass; the Very Reverend J. J. Cronin, C.M., president of St. Thomas Seminary, was deacon; the Reverend William Lonergan, S.J., of Regis College, sub-deacon; and the Reverend E. J. Mannix, assistant at the Immaculate Conception Cathedral in Denver, was master of ceremonies.   More than twenty priests of the diocese of Denver and numerous friends of the sisters and pupils were present at that Mass of thanksgiving.

In their white uniforms and veils the students formed an attractive and important part of the congregation since it was for them, for those who had preceded them, and for those who were to follow, that the school had been opened, and the hardships and anxieties of those first lean, hard years had been endured.   The white uniforms and veils of the students were symbolic of the ideals which the sisters entertained for those who were under their care.

After the religious exercises, the Fort Logan band gave an enjoyable concert.   In the afternoon the following students acted their parts well in *Anima,* a morality play: *Anima,* Alice Croke; *Innocence,* Mary Pearl Queen; *Scientia,* Anna Rittmayer; *Pride,* Evelyn L'Abbe; *Faith,* Genevieve Doyle; *Hope,* Helen Kehn; *Charity,* Gertrude Norman; *Poverty,* Ruth McFarlane; *Obedience,* Irene Johnson; *Humility,* Mildred Guireaud; *Purity, Despair,* and *Revenge,* Mary Reddin; the Senses—*Palatio,* Elone Brachvoegel; *Auditio,* Mary McDonald; *Visiona,* Dorothy Hatch; *Odora,* Erin LeBissoniere; *Sensa,* Marie Pryor.

Records of the school from its opening until its twenty-fifth year show that about 2,750 pupils had been in residence during those years.   A rough calculation of the students in both academy and college during the succeeding quarter of a century indicates about 7,500.

Those who received diplomas at the graduating exercises in June, 1917, were Anna Rittmayer, Genevieve Rittmayer, Mary McDonald, Dorothy Hatch, Evelyn L'Abbe, Gertrude Norman, Nancy Van Deusen, and Mildred Gireaud.

Carried out on the campus of Loretto Heights the next summer was a unique program. During the distressful condition of the country after the United States entered into World War I, the women of Colorado were vitally concerned about the share they could take in giving worth-while aid to the country in its need. Accordingly some of the patriotic women of the state organized a national service camp with their army tents pitched on that part of the western campus of Loretto Heights, extending between the club house and Pancratia Hall. The officers' quarters were to the south of these tents, on the top of the elevation near the tennis courts.

Concerning this venture, Ella Miriam Sullivan had this news item in the *Denver Post*:

Society is waxing very eloquent over the National Service school which will soon open at Loretto Heights, July 2, and it is considered the smart thing to register for the summer encampment. Thruout the east these schools have been wonderfully successful and attended by members of the most exclusive social sets, and judging by the number of prominent women who have signified their intention of enrolling and who are forming battalions of girls among their friends, the Denver school will step into the front ranks alongside those of the east. Mrs. Alexander Sharp will come from Washington to take charge. Among the prominent people who are on the committee of arrangements are Miss Lillian Hurd, Mrs. L. C. Campbell, Mrs. Verner Z. Reed, Colonel Getty, General Frank D. Baldwin, Henry M. Blackmer, Lucius Hallet, Dr. G. Walter Holden, Harold Kountze, Charles McAllister Wilcox, Clayton C. Dorsey, and Edward Bell Field, Jr.

The Fifth National Service School of the women's section of the Navy League did active work at Loretto Heights from July 2 to July 22, 1917. The purpose of this school was to give efficient training to women in caring for the wounded, feeding the hungry, and keeping things going while the men were actively engaged at the front. Although the two hundred women in training at the camp were under military discipline, it was never the intention of the officers to train women for active duty. The military training, which was incidental to the whole program, was introduced

Glimpses of Fifth National Service School
July 2 to July 23, 1917

Campus Views—Alma Mater

merely to insure efficiency through unquestioned obedience. While the women in the camp were being taught to give instant mechanical obedience to orders, they attained and maintained alert faculties through the physical benefit derived from the exercises and the simple habits which were of obligation. Since the service school trained for field duties under the Red Cross, two Red Cross courses were compulsory; so also were wigwag, military drill, and calisthenics.

During those war times, the federal government placed such high valuation on this training for women that it gave a large reservation on the Conduit Road near Cabin John Bridge, Washington, D. C., as a site for the First National Service School. The highest military and Red Cross officials assisted in the organization of the schools in various parts of the country. In the service school carried on at Loretto Heights, the army furnished the tents for the sleeping quarters; gas and electricity were supplied for the camp grounds, and for the convenience of those who were in training, a jitney service was installed from the Englewood carline to Loretto Heights. Mrs. Thomas Keely was appointed chief of the commissariat, which department purchased and prepared food for two hundred women for twenty days.

Living for the women in training was reduced to the minimum of essentials: they were given plain food, a tin basin of cold water for their ablutions, and, when their strenuous day was over, an army cot in a tent under the stars for their repose. If the women desired sheets for their cots, they were permitted to bring them from home; sheets, however, were considered an unnecessary luxury. Those who were to enter training were instructed to bring a handbag and a suitcase containing the bare living necessities.

Once the women donned the khaki, that was their uniform for three weeks; there was no changing to a tea frock or a jaunty sport suit for any occasion whatever. Their handbag contained only necessary toilet articles, all superfluities were forbidden; so, too, were cigarettes. Smuggling this article into camp was an act against discipline and those who did it were penalized. Stout drill shoes were worn during the day and a pair of large, loose slippers at night to rest tired, swollen feet and protect them from the earthen floors of the tents. The officers were insistent that the nature of the camp should be well understood; Loretto Heights camp was not to be a picnic party *de luxe*. The very purpose of conducting the school as a camp was to strip away the many time-consuming fripperies of so-called civilization. When freed from superfluous demands on their time, the women in training could devote themselves to the work of the Red Cross, civilian, and military courses which were offered.

Coordination of effort and concentration of energy were the chief accomplishments which the Fifth National Service School proposed to teach. Mrs. Alexander Sharp of Washington, D. C., supervisor and director, showed the advantages of such training: "The girls learn to do the same tasks at the same time everyday, day in and day out, whether they feel in the mood or not; they are obliged to cover a great deal of ground in a short time, and to do this they must concentrate; those in training learn true democracy since they must adapt themselves to the many dispositions of those with whom they work; bear a share of the load uncomplainingly; and acquire a fine sense of honor and personal responsibility which army routine gives."

A daily program of classes and duties kept the women fully occupied. This schedule was adhered to strictly: 6:30, rising, fifteen minutes for dressing; 6:45, military calisthenics; 7:30, mess; 8:00, police call; 8:30, inspection, tents in order; 9:00, military drill; 9:30 to 12:30, Red Cross classes under accredited instructors; 12:30, mess; 1:30 to 3:30, classes in wireless and plain telegraphy, typewriting and stenography, wigwagging and knitting; 4:00 to 5:00, lectures; 6:15, mess; 7:00 to 8:00, study hour and voluntary drills; 9:30, taps.

Some of the women were detailed to give aid in making surgical dressings at a Red Cross station in charge of Mrs.

W. G. Evans. Though no certificates were given for this work, or other official recognition, all were enthusiastic in endeavoring to make the bandages and dressings as perfectly as possible. The help given in this way to the Red Cross was of practical value since the dressings and bandages were sent to the front, where the demand for such articles was always great.

Life as lived in the Service Camp on Loretto grounds during those weeks in July, 1917, gave those in training a good idea of the life of a soldier while in camp. The four companies of women were under the direction of officers who were appointed according to their rank in competitive drills: commandant, Miss May Scotland; adjutant, Celeste Dorr; major, Mrs. Philip Chase; captains, Phyllis Campion, Nancy Hitch, and Dorothy Shomberg; first lieutenants, Dorothy Wood, Helen Campion, Eileen Ewing, and Anna Dillon; second lieutenants, Martha Wilcox, Louise Guldman, Katherine Ditmore, and Rosemary Quinn; sergeants, Florence Guldman, Kathleen Mitchell, Dorothy Kellerman, and Juanita Fruth; corporal, Margaret Owen.

The majority of the women appreciated this glimpse of army life even though the training was severe and demanded their full service and attention. When the time came, however, to break up camp, few were reluctant to give up this mode of life and return to their usual routine and garb. At the close of the service school, Colonel Robert N. Getty thanked the Sisters of Loretto for the many courtesies which had been extended to the officers and women of the school.

One can easily visualize what must have been the unusual conditions at this quiet seat of learning while the school was on the grounds: the campus dotted with the tents of the women in training; signs on all sides of a bustling camp life—the tramp of marching feet, the bugle calls and taps vieing with the convent bells, ringing at stated hours to call the sisters, permanently living at the Heights, to their various exercises.

After the service school broke camp, the quiet, well-ordered days were soon re-established in and around

Loretto Heights. On the third day of the annual retreat, the sisters received the sad but not unexpected news that their good father and friend, the Most Reverend Nicholas C. Matz, the second Bishop of Denver, had died that morning, August 9, at St. Anthony's Hospital.

Bishop Matz had been ordained for the Denver diocese, May 31, 1874, in the old St. Mary's Cathedral, by Bishop Machebeuf. Thirteen years later, Bishop Machebeuf, owing to failing health and the infirmities of age, petitioned Rome for a coadjutor to assist in the duties of the office which was weighing heavily upon him. Accordingly on October 28, 1887, the Most Reverend J. B. Salpointe, Archbishop of Santa Fe, consecrated Reverend N. C. Matz, in the same Cathedral where he had been ordained, Coadjutor Bishop of Denver, with the right of succession. Scarcely two years later, when Bishop Machebeuf died, July 10, 1889, worn out with his years of zealous, apostolic labors in the vicariate and diocese of Denver, the Most Reverend Nicholas C. Matz became the Ordinary of the see. In September, 1917, the gentle and learned Bishop of Lincoln, Nebraska, the Most Reverend J. Henry Tihen, was appointed third Bishop of Denver.

During the fall months of 1917, the students tried to do what they could to help in the national crisis by becoming members of the Loretto Auxiliary, which was composed of seventy students and thirty alumnae. The purpose of the organization was to knit for the soldiers. Knitting became the order of the day. Everybody was knitting, in season and out of season, sweaters, helmets, socks, and mufflers for the men in service. Miss Margaret Fallon, an alumna, was president of the Auxiliary, Mrs. William Matthews, secretary, and Mrs. Fred Schmidt, treasurer. Anna Fallon and Emily Cox, former students, were indefatigable workers for this worthy project.

Besides working zealously in knitting, the girls contributed generously in helping the Knights of Columbus of Denver in their efforts to raise their quota for the National War Fund. On March 4, 1918, Mr. James McSwigan, general chairman for the Denver Knights, wrote to thank the sisters and students for their checks of $75 and $165 respectively.

The sisters and students were honored when the Most Reverend J. Henry Tihen, the recently appointed Bishop of Denver, consented to deliver the commencement address and confer the diplomas upon the seniors at the closing exercises on June 11, 1918. The Honorable J. C. Gunter, Governor of the state of Colorado, was one of the honor guests on the occasion. After Bishop Tihen had delivered his learned and eloquent address—it will be remembered that Bishop Tihen was a master in oratory—he called upon Governor Gunter, quite unexpectedly, to confer the diplomas upon the graduating class. Bishop Tihen's gracious recognition of the Governor and the latter's affable acceptance of the honor elicited a burst of applause from the audience.

Those who were distinguished by having the highest dignitaries in the Church and state at their graduating exercises were Grace Bransom, Wilhelmina Cordano, Alice Croke, Irene Johnson, Helen Kehn, May Guireaud, Lucille Mannix, Pauline Nelson, Mary Pearl Queen, Patrice Richards, Muriel Turnbull, and Mary Shaw.

Chapter XVIII

LORETTO HEIGHTS COLLEGE OPENS

Under circumstances which might appear to the casual observer fortuitous but to the initiate as belonging to the great pattern designed by Almighty God, the Sisters of Loretto began their work of teaching in 1812. To this work the sisters have devoted themselves wholeheartedly, realizing that teaching and training the young were the means God had designed for their own sanctification as well as for the sanctification of the souls entrusted to their care. Since teaching was the purpose of their Society, the importance of preparing themselves for their calling was always understood. At an early date a normal or training school was established at the Motherhouse, where the young religious, before entering upon the duties of the classroom, were grounded in the content of the courses they were to teach and in methods of presentation. Later, after their duties in the classroom had become familiar to the junior teachers, the superiors arranged, wherever there was an opportunity of securing professors, that the sisters should continue at convenient times their higher studies; for the most part, however, there was no plan or sequence in these courses.

When the Catholic University of America admitted the sisterhoods to the regular sessions, a fresh impetus was given to higher education. The example set by this institution was soon followed by many Catholic universities throughout the country. The Sisters of Loretto, like the members of other teaching communities, availed themselves of these educational opportunities that they might be better prepared for their profession.

The influence of these institutions of higher learning began to be felt in the faculties of the secondary schools. Many of the sisters thought that the time was opportune for opening Catholic colleges, in order that those students of the high schools who wished to continue their education might pursue their work in a Catholic environment. Mother Praxedes, a woman of courage, zeal, and vision, the Superior General of the Sisters of Loretto, believing that the educational scope of the Lorettines should be enlarged, began to plan for the erection of a college. With Mother Praxedes to plan and dream was to execute. To the astonishment of many of the sisters of her own community, her dreams and plans began to materialize in the college which she was erecting in Webster Groves, Missouri. It took courage, it took faith to build at a time when the first World War was in progress, the outcome of which no one could foresee. In the fall of 1916 Loretto College, now known as Webster College, was opened, the first Catholic institution of its kind for women in or near St. Louis. The opening of this college was an educational venture, which appeared, no doubt, to many, premature and quite unnecessary.

Scarcely was Webster College well launched when Mother Praxedes became convinced that an institution for the higher education of the young women of Colorado and the adjoining Western states should be opened at Loretto Heights. In planning for this second college, the Mother General of the Lorettines and the local superior, Mother Clarasine, felt that the large, commodious administration building would accommodate, at least for a few years, both the academy and the college students.

Accordingly, with little preparation or forethought, Loretto Heights College was opened in September, 1918, with Mother Clarasine Walsh, president, Sister Dolorine Morrison, dean of the college, and Sister Vivian Edelen, registrar. Sister Dolorine had been connected with Loretto Heights for many years as teacher or directress; Sister Vivian had lived all her religious life, after the completion of her novitiate, at St. Mary's Academy, Denver. Both sisters were well acquainted with the city and its people; a knowledge which was useful in the difficult work which confronted them in this new venture.

Since the attendance in the academy department was quite large that year, very little space could be set aside for college classrooms or other necessary quarters. The outlook for establishing a college was not bright. Finally, an assembly room and a classroom—these were later thrown into one to form the present college library—a science room and library were furnished in the north wing of the building. Fortunately, the student body that first year was small: Mary Hayden, a sophomore, Alice Croke, Mary Donnelly, and Shellie Clark, of freshman rank. Sister Dolorine taught English and expression; Sister Vivian, history and mathematics; Sister Vitalis, modern languages and music; and Sister Bathildes, chemistry and Latin. As the work progressed many difficulties presented themselves; but the superiors were optimistic, and the sisters kept bravely at their duties, familiarizing themselves with college requirements and adjusting themselves to the demands of the work before them.

The college grew slowly both in students and faculty. In the second year new courses, which required additional professors, were added to the curriculum. Monsignor Richard Brady taught religion and church history; the Reverend William Brennan, C.M., Ph.D., of St. Thomas Seminary, was professor of philosophy; the Reverend Russell J. Kirschenheuter, C.M., also of St. Thomas Seminary, taught Sacred Scripture; Sisters Dolorine, Vitalis, and Bathildes gave additional courses in their departments; Sister Francisca taught English and education; and Sister Vivian added Greek to her previous schedule.

There was need of enduring courage during those first years; although there had been an increase in the registration, the school remained small. Perhaps it was well that the college grew slowly, for the soil was, in a way, being processed carefully, systematically, with scientific adjustment here and mathematical precision there, the whole being leavened with the spirit of Loretto. The planting was being done; the future would take care of the harvest.

Mother Clarasine, besides being president of the college, was superior of the community; these offices she held until she was elected Superior General of the Sisters of Loretto at the Foot of the Cross, in 1922, by the delegates to the general chapter of the Society. Mother Clarasine proved to be an efficient administrator. During her term of office at the Heights the emergency hospital was erected on the south campus and adequately furnished. This building has been used for years as a practice house by the students of the home economics department. Fire escapes were constructed on the north and south wings of the administration building; the chapel of Our Lady of Loretto was beautifully frescoed; and, finally, forty-five acres of land were added to the campus. This new ground was located southwest of the original tract purchased in 1888 by Mother Pancratia. The expenses incurred for these various improvements were all liquidated before the close of Mother Clarasine's term of office.

At the opening of the third year of the college, in the fall of 1920, the Very Reverend William Barr, C.M., Ph.D., president of St. Thomas Seminary, became professor of philosophy; the Reverend James O'Malley, C.M., also of St. Thomas Seminary, taught psychology; Sister Mary Edmond Fern was transferred from St. Mary's Academy in the city to direct the department of classical languages; and Sister Bernadita Bauckman became librarian and instructor in German and mathematics.

Miss Mary Hayden, daughter of Mr. and Mrs. Charles Hayden of Denver, was the first student upon whom Loretto Heights College conferred the Bachelor of Arts degree in June, 1921. Miss Hayden, having made her first year of college at Mt. St. Joseph's, Cincinnati, Ohio, entered Loretto Heights College as a sophomore in the fall of 1918. A specially gifted student, this first alumna of the college excelled not only in all her academic studies but also in music. After teaching one year at the Cathedral High School in Denver, Mary surprised her many friends by entering the Daughters of Carmel, in Los Angeles, where she received the name, Sister Céline of the Holy Trinity. She has kept close to her old school, Loretto Heights College, during the years which have passed since her gradua-

tion. The sisters at Loretto Heights recall with gratitude
that the first graduate of the academy, Katherine Casey,
now known as Sister Menodora, dedicated her life to God
as a Sister of Loretto, and the first graduate of the college
entered the cloistered life of Carmel.

The officers of the newly-opened college soon took
measures to secure necessary accreditation which the school
must acquire in order to have proper scholastic recognition. The first step taken in this direction was to obtain
the approval of the State Board of Education so that the
graduates who qualified might receive state teachers' certificates. In the spring of 1921, Mrs. Mary C. C. Brad-
ford, State Superintendent, Dr. Wm. H. Smiley, William
S. Roe, and four other members of the State Board of
Education visited the college, attended the classes which
were in session, examined the science department and its
equipment, the library facilities, and the courses of study.
The Board later gave its unanimous approval of the college.

As soon as the college was well established, courses
which would meet the educational needs of the sisters in
the vicinity were offered, for the first time, in the summer
session of 1921. The students who attended were for the
most part Lorettines in Colorado and other western states.
Every year since 1921, the summer courses have been attended not only by Lorettines but also by members of other
teaching communities. Many sisters, who on account of
their school duties are not able to attend the regular sessions of the college, have been enabled through the courses
offered at Loretto Heights on Saturday and during the
summer to complete their undergraduate studies and earn
the Bachelor's degree.

Monica Elizabeth Hayden, sister of Mary Hayden, was
the second graduate of the college. She also had completed
her freshman year of college in Cincinnati, coming to the
Heights in the fall of 1919 as a sophomore. The commencement exercises were held in the chapel on the morning of June 5, 1922. The Reverend Hugh McMenamin,
rector of the Cathedral in Denver, in the address for the
occasion gave well-merited praise to Miss Monica Hayden

who received graduating honors that morning. On August 2, at the closing exercises of the summer school, seven Sisters of Loretto received the Bachelor of Arts degree.

Mother Mary Linus Maier, who had long been associated with Loretto Heights, even from the early days, and had practically grown up with the institution as an efficient teacher of mathematics and other subjects, after an absence of a number of years, returned to her old home, in the summer of 1922, as superior of the community and president of the college. The valuable experiences which had come to her as directress at Loretto Academy in Las Cruces, New Mexico, and superior of the Loretto school in Bisbee, Arizona, and of Loretto Academy, Kansas City, Missouri, were of service in the position which she was then called upon to fill.

The officers of the college, as they studied the needs and requirements of the various departments, continued to expand the curriculum. In the second semester of the year 1922-1923, the Reverend Francis Walsh, who was an assistant at the Cathedral, became professor of sociology, a subject which he continued to teach for several years. Father Walsh later returned to his native East and after some years was raised to the rank of Monsignor. About the same time, he was appointed president of New Rochelle College, New York. Sister M. Valena Eppler became art instructor in the fall of 1922.

Within the scholastic year of 1922-1923, an advisory board was organized with the Most Reverend J. Henry Tihen, Bishop of Denver, as president and moderator. The Very Reverend William P. Barr, president of St. Thomas Seminary, the Right Reverend Monsignor Richard Brady, chaplain of the college, the administrative officers, and several members of the faculty formed the personnel of the board.

Three students received degrees in June, 1923, Mary Lucille Mannix, Mary Margaret Stout, and Catherine Cecilia Byrne. All three girls have distinguished themselves as teachers in the public schools of Colorado and other states. Mary Stout, after teaching for a few years, entered the novitiate of the Sisters of Loretto, receiving the name of Sister Miriam Jerome. At the completion of her years of religious training, she was missioned to New Mexico where she has continued her teaching.

While the sister members of the faculty were carrying on the regular work of the college, they were not neglecting to further their own studies to meet the requirements for higher degrees. Sister Mary Edmond and Sister Vivian attended the graduate school of Colorado University during the summer of 1923, taking courses in classics and history respectively.

Two college publications, the *Heightsonian* and the *Loretana,* began their existence during the school year of 1923-1924; the former was the college news sheet, the latter the yearbook. The date line for the first number of the *Heightsonian* was November 25, 1923; the yearly subscription was $1.25. The staff personnel was Sister Mary Dolorine, faculty adviser; Surilda Wilson, editor-in-chief; Helen Doyle, assistant editor; Elizabeth Marshall, advisory manager; Helen Hyland, college athletics; Delette Coy, Bernadine Hagan, Marie Fuite, assistant editors; Eileen Whisler, academic editor; Queena Aulgar and Ursula Fagan, assistant academic editors. The *Heightsonian* was a three-column, four-page, eight-and-one-half by eleven inch paper.

When the students of the college were planning their news sheet, the problem of naming the paper presented itself. A committee was appointed to choose an appropriate name for the paper which was in course of formation. After exhausting their ingenuity in vain, they decided to advertise, offering a year's subscription as a prize to the person suggesting the most suitable name. Enthusiasm ran high; naming the publication elicited interest among faculty and students. Sister Mary Vivian was awarded the prize for suggesting the name, *Heightsonian,* which the committee considered the most characteristic for a news publication of Loretto Heights College.

The college yearbook, the *Loretana,* was a revival of the *Loretto Annual,* a publication which was issued for a few years by the students of Loretto Heights Academy. The name *Loretana* was, perhaps, a corruption of *Loretto Annual;* whatever was the origin of the name, its significance is evident.

Sister Dolorine was the faculty adviser of the *Loretana* for 1924; Bernice McGroarty, editor-in-chief; and Delette Coy, assistant editor. This first yearbook records no other officers; the remainder of the work which the publication entailed must have been distributed among generous helpers.

As a matter of history that issue of the *Loretana* is an important volume among the college records. The dear, familiar faces of the seniors of that year look out from the pages, cheerfully and hopefully, on the world which then lay unconquered before them. The captions attached to each student's picture are interesting in retrospect; so, too, are the various offices held by those students who have since proved themselves loyal alumnae of Loretto and efficient women in their chosen fields. Margaret Sullivan, "One of the few immortal names that were not born to die," President of the Student Body and President of the Dramatic club. Helen Hyland, "The only silent woman in the world," President of the Class of '24 and President of the Athletic association, Athletic editor of the *Heightsonian,* and Representative of the Student Council; Surilda Wilson, "Yes, I'm always good; I always put off until tomorrow the things I shouldn't do at all," Vice-president of the Student Body, Editor-in-chief of the *Heightsonian,* President of the Literary club; Helen Doyle, "A noble type of good, heroic womanhood," Prefect of the Sodality, Treasurer of the Athletic Association, Assistant Editor of the *Heightsonian;* Mary Shovlin, "We hate to lose her, but the good of the world comes first," Vice-president of the Sodality, Business Manager of the *Heightsonian,* Chronicler of the Class of '24; Delette Coy, "Study all night for a quiz, then sleep past quiz time," Vice-president of the Class of '24, Secretary of the Sodality, Secretary of the Athletic Association, Assistant Editor of the *Loretana;* Marie Eaches, "She never allows anything to interfere with her education,"

Secretary of the Class of '24, Vice-president of the Dramatic club; Bernice McGroarty, "Age will not wither her, nor custom stale her infinite variety," Vice-president of the Athletic Association, Treasurer of the Mission Crusade, Editor-in-chief of the *Loretana*.

The students of both the college and academy were deeply interested in the celebration, November 14, 1923, of the golden jubilee of Mother Clarasine Walsh, the Superior General of the Sisters of Loretto at the Foot of the Cross, who had been, until 1922, the superior of the community at Loretto Heights and president of the college. The first issue of the *Heightsonian* carried this account of the jubilee: "In appreciation of Mother Clarasine's noble work carried on so successfully for many years, all the superiors of the various houses, laden with beautiful gifts and thoughts from the Loretto Sisters and girls, attended the celebration."

For some time the girls of the college had been informing themselves of the advantages and disadvantages of student government as it was functioning in many colleges. After due deliberation and consultation with the faculty, the students formally adopted this system on October 13, 1923, a date which marks the beginning of the first stumbling attempts at student government, a system not altogether new; for, from the opening of the college, the necessity of securing order and co-operation through the individual's sense of responsibility was inculcated. Margaret Sullivan, the first student body president, made this statement regarding the new form of government: "Since in all undertakings plans must be allowed to ripen, dreams must be developed slowly, only now is the college sufficiently established to warrant its adoption. The ideal of student government is to foster dependability in the members and bring faculty and students together in closer sympathy."

Members of the Student Council, the executive unit of the association, were elected. This body formed a sort of court which had jurisdiction in minor disciplinary matters; a Supreme Council, consisting of the president of the college, the dean, and the faculty, met regularly with the members of the Student Council to legislate on matters of major importance.

Students of Loretto Heights College were kept busy; the regular schedule required much of their time, but in addition to their studies many extra curricular activities claimed their attention: they were establishing student government, attending meetings of the athletic association, contributing to musical, dramatic, and literary clubs, and all the while trying to find time to live. Kathleen White, the regular contributor to the "Day Dogs' Diary" in the *Heightsonian*—"day dog" was the student vernacular for day student—wrote a rhyme which pictures the day students as they saw themselves in those days. Miss White explained that *Run,* the motto of the *D.D.'s,* was well chosen, because, as Byron said, "The life of a dog is one continual run after another":

> We run for front seats, we dress on the run:
> We run while we eat, we run for the car—
> We run through our texts while we're on No. 3;
> Again run for front seats in the busses we see.
> We run to our classes, we dash to our lunch,
> We run back at one, and land in a bunch,
> We run to the classroom, our lessons run o'er,
> Then run for coats and for the side door.
> We run for the car, to Englewood it runs us,
> To the trolley we run, and alight in a muss.
> We run to our homes, again run through our texts,
> Then run off to bed—where shall we run next?
> That Byron was right, you plainly can see.
> Don't you think that our motto fits us nicely?

In June, 1924, the number of students to be graduated shows an increase over the first years. Sarah Delette Coy, Helen Marie Doyle, Marie Shane Eaches, Helen Cecilia Hyland, Bernice Catherine McGroarty, Mary Agnes Shovlin, Margaret Josephine Sullivan, and Laura Surilda Wilson. Eleven Sisters of Loretto received degrees at the close of the summer school in August, 1924.

During the summer of 1924, Sister Mary Dolorine, dean of the college, and Sister Mary Vivian, registrar, received the degree of Doctor of Philosophy from De Paul University in Chicago, a well-merited recognition of their scholastic attainments. Sister Mary Dolorine's major subject was English and Sister Mary Vivian's history.

Doctor William P. Barr, C.M., who had been transferred to Perryville, Missouri, in 1924, was replaced in the philosophy department by the Reverend Marshall Winne, C.M., of St. Thomas Seminary. That same year and for several years after, the Reverend Matthew Smith, editor of the *Denver Catholic Register,* taught the students interested in journalism the secrets of successful newspaper writing. Sister Mary Romula Dea was appointed to the college faculty in the fall of '24 as an instructor in English and education and served as librarian.

Mother Mary Linus had been an efficient president of the college from the time she took over its duties in 1922. It was with regret that the faculty witnessed her departure, in 1925, to assume the same duties of superior and president at Webster College, Webster Groves, Missouri. Mother Eustachia Elder, director of the department of chemistry at Webster College, was appointed superior and president at Loretto Heights, a position she held until her death in 1929.

The first important matter to claim the attention of Mother Eustachia was the accreditation of the college by the North Central Association of Colleges and Secondary Schools. Great credit is due to Mother Eustachia for her efforts in securing the necessary recognition of the college. An amount of correspondence was carried on; questionnaires were answered; and, finally, the North Central Association appointed Doctor Reed of the University of Nebraska to examine the college, its teaching staff, its records, buildings, and equipment. As the result of his inspection, Doctor Reed recommended the college for admission to the North Central Association, with the recommendation that, as soon as possible, college and high school should be completely separated. At the annual meeting of the Association in March, 1926, Loretto Heights was placed on the list of accredited colleges. Sister Mary Dolorine and Sister Mary Vivian, who attended the meeting in Chicago, sent the encouraging news to Mother Eustachia, who was eagerly awaiting the outcome of the request for accreditation. Both faculty and students were cheered by this recognition of the college which was of prime importance especially to those students who were planning to enter the teaching profession after receiving their degrees.

Sister Dolorine, dean of the college, took pleasure in making the days preceding graduation eventful for the seniors of each year. The crowning of Our Lady of Lourdes in the grotto on the last Sunday in May, the consecration of the graduates to Mary Immaculate, class day programs, the religious and student ceremonies of Baccalaureate Sunday—all these exercises, scheduled for the closing days, were impressive and colorful. Commencement was the crowning day for the seniors.

After the senior play, senior music recitals, and all other final programs, Mary Margaret Carraher, Ethel Catherine Doss, Mary Madeleine Gibbons, Margaret Lucille Lucy, Anne Delia New, and Margaret Elizabeth Vinton received Bachelor of Arts degrees in June, 1925; Mary Adele Clements, the first Bachelor of Music degree among the girl students. At the close of summer school, two Sisters of Loretto received degrees.

For several years in the '20's, the Knights of Columbus manifested their interest in the college by sponsoring an oratorical contest. The number of final entrants was always sufficient to make the winning of the gold medal award, donated by Mr. Joseph A. Stanko, in memory of his little son, J. Richard Stanko, a much coveted honor. On March 14, 1926, Madonna Campbell of the class of '26 was the successful competitor.

The students in those days were quite interested in the art of public speaking. Girls who had special ability in oratory formed part of a group or groups, usually there were several, which toured the state each spring, in order to make the institution and its work better known to the people of Colorado. These educational tours served as an incentive in several departments; talented students in music, voice, and speech formed the trio or quartette which advertised the college in a practical way.

Madonna Campbell, her sister Evelyn, Marie Fuite, Margaret Carraher, Margaret Vinton, and Mary Kelly were a few of the students selected for these tours. The Knights of Columbus of the state of Colorado are remembered gratefully for their co-operation in this activity of Loretto Heights: they arranged reception committees for the college girls and their chaperons and secured auditoriums and appreciative audiences in the cities visited.

The Denver Knights of Columbus gave a further proof of their interest in the spring of 1926. The Knights in charge of the *Record,* one of their publications, entrusted the editing of the March issue to the students of the journalism class. The girls, feeling their responsibility in getting out a real magazine, put their best efforts on the paper.

Bachelor of Arts degrees were granted in June, 1926, to Ida Ann Uerling, Mary Ellen Mitchell, Bernadine Elma Hagan, Mary Cecilia Sullivan, Iverne Cecilia Hickey, Clare Frances Biglin, and Margaret Madonna Campbell; Isabelle Agnes O'Drain received a Bachelor of Music degree. At the close of the summer session of that year, four Sisters of Loretto received the Bachelor of Arts degree, and two received degrees in music.

As the needs of the students developed from year to year, the curriculum and the teaching staff were enlarged. Sister Ann Francis McArdle became librarian in the fall of 1926 and instructor in education. Other professors and instructors were added at the beginning of the scholastic year, 1926-1927: the Reverend Paul Misner, C.M., Ph.D., professor of philosophy; the Reverend Joseph O'Heron, sociology; Sister Antonina Ryan, biology; Sister Celestine Casey, English language; and Sister Teresa Marie Hentzen, director of the music department. At the close of the summer of 1927, Sister Rose Margaret Cook received the Master of Science degree from the University of Notre Dame and became director of the department of mathematics and physics.

In June, 1927, the largest class, up to that time, in the history of the college was graduated. The first students to receive the honor of *summa cum laude* were Marie Genevieve Fuite of Grand Junction, Colorado, and Mary Ann Taylor of Cheyenne, Wyoming. The other eight who received degrees that June day were Eileen Joanna Barry, Helen Irene Cannon, Mary Margaret Kelly, Mary Evelyn Campbell, Loretto Agnes McGrath, Eileen Francis Solis, Patricia Fabiola Ross, and Margaret Bensberg On August 2, four Sisters of Loretto received Bachelor of Arts degrees, and two received degrees in music.

These first nine years were years of earnest endeavor on the part of faculty and students. The regular schedule of classes was diversified by student programs, clever plays given from time to time by the members of the dramatic association, lectures by well-known speakers, and devoted work for the home and foreign missions—all these contributed to the mental and spiritual development of the students and formed an important part of their training.

Chapter XIX

PANCRATIA HALL GRACES CAMPUS

During the opening year of Loretto Heights College, since the students were few in number, Sister Dolorine carried the duties of the dean and directed the activities of the academy. In the fall of 1919, Sister Francisca Engles was appointed directress of the academy, a duty which she performed faithfully until 1927 when she was transferred to the college as a full-time teacher.

Loretto Heights Academy during these years was, above all, a school of high ideals and scholarship where the students were taught to know and love the good and the beautiful. While Sister Francisca retained all the worthwhile traditional customs, she added extra-curricular activities which brought further expansion and progress.

The atmosphere and high moral tone of the school were no doubt instrumental in arousing interest in the doctrines of the Catholic Church among many of the older girls who were not Catholics. Twenty baptisms and fifty-seven confirmations are recorded in the chaplain's *Registrum*, a goodly number to receive these sacraments, when compared with the total registration of the school. Sister Francisca, in recalling the academy as she knew it, wrote: "To me these conversions constitute the most outstanding incidents of those years, since they show God's blessing upon the school, and indicate that our work justified its existence; and that it was fulfilling one of the ends for which it was established."

Students of the academy who were graduated during the next decade, from 1919 to 1929, were distinguished for ability and leadership in many fields. Though each girl deserves to be written into a sheaf all her own, which would prove the appreciation of her one-time teachers, not more than a mere listing of successive classes can be given here.

In the class of 1919 are found the names of Edna Ferris, Frances Conway, Ruth McFarland, Virginia Rice, Dorothy Platt, Martha Manty, Phyllis Udick, Claire Corning, Hannah Gross, and Cecilia Gallegos. The seniors to receive diplomas in the following June, 1920, were Corinne Espinosa, Elsie Mahoney, Virginia Paradise, Lucille Croke, Helen Doyle, Florence Donnelly, Marjorie Grimes, Mary Reddin, Mary McGregor, Frances McGarry, Belinda Salazar, Marie Eaches, and Erin La Bissoniere. Mildred Pauline Hite's name appears on the school record as a member of that class of '20 but Pauline, as she was usually called, was absent on commencement day to the great grief of her teachers and classmates. A short time before the close of school Pauline became suddenly ill; and, in spite of all the efforts of doctors and nurses, she died, after three days illness, of appendicitis, on May 17, 1920, the only student in the history of the institution to die at Loretto Heights.

Since they numbered fifteen, the members of the class of 1921 loved to call themselves the decades of the rosary. The members of that living rosary were Georgena Burns, Lolalee Tomblin, Margaret Smith, Rose Marie McGinley, Catherine Rose, Maryette Fitch, Hester Holland, Pauline Whitman, Vivian Wilson, Sara O'Keefe, Thelma Everitt, Elizabeth Offerman, Margaret Dunn, Rosylyn Vurpillat, and Kathleen Andrew.

In June, 1922, sixteen girls formed the graduating class, the members of which were Katherine Ryan, Alice O'Neil, Marie Hamilton, Louise Paggi, Ida Chase, Helen Croke, Alice Powers, Genevieve Funk, Bernadine O'Neil, Treva Williams, Shirley Wood, Bernice Mecum, Anna Scariano, Dorothy Doyle, Josephine Schneible, and Anne Prendergast.

The class of 1923 had the following roll call: Dolores Strutzel, Margaret Brown, Virginia Porter, Rosella Johnson, Florence Henry, and Helen Stahl.

Making up the class of 1924 were these students: Theresa May Hample, Ursula Fagan, Mildred O'Neil, Enaze Porter, Eileen Whisler, Mary Keegan, Mary Tracy,

Helene Hall, Queena Aulgur, Juanita Hagan, Angela Ayola, and Eulalia Reagan.

Ranking in numbers next to that of 1926 was the class of 1925: Corrine C. de Baca, Catherine Clements, Catherine Croke, Helen Doyle, Ruth Ellis, Ada Emerich, Bernice Garwood, Charlene Garwood, Mary Charlotte Hannig, Evelyn Kipferl, Eleanor McKelvey, Mary O'Loughlin, Elizabeth Swift, Charlotte Temple, Helen Tubbs, Evelyn Waldo, and Julia Wooldridge.

The class of 1926 was the largest in the history of the academy. The graduates of that year were Margaret Barney, Ethel Beringer, Mary Cassidy, Marguerite Dolan, Marjorie Edman, Alice Jane Evans, Kathleen Feeney, Sally Fisher, Elizabeth Gartland, Mary Elizabeth Gaule, Sidney Graybeal, Marguerite Hall, Bernice Lattin, Mary Ledford, Naomi Lilja, Emily McKeon, Madeline Milan, Lena Rogers, and Alice Staunton.

During the next scholastic year the seniors again formed a complete rosary chain. The students to receive diplomas in 1927 were Margaret Allen, Rachel Berry, Louise C. de Baca, Helen Chambers, Rose Doyle, Dorothy Duffies, Madeleine Erickson, Helen Fairfield, Hilda Gallagher, Paula Garcia, Mary Heffron, Catherine McMullen, Leanore Ostrander, Marie Pigeon, and Isabel Ward.

In 1928 the students to complete their academic course were Prue Avery, Mae Carney, Dorothy Coon, Marguerite Baca, Dorothy Ennis, Mae Irene Gish, Helen Gallagher, Eunice Lopez, Laberta McClung, Helen McGraw, Louise McMahon, Marquette Spence, and Mercia Walker. Sister Mary Urban McFarland was directress during the scholastic year 1927-28.

Mother Eustachia Elder, the local superior at the Heights from 1925 to 1929, who had been largely instrumental in having the college accredited by the North Central Association of Colleges and Secondary Schools, did not lose sight of the necessity of separating the college from the high school and grade school. From the time the college had been placed on the accredited list, Mother Eustachia was concerned with plans for the new building. Finally, at the beginning of 1928, definite steps were taken to effect these plans: architects were consulted, blueprints were made, contractors were interviewed, bids were received, faculty members were brought into conferences, plans were made and remade—all this before the work of building could be entered upon.

In January, 1928, a Building Fund Campaign was formally opened at a banquet at the Albany hotel in Denver. This was attended by business men of the city and friends of the Sisters of Loretto, who were vitally interested in the building project. The members of the finance committee explained their plans for raising at least $75,000 as a contribution of the people of Denver toward defraying part of the cost of the new building. Besides the directors of the "drive," there were volunteer workers called "gleaners," who were to take over much of the drudgery of the house-to-house contacts. The "drive" was to extend over a brief period of time. When the various committees had received their instructions, the work was begun and carried through on a definite time schedule.

At the close of the campaign, a "victory" dinner was given to the men and women who had taken an active part in bringing the "drive" to a successful close. While the original goal of $75,000 was never realized, a good sum, $55,000, was contributed through this concerted effort. To the generous donors of that sum, the Sisters of Loretto were deeply grateful and will always be indebted. The girls of the college gave $500 to the building campaign, quite an acceptable and generous gift from students who were limited in their allowances.

Ground was broken for the new building October 24, 1928. Everyone present, faculty and students, participated in the ceremony of removing sufficient soil to form a cross to mark the site. Mother Mary Olivette Norton, Superior General of the Sisters of Loretto, who had come from the Motherhouse for the ceremony, was the first to use the spade in the process of digging; Mother Genevieve Wheat, Treasurer General, was the next to remove the soil; Mother

Eustachia, superior of the community and president of the college, Sister M. Dolorine, the dean, and members of the faculty of both schools helped to deepen the cross. The last to use the spade was little Carol Southern, the youngest child in the academy.

The Very Reverend William M. Brennan, C.M., president of St. Thomas Seminary, the speaker for the occasion, congratulated the Sisters of Loretto on the work in education they had already accomplished in the state of Colorado and spoke of the significance of the ceremony they had just witnessed for the advancement of education.

During the winter months, the work of construction which was begun immediately was retarded. With the coming of spring, the number of workmen was increased and the walls began to rise. The sisters gave enthusiastic attention to the progress of the building; they watched, apparently, every brick as it was laid in place, rejoicing when the work seemed to make headway and grieving when there was a delay. And there were delays.

Especially interested in the progress of the building were the girls of the high school. *The Pancratian* in an early issue of 1930 carries an article which gives evidence of their enthusiasm:

At last Pancratia Hall has reached that stage in its development when it is possible for even school girls to visualize how it will look next September when it is finished and furnished and filled with happy students. Every afternoon eager groups roam through the halls selecting rooms for next year, planning desk locations in the beautiful study halls, and making reservations on the use of the candy kitchens.

During the summer of 1930, all the finishing touches were put on the new building which was finally ready for occupancy at the opening of the fall term. The initial cost of Pancratia Hall was estimated at $225,000; when the building was finished these figures had been increased to $298,171. This latter amount was further increased by unavoidable expenses incurred for constructing a tunnel in connection with the irrigation system; for the subway which serves not only as a conduit for steam and water pipes but as a passageway between the buildings; for a water tank, having a capacity of 50,000 gallons, which supplies all buildings on the campus; for remodeling and refurnishing the administration building and completing the equipment and furnishings of the new school—all these expenditures made a total of $350,000.

According to the contract the building should have been completed much earlier than it was. The members of the class of 1929 of Loretto Heights Academy had no regrets about spending their last year in the classrooms and haunts so full of happy memories. Sister Mary Edgar McCall was directress from September, 1928 to June, 1930. The members of her first senior class were Martha Berger, Rosemary Cassidy, Susan Cassidy, Margaret Cole, Margaret Hesse, Trinidad Lopez, Wilma Meyer, Clara Mueller, Laura Oswald, Marguerite Roy, Margaret Runsteller, Pauline Smith, Ruth Thomas, and Josephine Wardell.

Still another year passed before the new building was nearing completion. On June 4, 1930, the last class of seniors, the thirty-ninth graduating class, to have the honor of completing their studies in the historic building, were, according to academy records, Helen Bugas, Marian Church, Catherine Eichoff, Fay C. Hougham, Patricia Kenehan, Irene Kohler, Catherine McClure, Grace L. Mahoney, Helen McKelvey, June Mawhor, Julia L. Smead, and Virginia A. Vyse.

The summer of 1930 was one of intense activity for the faculties of both schools: the main building was undergoing a complete renovation and remodeling in order to fit it for the growing needs of the college; the high school department was being transferred to the fine new fireproof building, Pancratia Hall, a fitting monument to the memory of Mother Pancratia, that valiant woman who by her zeal and devotedness had contributed so generously, through long years, to the advancement of Catholic education in Colorado.

In August of that year, Sister M. Modwena Doyle was appointed directress of Pancratia Hall, a position which she held for four years. To her wise educational policies the school owed much of its progress after its removal from its old quarters in the main building where it had functioned since 1891.

For some weeks previous to the dedication of the building, Sister Modwena and the high school faculty were busily preparing for this impressive ceremony. Particular attention was given to the furnishing of the beautiful chapel. The parents and friends of the sisters were generous in donating gifts for the home where Christ was to dwell. The main altar was erected in memory of Mr. and Mrs. David McGarry, the parents of Sister Francis de Sales; the altar railing and chalice were gifts of Miss Frances Keefe in memory of her parents, Mr. and Mrs. John A. Keefe, one of whose daughters, Sister Frances Loretto, was then music teacher in the high school department; Mrs. John Reddin, mother of Sister M. Cecille, another member of the faculty of the new school, gave the statue of Our Lady; the statue of St. Joseph was donated in memory of Mr. Francis J. Lyons, brother of Sister Peter Joseph, teacher of voice; the beautiful sanctuary lamp was the gift of Mr. and Mrs. J. G. Wirthman of Kansas City, brother and sister-in-law of Sister Mary Rosalie, a devoted member of the community at the Heights; the parents of Sister Mary James, Mr. and Mrs. James Dowd of St. Louis, donated the ciborium; Mr. and Mrs. Edward O'Toole, also of St. Louis, the parents of Sister Frances Jane, gave two gold vases for the main altar.

Mother Praxedes Carty, superior of Loretto Academy, El Paso, Texas, and former superior of Loretto Heights Academy from June, 1894 to March, 1896, and later superior general of the Sisters of Loretto, donated a missal stand and a beautiful burse. Miss Blanche Rayle, a teacher in the Southwest, who attended for several years the summer sessions at Loretto Heights College, gave the golden candlesticks and crucifix for the main altar in memory of Mother Clarasine, former superior of Loretto Heights and, later, successor of Mother Praxedes as superior general of the order. The class of 1930 of the academy gave two pair of gold vases for the altars of Our Lady and St. Joseph; the juniors and seniors of 1931 donated the Stations of the Cross, and the class of 1932 donated the censor and stand.

The girls of Pancratia Hall loved from the very beginning the beautiful little chapel to which they had contributed so generously. One of the issues of *The Pancratian*, the school paper, gives an interesting and accurate description of the new chapel:

The chapel of Christ the King is so situated that the rays of the rising sun play about the altar during the holy sacrifice of the Mass. The altar, rectangular in shape, without spires or niches, is a dark cream color. A lamb, surrounded by a halo of gold, decorates the front of the altar. The tabernacle door, unique in design, is embossed with two angels kneeling before a cross. The candlesticks and sanctuary lamps are of Gothic design. At the left of the main altar is the Blessed Mother's statue, beautiful in its simplicity; purity and holiness are portrayed in the statue of St. Joseph at the right. The communion railing is of marble, trimmed in gold, following the Gothic plan. The ceiling is made of beams stained dark, as are the pews and other woodwork. The walls are dark cream, matching the altar. A quiet atmosphere of peace and restfulness reigns in the chapel of Christ the King.

The dedication ceremonies of Pancratia Hall began at 10 o'clock on September 18, 1930. After blessing the new chapel and dedicating it to Christ the King, the Most Reverend J. Henry Tihen, Bishop of Denver, celebrated Pontifical High Mass, assisted by the Very Reverend William M. Brennan, C.M., president of St. Thomas Seminary, deacon, and the Very Reverend Aloysius A. Breen, S.J., president of Regis College, sub-deacon. The students of the high school sang the Mass under the direction of the choirmaster, the Reverend Russell J. Kirschenheuter, C.M. The chapel was filled to its capacity by visiting clergymen from various parishes of the city and state, Sisters of Loretto from many houses in Colorado, and friends of the institution.

At noon a banquet was served, in the large dining hall of the new building, to the clergymen in attendance at the ceremony and to the officers of the building campaign who had contributed both time and money to the fund raised for Pancratia Hall.   More than forty guests were present at this function.

At two in the afternoon, His Excellency, the Most Reverend Bishop, began the impressive ceremony of dedication, assisted by the Right Reverend Monsignor Godfrey Raber, Vicar General of the diocese, and the Right Reverend Joseph Bosetti, Chancellor.   The Bishop with his assistants, forming a procession with the sisterhoods who were present, went from room to room, from floor to floor, blessing each part of the interior of the edifice; then passing to the outside of the building, His Excellency continued the ceremony, making the circuit while blessing the walls.

After the dedicatory services, prominent officials and laymen of the city of Denver took part in a civic program. On a platform erected for the occasion on the east campus in front of Pancratia Hall, dignitaries of Church and state were seated.   Mr. Herbert Fairall, the chairman, introduced the speakers.   Mr. B. T. Poxon, secretary to the Honorable William H. Adams, Governor of Colorado, spoke as the representative of the state; Mr. John T. Barnett, a distinguished Denver lawyer, who had been chairman of the Building Fund Campaign, paid tribute to the life and memory of Mother Pancratia Bonfils, stressing the educational work she had entered upon at so early an age in the city of Denver and declaring that the edifice just dedicated was the fulfillment of her lifelong dream for the schools she had helped to build on the Western frontier. The Most Reverend J. Henry Tihen closed the program by explaining briefly the significance of the religious ceremonial of the day.   His Excellency commended the Sisters of Loretto for their contribution to Christian education and congratulated the people of Colorado on having such an educational center for the training of their daughters.

The dedication of Pancratia Hall was an eventful day for the sisters at the Heights; a day that was reminiscent of that other day when the large imposing main building had been set aside by the ceremony of holy Mother Church as an abode of Catholic learning, on the feast of Our Lady of Loretto, December 10, 1891. The day on which Pancratia Hall was dedicated was not the happy conclusion of the building program, for the greater part of the debt which had been incurred had still to be liquidated, but in the joy of that day on which they saw their plans and dreams of years in visible form in this beautiful new structure, the sisters forgot for the moment the new financial burden which had been incurred in the project just completed. The announcement of the opening of the new edifice at the beginning of the fall term, September, 1930, gives a fair description of the building:

Pancratia Hall, the new academy structure, thoroughly fireproof and modern in every detail, will be ready for occupancy in September, 1930. Ideal living conditions and every facility for furthering the education of young girls are provided in this carefully planned building. Classrooms, study halls, and laboratories are large, cheerful, and well lighted, automatically ventilated and equipped according to the most recent educational standards.

The high school pupils will be housed in two wings of the building apart from the younger girls. Each pupil will have a single private room, adequately furnished and supplied with hot and cold running water or with an adjoining private bath. Bright well-ventilated dormitories, having adjacent dressing alcoves, each fitted with a stationary wash bowl supplying running water, a dressing table and wardrobe accommodations, are provided for the younger children who require more personal supervision.

Social rooms, fudge kitchens, and a provisional gymnasium for indoor activities; courts for tennis, volley ball, and roller skating, a hockey field and fully equipped playground for outdoor exercise take care of every recreational need.

While the sisters experienced a certain amount of joy when they saw Pancratia Hall finished and dedicated, yet that day was not a perfect day, nor was the joy a perfect joy. "There is nothing perfect on all sides," wrote Horace, the great Roman poet. All through the dedication ceremonial, many of the sisters kept thinking of the superior who had been so deeply interested in planning for the new high school. It was Mother Eustachia who had brought to the attention of the higher superiors at the Motherhouse the need of immediate action with regard to the building project. She had entered enthusiastically into all the necessary preliminaries: the selection of architect and contractors, the choice of the site, the organization of the building fund campaign, and the meetings held in the city to arouse civic interest. She had seen the ground broken, the foundation laid, the first few rows of brick placed, then suddenly toward the end of January, 1929, her physician told her that she must spend a few days in the hospital for an examination—no more than a few days; after a short time she would be again at her post, supervising and attending to all necessary details. Mother Eustachia never returned from the hospital. During months of lingering illness, she lay on a bed of suffering, still interested in the building, anxious about its progress, not realizing that her work was done, that another would finish what she had begun. The weeks dragged into months—over six long months she suffered. Mother Eustachia died August 20, 1929, after serving for four years as superior of the community and president of the college.

Mother Mary Edith, the Mother Vicaress, came from the Motherhouse to take over the supervision of the building, during what was at first supposed to be the temporary illness of Mother Eustachia. After the close of school in June, Mother Mary Edith returned to the Motherhouse; and early in July, Mother Consuelo Baumer was sent to supervise the building and take charge of the community. It was no easy task that was suddenly placed upon Mother Consuelo. With a great trust in Divine Providence this religious went into the work that was assigned, trying to the best of her ability to inform herself of details which at first seemed labyrinthine.

After the excitement of the formal opening of the school was over, the faculty and students settled down to the important work of establishing themselves properly in their new quarters. While preserving all the treasured traditions which were their inheritance, the faculty knew that it would be necessary to introduce changes which might be worth preserving as precedents for future years. That the students realized, to a certain degree, that they were responsible for the policy of the school may be gathered from their comments on this subject in one of the issues of their school paper:

The year—the first glorious months of Pancratia's existence—is drawing to a close. There are none who will deny that it has been a success. It has set standards and these ideals must inevitably live on. The Pancratia Hall girl will ever stand for what she has proved herself to be—she is a Loretto girl. While Pancratia possesses the traditions of an old school, yet she delights in the charming individuality of the new one. The making of a school is no trifling matter. It belongs not to teachers alone but to scholars as well.

Sister Modwena Doyle, directress of Pancratia Hall from August, 1930, to August, 1934, wrote of those four years:

The events of the first years were centered around the adjustment of the school to its larger quarters, a continuation of the old cherished traditions, and, of necessity, the establishment of a few precedents for the future. Of these I consider outstanding the first procession in the beautiful chapel of Christ the King, ushering in the month of May and the crowning of the statue by Dorothy Karasiewic, the prefect of the sodality. The first Mass in the chapel on the feast of Christ the King was an event. May 12, 1931, the feast of St. Pancratius, marked the first observance of Pancratia day—green and white day—one special observance of which was the visit of the student body to Mother Pancratia's grave, reciting the rosary as they proceeded. In 1933, *The Pancratian* received the honor of being judged the best paper of its class in the state contest conducted by Colorado University. In another contest, conducted by the *Queen's Work*, Mary Kate Bland won a cash award for a short story.

The successive directresses who sponsored the academic and social activities of the students of Pancratia Hall were Sister Modwena Doyle from 1930 to 1934; Sister Helen Clare, 1934 to 1935; Sister Mary Romula Dea, 1935 to 1936; Sister Marie Lourde Conboy, 1936 to 1941.

As a matter of historical data the various students who finished their high school courses in Pancratia Hall are listed here. The members of the class which finished in June, 1931, were Leonore Carney, Edith Dunn, Ruth Hughes, Rose Nelson, Esther Thomas, Edna Mae Weller, Eileen Vezina, and Dorothy Karasiewic.

Lucille Allen, Charlotte Beeby, Florence Burke, Margaret Dahl, Eugenie Guindon, Dolores McConnell, Rosalie McBride, Marie Rosa Ortiz, and Mary Margaret Tobin formed the class of 1932.

Ruth Church, Theresa Connolley, Mary Kate Bland, Dorothy Aley, Helen Deutsch, Eleanor Esser, Mildred Hines, Marian Lower, Mary Kathryn Russell, and Helen Tobin finished in 1933.

The first students who had spent their entire four years at Pancratia Hall were the senior class of 1934: Jean Baumer, Genevieve Mollands, Cassilda Romera, Mary Elizabeth Schreiber, Eleanor Swezy, and Ellen Rita Milan.

Ten students were graduated in June, 1935: Laurette Allen, Elizabeth Jane Bent, Laura Mae Givan, Martha Jane Kaiser, Blanche Knights, Bernice Evans Lyon, Mary Agnes Milan, Lucila Ortiz, Mary Cecille Romera, and Lina B. Roybal.

The same number of students formed the class of 1936: Louise Doherty, Margaret Durocher, Gladys Givan, Jennie Lege, Mary Josephine Lege, Kathleen McDonald, Magdalene Ortiz, Violet Roybal, Rafaelita Simpson, and Shirley Marie Sullivan. Sister Romula, directress during the year 1935-1936, when interviewed, said that the girls were good students, enthusiastic both in work and in play; the usual round of entertainments and social parties took place, giving pleasant variety to the regular routine of the school calendar. Sister Romula remembered her year at Pancratia as a happy one. ''The sisters of the faculty,'' she said, ''were lovely, and so were the girls.''

The class of 1937, Pauline Guindon, Anna Margaret Zook, and Dorothy Jean Stoval, though limited in number has been remembered for its high scholarship.

Four students, Helen Madeleine Gordon, Margaret Jean Irvin, Shirley Kalotta, and Lorraine Gasser, finished in June, 1938.

In June, 1939, seven girls received diplomas from Pancratia Hall: Isabelle Gomez, Katherine Esther Gust, Bonnie Daisy Kolb, Betty Jo McConnell, Marie Amanda Pena, Martha Adelana Yantarno, and Betty Norine Zinn; and in June, 1940, Mary Katherine Brown, Peggy Jane Keown, Ana Avelina Pena, and Bonnie Jean Meyers.

In June, 1941, the last seniors to be graduated from Pancratia Hall were Ophelia Gomez, Ruth Elizabeth Graber, Sara Jane Greer, Dixie Lee Howard, and Constance Kanable.

The commencement exercises in June, 1941, were marked by an occurrence unique in the history of Loretto Heights: Sister Menodora Casey, a member of the first class to be graduated from the school, attended the closing ceremony. The Reverend William Higgins, Pastor of St. Philomena's Church, delivered an eloquent address to the graduates. Father Higgins spoke of the inspiration which the seniors should derive from the presence of that first graduate of their time-honored school, who forty-nine years before had received the laurel wreath as the insignia of her graduation. "This first graduate of Loretto Heights," Father Higgins said, "dedicated her life to the educating of other young girls in the way of ideal womanhood, influencing her students, numbering into the thousands, to good. But whatever vocation you embrace, my dear graduates, have always in mind you have been Loretto trained; that training has left an indelible mark upon you. Be true to your teachers and to your parents, who chose Loretto for your school."

There was a tinge of sadness permeating the exercises of that commencement day: Pancratia Hall was to be closed. That school, a continuation of the academy which had begun its work out on Loretto hill in 1891, had a glorious history in those fifty years of its existence.

The reason for closing the high school department was obvious. Since the college was expanding from year to year, it was deemed wise to close Pancratia Hall, an exclusive boarding school with a small enrollment, in order to provide living quarters for the increased number of college boarding students. The decision to close the high school, reached after careful deliberation, was made with a certain degree of regret.

That last year, the faculty at Pancratia Hall were Sister Marie Lourde Conboy, directress; Sister Mary Zilda Hammond, Sister Berenice Cromwell, Sister Columba Higgins, and Sister Francis Aloys Hunleth. Sister Teresa Marie and Sister Peter Joseph of the college music department taught the students music and voice. It can be said in all truth that the sisters of the faculty conducted Pancratia Hall in a manner as ideally Loretto as Father Nerinckx, their holy Founder, could have wished.

Chapter **XX**

THE MARCH OF TIME

While plans were being formed and executed for the expansion of housing conditions at Loretto Heights, the college was continuing to develop. The marked increase in the number of resident students in the fall of 1928 was an incentive for the superior and administrative officers to feel justified in pushing forward the building plans. There were definite signs of increase and progress.

Shortly before the opening of the fall session of 1928, an Otis elevator was installed in the administration building through the benefaction of Mrs. Julia M. Anderson, Mrs. Alcetta Green Hepburn, and other good friends of the school. It was only after the elevator was giving service that the sisters realized what hardships had been endured through the years, especially by the sick and ailing, in climbing the many flights of steps. The Sisters of Loretto are required by rule and custom to pray daily for benefactors. The friends who contributed so materially to the welfare of the sisters surely deserve many an extra prayerful remembrance from the beneficiaries of their gift.

The freshmen of the year proved to be particularly talented in histrionics and took pleasure in providing many clever entertainments for their appreciative audiences. Early in the year, Helen McGraw, president of the freshman class, as "King Hollywood," was the center of a brilliant play. The king, dressed in the style of Louis XIV, presided with calm dignity over his royal court and set the heart of many a young girl aflutter. Dainty "chorines," performing according to the king's whims, proved that even the staid ruler of a kingdom can be affected by beauty and the "varsity drag."

Commenting casually on the dramatic talent of the freshmen, the sophomores said: "The freshmen are good in their way but they have much to learn. When they can present something as good as the *Sophomore Revue,* we shall accept them." Miss Alvena Leversedge, a talented sophomore, directed the *Revue* which was presented November 5, 1928. Clever girls performed in ten acts, each act vying with the other in wit and execution. The whole class appeared in their original song "The Sophomores," the words of which were written by Agnes Fladung and the music by Alvena Leversedge. "The Country Hick," cleverly portrayed by Julia Kenehan, showed freshman worries such as alcoves, food, dates, and lessons. Politics also entered into the *Revue.* "The Night Before," by Emma Busch and Mary Leslie, was a witty parody on the presidential election just over. Miss Busch impersonated to the most minute details the victorious candidate, Herbert Hoover; Miss Leslie gave a remarkable imitation of Governor Smith's oratorical mannerisms and personality. "Variety," the last act was a fashionable parade which displayed the proper costumes for college activities.

One of the most active and efficient student organizations on the campus is the Press Club. It dates its origin back to the early months of 1929. The school paper carried this information of the organization of the club:

For several days around the first of January, it was whispered by two or three; it spread through the college; it was debated by a certain class; and now it is a reality— Loretto Heights is going to have a Press club, an active club composed of twenty-five charter members. The purpose of the club is to boost the "Heightsonian," to obtain funds necessary for each publication, and to have a good time socially. The last purpose is an incentive to all. But membership must be earned—every member must have and maintain an *A* or *B* average, and she must be a competent and willing worker.

Begun with such standards and objectives, the Press Club is still functioning strongly; during the years which have intervened, it has carried out the original plans and ambitions. Its slogan has been: "Our charter members made a magnificent beginning; we can't let them down."

This club has sponsored contests of various kinds—song, poetry, popularity.

On February 23, 1929, the first social meeting of the Press Club took place in the Union Station Dining Room. The guest speaker, Mr. Joseph Emerson Smith, the dean of journalism in Colorado, addressed the club on "The Romance of the Newspaper." In his talk Mr. Smith spoke of the growth of the *Denver Post* and discussed many topics of interest, especially to the Denver students in journalism. The interest which Mr. Smith and his esteemed wife, Mrs. Eudocia Belle Smith, have taken in the young journalists at Loretto Heights dates from that meeting. To encourage the embryo writers in this field, Mr. and Mrs. Smith have presented for several successive years a loving cup to the student doing the most outstanding work in the department. The recipients of this award have been Margaret Dunphy, '34; Jane Carroll, '35; Lucille Edwards, '36; Maxyne Rogers, '37; Ellen Rita Milan, '38; Dorothy Starbuck, '39; Veronica Gegan, '40; Patty Ann McLaughlin, '41; and Kaye Blodgett, '42.

The "Killarney Players," the freshmen of that year, displayed unusual talent in their presentation on March 14, 1929, of an Irish operetta, "The Wishing Well." The romance of old Ireland was charmingly portrayed by Helen McGraw as "Terence O'More," and Marie Trenchak as "Lady O'Donnell." Other members of the cast who contributed to the success of the entertainment were Meada Thornton, Anna McGlone, Mercia Walker, Clara Cella, Lucille Riede, Marianna McCann, Marie Stillhammer, Louise Bessler, and Elizabeth O'Meara. A chorus of students formed the neighboring gentry and families, and six girls appeared in fairy scenes and dances. Forty-six freshmen produced the operetta which was long the talk of the campus.

In May, 1929, it was announced in the daily press that Mr. Frederick G. Bonfils would grant one hundred scholarships to be awarded to ambitious youths in midwest states. Six educational institutions within the state of Colorado were to be beneficiaries in this grant: Loretto Heights College, Regis College, Colorado College, the University of Denver, the University of Colorado, State Teachers College, and Colorado State College of A. and M. Arts. These scholarships included tuition, books, laboratory fees, matriculation fees, student assessments, and material costs. Students were required to pay their living and traveling expenses. The scholarship had a money value of about two hundred and fifty dollars, quite a financial aid to those who could not otherwise attend college. Several students at Loretto Heights College have been benefited by these scholarships.

The regular routine of the college schedule was lightened from time to time by affairs which served as pleasant interludes to both faculty and students. Sister Dolorine, dean, and Sister Vivian, registrar, combined a professional duty with pleasure when they made a trip to distant Seattle, in the spring of 1929, to attend a meeting of registrars. Later in the term the senior play, *The Rivals* by Sheridan, was presented to appreciative audiences in a manner which reflected credit on both performers and coach.

Dramatic groups of the college had always attracted attention for their clever productions. At least twice each year, the "Loretto Players" gave evidence of remarkable talent and training in the plays which were given in the little theater. This work was under the direction of Sister Dolorine Morrison, whose special talent was in the field of dramatics. It would be impossible even to outline briefly the many interesting programs presented through the years, timely, entertaining, and professional. Shakespearian plays, both comedy and tragedy, "Joan of Arc," "Pride and Prejudice," "Old Woman Sea," "The Sight of the Blind," and the "Cradle Song" are but a few of the many which have been a credit to the Speech department.

The usual round of activities took place at the end of the term and brought June, 1929, and the coveted diploma to a fine class of seniors. Bachelor of Arts degrees were granted to Catherine Mary Bailey, Rosalie Helen Buchmann, Mary Judge, Mary Katherine Reardon, Evelyn Laura Taylor, Regina Helen Black, Marie Kathryn Coffey, Loretto Ann Cook, Rosemary Agnes Dolan, Bessie Driver, Trinidad

Garcia, Elizabeth Haas, Julia Wooldridge, Hazel Lindstrom, and Mary Ida Petros.

Transportation to and from Denver remained a problem still giving thought to the college officials. The nearest car line was three miles distant. As the number of students increased, the sisters were convinced that the only solution for this handicap was a school bus of their own which would come and go at convenient scheduled hours. This was the first pressing need which was brought to the attention of Mother Consuelo, the newly-appointed superior. When the difficulty of transportation was discussed with friends of the school in Denver, they, realizing the importance of immediate action, made a donation sufficiently large to encourage the superior to place the order for the construction of the bus.

It was welcome news when the announcement, "All Aboard for Denver," informed the students that with the beginning of the fall term free transportation would be furnished to and from Alameda Avenue. When the "Loretto College Bus" was finished and driven through the campus, it aroused about as much local interest as did the first Baltimore and Ohio railway train. The "green bus" has been doing faithful service ever since its first maiden trip. How many students it has carried back and forth; how many conversations it has heard; how many student views it has recorded. What information that bus could give if it only could speak as it goes!

For the convenience of the soldiers at the near-by fort, a tramway bus to Fort Logan began to operate in 1941. It was hailed with enthusiasm by both faculty and students as its route on Federal Boulevard passes Loretto Heights. Owing to the rationing of gas by the government the old green bus makes but one trip a day, in the early morning, when the tramway's schedule does not serve students due at the first period classes.

Several new professors and instructors were added to the faculty in September, 1929: the Reverend T. V. Cahill, C. M., the Reverend R. V. Bayard, C. M., the Reverend

Harold V. Campbell in the department of religion; Sister Ann Francis McArdle returned from St. Mary's Academy, where she had been directress, to be instructor in education and first dean of women at the college; Sister Constantia Schaub was appointed librarian in addition to her duties as postmaster.

The office of president, which had been left vacant by the untimely death of Mother Eustachia, was not filled until the second semester. On February 19, 1930, Sister Mary Edmond Fern, who was in her second year of absence from the college, completing her studies for the doctorate at St. Louis University, was appointed president. Sister Mary Edmond completed the semester at the university, and, with the exception of representing the college at the North Central meeting at Stephen's hotel in Chicago in March of that year and performing some minor duties, *in absentia,* did not take over the office until her return in June.

Thirteen were graduated that year from the college on June 2. Jewel Keating received a Bachelor of Music degree; Bachelor of Arts degrees were conferred on Helen Mary Finn, Mary Elizabeth Gaule, Mary Louise Black, Muriel Eileen Fuite, Rose Agnes Clinton, Margaret Mary Keaney, Mary Evelyn Ryan, Norma Dearhamer, Mary Elizabeth Donnelly, Olive Mary Horner, Madeline Cecelia Milan, and Mary Agnes O'Connor. The Most Reverend Cyprian Bradley, Abbot of the Benedictine Monastery at Canon City, was the commencement orator. At the close of summer school, on August 2, seven Sisters of Loretto received Bachelor of Arts degrees, and one, a Bachelor of Music.

During the summer of 1930, the administration building was a scene of great activity. Carpenters, painters, and plumbers were busily engaged in remodeling and renovating the building. After the high school was transferred to Pancratia Hall, many changes were made to meet the requirements of the various departments. On the main floor two classrooms were thrown into one to form the present library; former dormitories on the third floor were transformed into science suites; the sisters' community room was removed to the opposite wing to give place to the present classics room; the administrative offices were decorated and furnished and also the council room. Much of this work was supervised by the newly appointed president, Sister Mary Edmond, who at the same time was deeply engrossed in writing her doctoral dissertation. Each sister contributed generously in helping to complete the work, especially in her own department. At the opening of the fall term, when the students returned, the interior of the college had been entirely renovated. The cost of making these improvements was heavy, but succeeding years have proved that the changes were all well planned and timely. Mother Consuelo, the superior, was bearing a double responsibility during those days when Pancratia Hall was receiving the last finishing touches and the college building was being remodeled.

The faculty was increased that fall by the addition of several instructors. Sister Carmela replaced Sister Antonina as instructor in biology; Sister Roberta became instructor in French; Sister Theodore, in English; and Miss Margaret Killeen, instructor in physical education.

Until the fall of 1930, Sister Dolorine, besides being director of the English department, had trained all the classes in dramatic art. Mrs. Margaret Mitchell Burke of Akron, Ohio, an accomplished teacher in speech, conducted the work in that department from September, 1930 to June, 1932. The "Loretto Players" under Mrs. Burke's instruction maintained their high standard in dramatics. "The Merchant of Venice," presented in May, 1931, was particularly fine.

Sister Rose Margaret Cook and Sister Frances de Chantal McLeese were granted a leave of absence in the fall of 1930 to pursue graduate work at St. Louis University. Sister Rose Margaret began her work for the doctorate in mathematics, Sister Frances de Chantal, her master's work in chemistry.

Great was the surprise of the people of Denver and Colorado when they learned from the press on January 11, 1931, that the Most Reverend J. Henry Tihen, on account of failing health, had submitted to Rome his resignation as bishop of the diocese. On April 22, 1931, the news was flashed through the Associated Press that the Right Reverend Monsignor Urban J. Vehr, rector of Mt. St. Mary Seminary, Norwood, Ohio, had been appointed bishop of Denver to succeed the retiring prelate. Monsignor Vehr, a native of Cincinnati, had received his education at St. Xavier's University and his training for holy orders at the local Cincinnati seminary. He was ordained May 29, 1915. After doing parish work for some years, he was chaplain at the Motherhouse of the Sisters of Charity at Mt. St. Joseph on the Ohio and a member of the faculty at that college. Bishop Vehr pursued his graduate work at Notre Dame and the Catholic University of America where he received the Master of Arts degree in 1924; in 1928 he received the doctorate in Canon Law at the Angelico University in Rome.

After his consecration on June 10, in the Cathedral of Cincinnati by the Most Reverend John T. McNicholas, Archbishop of that city, the newly-consecrated bishop with an escort of high dignitaries of the Church arrived in Denver on the morning of July 16, 1931. The retiring Bishop, the Most Reverend J. Henry Tihen, was celebrant of the Mass at which Monsignor Hugh McMenamin, rector of the cathedral, read the brief appointing the Most Reverend Urban J. Vehr Bishop of Denver. The last official sermon of Bishop Tihen was his welcome to the diocese of the newly-appointed Bishop. At the close of the Pontifical Mass, the youthful Bishop, who was now the head of the diocese, entered the pulpit and delivered his greeting to the clergy, religious, and people of Denver and Colorado who thronged the Cathedral of the Immaculate Conception. Bishop Vehr's message to his people on that day is summed up in his statement: "I give myself absolutely to the service of the Church through the priests and people committed to my care"—a promise which has been faithfully kept.

A few days after his installation, the Most Reverend Bishop Vehr paid an informal visit to the sisters at Loretto Heights. His first official act was to preach the sermon at the requiem High Mass sung at the obsequies of Sister

Edwina Casey, sister of Sisters Menodora and Celestine Casey. Having come to visit Sister Celestine at the Heights, a few days before the opening of the annual retreat, Sister Edwina became seriously ill on August 2, and, after some days of intense suffering, died at St. Joseph's Hospital on August 8. Bishop Vehr in his sermon spoke earnestly and consolingly on the meaning of life and death, especially for a religious. He recalled the words of Christ to Martha, who was grieving over the death of her brother: "I am the resurrection and the life; he that believeth in me, although he be dead, shall live."

On June 2, 1931, Sister Mary Edmond Fern and Sister M. Francisca Engles received the degree of Doctor of Philosophy at St. Louis University; the former in the fields of Latin and French, the latter in philosophy and education. On the same date Sister Frances de Chantal received the Master of Science degree in chemistry.

At the commencement exercises at Loretto Heights on June 2, 1931, the following students received the Bachelor of Arts degree: Grace Agnes Bryan, Mary Patricia Cassidy, Rose Marie Doyle, Agnes Agatha Fladung, Hilda Mary Gallagher, Josephine Bernice Lattin, Mary Elizabeth Leslie, Alvena Leversedge, Marie Elizabeth McNamara, Mary Margaret Moffitt, Mary Ann O'Connor, Helen Mary Sullivan, Jane Winburn. Three Sisters of Loretto finished their course in the summer of that year and received the Bachelor of Arts degree at the close of the session, August 2, 1931.

In the fall of 1931, Sister Germaine Fogarty was appointed instructor in physics and mathematics; and Sister Francis de Sales McGarry, instructor in Spanish.

Early in January, 1932, a scholastic honor came to the college from the Department of Education of the State of New York. When Miss Margaret Sullivan of the class of '24, who was completing her graduate studies at Columbia University, applied for a teacher's certificate from the department of education in New York, the officials of the University of the State of New York communicated with the president of Loretto Heights College. After question-

naires had been answered and submitted, the president of
the college received the following official notice, dated January 11, 1932, from H. H. Horner, Assistant Commissioner
for Higher and Professional Education of the Department
of Education:

It gives me pleasure to inform you that this Department has today approved the courses of study offered by
Loretto Heights College leading to the Liberal Arts degrees of Bachelor of Arts and Bachelor of Science and
Home Economics, the technical degree, Bachelor of Music,
and has registered these degrees.

The Liberal Arts courses are fully approved for credit
toward all credentials issued by this department for which
a Liberal Arts College education is a prerequisite. For
the specific requirements of each of these credentials, reference is made to the professional handbooks and the circular
announcements issued by this division of the State Educational Department.

During the second semester of the scholastic year 1931-
1932, the most outstanding event was the observance by the
college of the nation-wide celebration of the bi-centennial
of George Washington. The various departments vied with
each other at the student assemblies each week in portraying
in a decidedly original and clever manner some phase of
American history directly connected with the first President
of the United States.

The Student Council conducted the premier program of
the series. The guest speaker for the occasion was His
Excellency, the Most Reverend Urban J. Vehr, who addressed the assembly of faculty and students on "Patriotism, a Duty to God and Country." At the close of the
Bishop's inspiring talk, a shadow picture was brought to
light—a miniature of Loretto Heights College, the American flag, and George Washington comprising the silhouette
in the background. The martial music of the Fort Logan
band gave a patriotic and military color to the program.

At the close of the assembly, the president of the Student Council, Helen McGraw, challenged all contesting departments to give a program more interesting, more educational, or more directly pertaining to George Washington than the one which their organization presented on February 18. The departments accepted the challenge; the weekly entertainments exhibited ingenuity on the part of the students and knowledge of past events. *The Heightsonian*, March 24, 1932, gives an interesting account of the contribution of the Alethian club:

Thursday, March 10, the Alethian club had its turn. Lovers of literature were encouraged to attend by the announcement, "Something different." Miss Marjorie Cannon wrote and directed a one-act play, "A Visit to Mount Vernon." Two girls from Loretto, Centennial and her sister Bi, longing for adventure in the realms of long ago, plan a visit to the Washingtons. Martha and George are peacefully happy in the quiet of their colonial home, away from the rush and changes of every day twentieth century life. It was an awakening when the two peppy collegians, full of news and enthusiasm, broke in upon them. Imagine the surprise of the first President when he hears that nation-wide celebrations are being held in commemoration of the two hundred years which have passed since his birth; of the honor and admiration, the reverence in which men hold him, naming him "Father of his Country."

He and his wife listen with interest to the story of present day politics, marvelling at the changes which have taken place since an active public ceased for them. The Loretto girls stress, too, the differences between the literature of today and that known and read by those who lived at the time of the country's birth. The inventions of science, television, and radio are incomprehensible to the Washingtons, but the foresight of their two visitors dispels incredulity on their part. A small radio is set up and from station *Loretto* comes the voice of Reverend H. L. McMenamin, addressing Loretto students on the influence Washington indirectly had on literature.

A later issue of the school paper records an equally clever program which linked the far-distant past with the making of American history:

The program for the Bicentennial Celebration held on Thursday, April 7, consisted of a clever play written by several members of the Classical club, an adaptation from Vergil's sixth book of the *Aeneid*. Miss Mary Collins gave the prologue, as was the custom in old Roman plays. The first scene depicted a slave teacher returning home from school with his two boy charges, who were discussing the authors of the day. In the atrium of the Roman house, anxiously awaited the mother, Flavia, and her two small daughters. The boys, when they arrived, told their mother the happenings of the day and what they had learned about their favorite author, Vergil. Presently the curtain was drawn back showing the meeting of the mortal, Aeneas, with his father, Anchises, in Elysium. Around them were gathered the souls of great men, living and dead. Anchises prophesied concerning the lives of future Romans. As he talked, figures of future heroes emerged from the hazy background and spoke to them: Romulus and Numa, Brutus, Caesar, Augustus, Charlemagne, Alfred the Great, Charles V, and finally the great George Washington who gave a stirring talk on the influence of the Roman Republic on present day civilization and especially on its code of laws.

Several of the students entered the National George Washington Bicentennial Oratorical Contest, an important part of the celebration throughout the country which was open to all colleges and universities. In the elimination contest at the college, February 17, at 2:30 in the afternoon, Lucille Riede was awarded first place by the judges: the Very Reverend Joseph A. Herbers, S. J., president of Regis College, Mr. Joseph Newman, favorite entertainer and teacher of speech, and Mr. Joseph P. O'Connell, a Denver attorney.

In developing her theme, "Washington, the Exemplar of American Ideals," Miss Riede said: "Our country should look to the ideals of Washington and from such ideals weave into the structure of our destiny not only noble thoughts and aspirations but practical principles that will carry us to a perfect democracy—a closer unity, a truer independence, and morality based on religion."

Miss Riede represented her college in the state oratorical elimination contest on Sunday afternoon, March 13, at the Woman's Club auditorium in Denver. The first place was given to Mr. Fred Couey of the State Teachers College, Greeley; Miss Lucille Riede tied for second place with Mr. Delbert Ross of the University of Denver.

Fourteen graduates received their sheepskins on June 1, 1932. Bachelor of Arts degree: Regina Louise Bessler, Louise Marie Cheshire, Mary Cecilia Collins, Helen Agnes Gallagher, Charlotte Mae Hamburger, Anna Margaret McGlone, Elizabeth Loretto O'Meara, Marie Helen Stillhammer, Claire Ellen Sullivan, Marie Julitta Trenchak, Frances Margaret McCarthy, and Lucille Margaret Riede. Bachelor of Music degree: Mary Agnes Galvin and Helen Jane McGraw.

The International Federation of Catholic Alumnae held its tenth biennial convention at the Brown Palace Hotel in Denver, from August 27 to September 1, 1932, under the direction of Mrs. Philip A. Brennan, president of the association. The ideal of this commendable association is expressed by the motto, "Every Catholic child in a Catholic school"; its aim is to carry out its second purpose, namely, to further Catholic education. Mrs. Brennan and her officers had prepared a well-organized program on which were represented the different departments which function in the federation. In carrying out the program, Mrs. Brennan was aided by Mrs. S. Paul Stock, the local chairman, who at that time was the governor of the Colorado Chapter of the International Federation of Catholic Alumnae, and by Grace Kenehan, local secretary of the I.F.C.A.

Sister Dolorine Morrison, dean of Loretto Heights College, read a paper entitled "Our Catholic Heritage," which later appeared in the December issue of the *Quarterly Bulletin* of the association; Sister Mary Borgia Clarke, dean of Webster College, gave an interesting paper on "The Catholic Graduate's Place in the Parish."

On Sunday afternoon, August 28, the Alumnae of Loretto Heights College were hostesses to the members of the Federation at an elegantly appointed tea. Mother Consuelo, superior of Loretto Heights, Mother Praxedes, superior of Loretto Academy in El Paso, and former superior general of the Lorettines, the president of the college, Sister Mary Edmond, Miss Katherine Kenehan, past president of the Colorado Chapter of Federation, and members of Loretto

Heights Alumnae stood in the receiving line as hundreds of guests arrived after their sight-seeing tour through the Rocky Mountain parks. Members of the Loretto League, the Alumnae, and the Mothers' Club poured at the various tea tables.

Presidents of colleges have often their duties prearranged for them by established customs. In conforming with one of these, Sister Mary Edmond issued an annual message at the commencement of the first semester each year. The greeting to the students in September, 1932, follows:

Although you are aware of the happiness which your presence here in college brings to all who are vitally interested in your welfare, yet I gladly avail myself of this opportunity to assure you formally of the hearty welcome which is yours, of the interest each member of the faculty has in you, and of my own deep personal desire that this may be the most fruitful year of your school life. To the students of the past one, two, or three years, the opening of school should mean a coming home, a taking up again of the threads of your college life in order to continue the tapestry which will be finished when you answer *adsum* to the final roll call. For you freshmen, this is the beginning of a four-year quest after knowledge and truth. May you be sufficiently clear-sighted to recognize that this is your chance and courageous enough to follow along the path of endeavor, even though at times it may seem difficult. To all this year of higher studies means the assuming of grave responsibilities.

This college is yours; everything within it is for your use, comfort, and improvement. You will find the faculty devoted, highminded, sympathetic, generously giving their time, their interest, themselves, to the enriching of your lives; to them you will give your co-operation, your very best, mentally, physically, and spiritually. In your contact with other students be determined that you will reflect credit upon yourselves and upon those who are sponsoring your higher education. With Epictetus I say to you: "In all the affairs of life, let it be your great care not to hurt your mind or offend your judgment. And this rule if observed carefully in all your deportment, will be a mighty security to you in your undertaking."

Toward the close of August, 1932, several changes were made in the college faculty. Sister Ann Francis, instructor in education and dean of women for three years, was appointed superior of St. Mary's Academy, Denver; Sister M. Georgetta Hoermann, instructor in the classics department for three years and for many years an efficient teacher in the academic department, was missioned to Colorado Springs as principal of St. Mary's High School; and Sister M. Carmela of the biology department was transferred to Lebanon, Kentucky, as superior and principal of St. Augustine's High School; Sister Francisca Engles became dean of women; Sister M. Aloyse Ellingson, who had recently received the Doctor of Philosophy degree in biology at St. Louis University, was appointed director of the biology department; Sister Isabella Marie Foley, instructor in Latin; Sister Rebecca Burke, instructor in home economics; Sister Mary James Dowd, instructor in music.

Much of the attractiveness of the campus today is the result of an experiment which Sister Aloyse Ellingson carried on for a few years in connection with the planting and rearing of trees indigenous to Colorado. Hundreds of seedlings were placed in nurseries on the south side of the campus, near the home economics practice house. From time to time Sister Aloyse transplanted these young trees to various places on the grounds. Now after a period of ten years, the landscaping which was done at that time contributes in no small degree to the beauty of the natural scenery.

The usual round of extra-curricular activities took place during the scholastic year. The one which attracted most publicity was the participation of Loretto college students in the model League of Nations. The International Relations Clubs of the Rocky Mountain region held their second annual conference in Denver, November 11 and 12, 1932. This took the form of a model League of Nations which met at the Colorado State Capitol to discuss the Lytton report on the Manchurian question. Loretto Heights and the School of Mines represented Russia. The following students were delegates from Loretto Heights College: Regina Montgomery, Winifred Espy, Mary O'Donnell, Geraldine Sullivan, Phoebe Pulver, Magdalene Klausner, Margaret Connelly, Catherine Floyd, Isobel Mahoney, and Mary Alma Fregeau. This state with the United States was extended a special invitation to attend the conference. It was a fine experience for the International Relations Clubs. Had it been a real conference to which the eyes of the world were turned, the youthful delegates could not have been more earnest in presenting data or better prepared for the discussions.

After distinguishing themselves in many activities, the class of 1933 completed the scholastic year on June 6. The Bachelor of Arts degree was conferred on Marjorie Mary Cannon, Laura Winifred Espy, Mary Geraldine Grey, Mary Magdalene Klausner, Mary Ellen Maginnis, Regina Isabella McMindes, Virginia Elizabeth McMindes, Isabella Martha McNamara, Regina Miriam Montgomery, Marcella Anna Murphy, Mary Margaret O'Donnell, Mary Jane Peconi, Pauline Katherine Smith, and Geraldine Margaret Sullivan. This class was increased in number when four Sisters of Loretto received degrees at the close of the summer session, August 2, 1933.

At the beginning of the year 1933-1934, Mrs. Regina W. Wachtel, a graduate of the University of Iowa, with a master's degree in speech and a minor in English, became director of the department of speech. Mrs. Wachtel remained at Loretto Heights College as instructor in dramatics and speech and moderator of one of the active campus clubs, "Wigs and Patches," until June, 1939. Mrs. Gene Wachtel will always be remembered by the students whom she taught during those years.

Sister Francis de Sales and Sister Frances Therese matriculated at the University of Colorado in September, 1933. The former began graduate study in the Spanish department; the latter, who had received in June, 1933, the Master of Arts degree from St. Louis University, continued graduate work in the field of education. Sister Mary Norbert Parsoneault began work in art at the Chappell House in Denver; and Sister Pancratia Madarasz at the Library

School of the Denver University. Sister M. Ethelbert Owens was appointed instructor in the Spanish department.

Scarcely had the first semester begun, when both faculty and students were shocked by the sudden death on October 5 of Sister Constantia Schaub. Sister Constantia was busy formulating plans for the library when she was stricken with a heart attack. After a very short illness of a night and a day, Sister Constantia succumbed. She had spent nearly all her years in religion at Loretto Heights, a careful, earnest teacher, a fervent religious; she worked to the very end for the interests of the place she loved so well. *The Heightsonian*, October 20, carried this expression of student opinion and appreciation:

We loved her for her steady sympathy, her eagerness to help, her patience. We'll miss her smile, her suggestions, even her warnings about silence in the library.

Although the school year is scarcely a month old, all the new students knew Sister Constantia, at least by sight, while the older ones will miss her indefatigable efforts to serve their needs. Sister was postmistress and librarian, and filled both positions well. We are sorry she is gone, but maybe God wanted someone to sort the mail in Heaven, or perhaps Heaven's library needed cataloguing, and so God decided to employ Sister Constantia. When she reached Heaven we know there must have been a host of souls who came to tell her that they were there because she helped to show them the way through good reading. Sister helped us to know the good from the harmful and we thank her for it.

Sister Constantia's own life was a book of highest inspiration bearing the title, "All for God."

At the cap and gown ceremony on Sunday afternoon, October 15, the Right Reverend Monsignor Matthew Smith, editor of the *Denver Register*, addressed the students on the need of Catholic leadership. Monsignor Smith outlined the means by which leadership might be attained and emphasized the fact that a leader should be a constant reader of good literature.

Delegates of the International Relations Clubs of the Rocky Mountain region held their third annual meeting at the Brigham Young University, Provo, Utah, November 3 and 4, 1933. Seventy-two representatives from twelve colleges were present. Four students of the International Relations Club represented Loretto Heights College at the conference: Margaret Connolley, Catherine Floyd, Mary Alma Fregeau, and Isobel Mahoney. The Loretto girls were entertained hospitably at the college of St. Mary's of the Wasatch, Salt Lake City, before going to Provo.

Through the Press Club, Loretto Heights presented eight broadcasts during the year. The first of the series was given November 7, at 6:45, over the station KLZ, the last over the same station, April 7. The journalism students wrote the scripts which set forth the aims and actual work of eight departments in the college. The instructor in the speech department, Mrs. Regina Wachtel, directed the voice work. Mrs. Eudocia Belle Smith was the announcer at all the programs.

The Advisory Board and the Mothers' Club were merged at a joint meeting on November 18, 1933, into an organization to be known as the Loretto League. The Advisory Board had its origin in January, 1931. Invitations to a preliminary meeting had been sent out by the president of the college to a limited number of Denver women who were interested in higher education. The object was to discuss the feasibility of forming an organization, advisory in nature, which would have for its purpose the furthering of the interests of the college. A good number of representative women attended the meeting in the Gold Room of the college. The officers of the college outlined the objectives of the organization which they had in mind. Discussions followed; ways and means of co-operating with the college were proposed; the result of the meeting was a unanimous vote to form an Advisory Board which would function tentatively for a time before deciding upon definite plans. In the beginning membership in this organization was limited, but as its scope was enlarged the attendance increased until it became too numerous to serve as an advisory council. The members who were active on the Advisory Board believed that more would be accomplished by a larger unit such as the Loretto League.

In the following January, 1934, the officers of the Loretto League sponsored their first series of lectures to establish a Foundation Fund for the education of worthy students at Loretto Heights College. Mr. Benjamin Masse, S. J., of the department of English of Regis College, was the first guest speaker. His subject, "The Dawson Synthesis," was developed in three lectures, which were given at the Brown Palace Hotel. The Loretto League has remained an active organization for more than ten years.

The second semester had a well-filled extra curricular schedule. Each activity had a place on the program since each gave an opportunity for training in leadership in many fields. The Catholic School Press Association convened for the first time at the college, February 24, 1934. The daily press gave publicity to this venture; the college paper carried an enthusiastic account of the day's proceedings: "What a convention! Loretto Heights College was the scene of the most enthusiastic conclave that has taken place there for many a day." This was the first convention of its kind ever held for Catholic colleges and schools in Colorado. That the convention was timely and effective is proved from the fact that it has continued to be a yearly affair with an ever-increasing attendance.

With the experience of nine Press Conventions, Loretto Heights College and the other twenty-six member schools of the Association of Catholic School Press Relations have gained confidence in themselves, their deans and principals, and their respective schools. In this novena of conventions, beginning in February, 1934, over three thousand delegates have met at Loretto Heights to discuss things journalistic and what the Catholic young people can do through the press to promote Catholic Action in accordance with the wishes of the Holy Father.

"Journalism demands," quoting the Illinois code, "of its individual members sound moral character, honesty of purpose and performance, courtesy and consideration with each other and the public." With this in mind, the college Press Club through these conventions is bringing fine Catholic youths into a closer scholastic relationship than any other phase of activity that might exist among Catholic colleges, and the high school contingents. As this book goes to press plans for the tenth annual press convention of the A. C. S. P. R. in February, 1943, are being formulated. Regina Reitemeier, '43, is chairman of the college student contingent for the conference; and Betti Rose NanKeville, secretary. The winners of silver loving cups in popularity contests, sponsored by Journalism Department, were Jewel Keating, 1929; Helen Jane McGraw, 1931; Catherine Floyd, 1933; Mary Nieters, 1934. The Pohndorf Award was given to Mary Kathryn Hagerty, 1942, Press Club President for two consecutive years 1941-1942.

The Women's Athletic Association of the Rocky Mountain Conference met in Denver May 6, 1934. Delegates and physical education teachers from Denver University, University of Colorado, Greeley State Teachers College, Colorado State College of A. and M. Arts at Fort Collins, State University of Laramie, Wyoming, and Loretto Heights College were guests at a luncheon served in the two student dining rooms. The event was the annual "play day" of the Women's Athletic Association of the Rocky Mountain region, to which the Denver University and Loretto Heights College were joint hostesses. All the athletics and games took place in the gymnasium of Denver University in the morning of play day; at 1:30 luncheon was served at Loretto in the beautifully decorated dining rooms, by students of the Home Economics department. Entertainment was furnished during the luncheon by the college Glee Club.

After the luncheon, the delegates made a tour of the buildings; at three o'clock they met in the auditorium for their business meeting and presentation of an impromptu program.

At the commencement exercises, the address to the graduates was delivered by the Very Reverend Thomas D. Coyne, C. M., president of St. Thomas Seminary. Right Reverend Monsignor Brady presented the candidates for degrees to His Excellency, the Most Reverend Urban J. Vehr, who conferred the Bachelor of Arts degree on Mar-

guerite Bisbing, Rose Mary Bradasich, Elizabeth Evelyn
Briggs, Helen Elizabeth Collins, Margaret Mary Connelly,
Elizabeth Frances Cullen, Catherine Agnes Floyd, Maria
Gazzolo, Mary Elizabeth Hanson, Patricia Jane Lucy, Mary
Frances Nieters, Ruth Frances Peterson, and Sarah Wil-
liams; Regina Marie Coll, the Bachelor of Literature degree.

Sister Francis de Sales McGarry received the Master
of Arts degree at the University of Colorado, June 11, 1934.
Her major subject was Spanish, her minor, French.

Graduating exercises on August 2, at the end of the
summer session, was the formal close of the scholastic year.
Four Sisters of Loretto received degrees.

Chapter XXI

COMPLETING TWENTY-FIVE YEARS

In the summer of 1934, Sister M. Francisca Engles, director of the philosophy department at Loretto Heights College and dean of women from 1932, was elected second assistant to the Superior General by the delegates to the general chapter. In addition to the duties of that office, Sister was given supervision of the high schools and colleges of the order.

In the early part of August, 1934, Mother Ann Francis McArdle, superior of St. Mary's Academy, Denver, was appointed superior of the community at Loretto Heights and president of the college; the offices of superior and president were vested in one person as had been the custom prior to the appointment of a president in 1930.

Toward the close of that same summer, another change was made in the personnel of the college. Sister M. Dolorine Morrison, who had lived thirty-seven years at the Heights—but not continuously—and had served in various capacities, teacher in the academy, directress in the academic department, later dean of the college, director of the English department, and, for several years, of dramatics, was transferred to the speech and English departments of Webster College. Sister Dolorine had been so long identified with Loretto Heights College that it seemed strange to the students on their return to school not to find her there busy, as in former years, with many activities.

Sister Frances Therese Halloran was appointed dean of studies and Sister Roberta Hardesty, dean of women. The Reverend Charles Convery, C.M., S.T.D., joined the faculty as professor of philosophy. Sister Mary Norbert Parsoneault continued her studies in art and Sister M. Pancratia Madarasz, her work for a degree in library science at the Denver University School of Librarianship. Sister

Francis de Sales McGarry and Sister M. Rebecca Burke were granted a leave of absence, the former to begin work for the doctorate at the Catholic University of America, the latter to pursue graduate study in education and home economics at the Colorado State College of A. and M. Arts.

It was not as a stranger that Mother Ann Francis assumed her duties as superior and president of Loretto Heights College since she had lived there on two former occasions. With a certain amount of knowledge, therefore, of the college and its faculty, the newly-appointed president entered upon her duties. At the beginning of the scholastic year this cheery message greeted the students:

At the opening of each new school year, as you approach your college administration building, you read on the arch over the doorway: *Fides, Mores, Cultura.* At the beginning of this year may I invite you to read the motto with a deeper sense of its significance?

As you pass through the doorway beneath this motto, you will naturally expect to be shown the way to the things which will help you to strengthen your faith, your morals, your culture. The college will set the signal lights along your route by placing before you sound and inspiring ideals of conduct and character, and she invites you to make your own choice of the finer things of life, to direct yourselves, to weigh and compare values correctly, to get a true conception of the real meaning of a college course.

Your own course of actions will result in the deposit of certain securities in the bank of life, securities that may be drawn on later proportionately as you deposit. Your college life is a period of your own development. May you achieve the traits of character and mind that will give to you joy in living and will give to others service.

I have heard that service is the rent you pay for the space you occupy. May you always be able to pay that rent, and may the motto of your college: *Fides, Mores, Cultura,* be engraven not only in the stone above the doorway but also upon your hearts. Your instructors are interested in you, your work, your welfare, and ask God to bless you this year and always.

The usual round of activities claimed the attention of the faculty and girls during the year. The first student extra-curricular event was a trip to Chicago. Five delegates, Margaret Dunphy, Lucille Edwards, Marcella Colburn, Jeannette Gies, and Margaret Fitzpatrick represented the journalism department at the convention of the Associated Collegiate Press and National College Press Association, held at De Paul University, October 11, 12, and 13, 1934. At the sessions of this convention, the students heard prominent speakers discuss every phase of practical journalism. The girls found time to see some of the worth-while sights of the big city and spent a day at the Century of Progress Exposition.

When these five set forth to Chicago to attend that convention, they established a precedent for their successors. Year after year since then, the youthful editors have planned attendance at this convention as part of their year's work. Jane Carroll, Ellen Campbell, Marcella Colburn, and Lucille Edwards represented their school at the meeting held in the same city October 17, 18, 19, 1935. Maxyne Rogers, Ellen Rita Milan, and Catherine Thackrey traveled to Louisville for the convention at the Brown Hotel, October 29, 30, 31, 1936. The University of Cincinnati was the host to the nation's colleges when their representatives convened November 3, 4, 5, 1938, to attend the meeting of the Associated Collegiate Press. Dorothy Starbuck, Maxine Davis, Gladys Givan, and Madelyn Nickolds were the privileged representatives that year. In 1939 Patricia Ann McLaughlin, Anne Elizabeth Monaghan, and Gladys Givan went to Des Moines for the annual press conclave on October 26, 27, and 28.

The International Relations Club has taken an active part in the annual regional conferences. Student participation in these meetings has served as an incentive to the members of the club to keep themselves informed on vital political issues. When the University of Denver was host to the conference October 18, 19, 20, 1934, Loretto Heights College had open house for the delegates on the afternoon from the state represented the University of Denver, Uni- of October 19, from four to six. Members of the college International Relations Club served tea in the reception and council rooms to more than one hundred guests. Delegates versity of Colorado, Colorado College, Denver University School of Commerce, and Grand Junction State Junior College. Out of state guests were from the University of Utah, Brigham Young University, Snow College, Utah, University of Wyoming, and University of Montana.

These regional conferences have been held annually for some years, either in Colorado, Utah, Wyoming, or Montana, the Rocky Mountain states. The club was established by the Carnegie Foundation to enable college students of the United States to study from an unbiased viewpoint the fundamentals, laws, and principles which govern international relations. Loretto Heights College was among the first to establish a local club. Delegates from Loretto have participated in the annual regional conference from the time it was inaugurated. In 1936 Miss Margaret Fitzpatrick of the class of '38 was elected regional recording secretary and in 1937 Miss Virginia Vollmar of the class of '39, regional vice-president. The International Relations Club of the college, besides being a member of the Rocky Mountain Conference of International Relations and the Carnegie Endowment for International Peace, is a member of the Catholic Association for International Peace.

Other clubs and societies form an integral part not only of extra-curricular activities but supplement in many cases the regular work of the class room. The Catholicity Club, Athletic Association, B Sharp, Choral, Classical, Dolora Choir, Dramatic Art, El Circulo Espanol, La Confrérie Joyeuse, Orchestra, and Riding Club are all media through which the students cultivate initiative and leadership.

But the most important of all the organizations on the campus is the Sodality of Our Lady. The students at Loreto Heights have always considered membership in the Sodality a special honor. The history of the Sodality of Our Lady at Loretto deserves to be written in a special treatise. Many sodalists, present and past, acknowledge that here at Loretto they learned the happiness of keeping close to Mary, their Mother.

At the commencement exercises, June 5, 1935, the Very Reverend Robert M. Kelly, S.J., president of Regis College, addressed the graduates. The Right Reverend Monsignor Richard Brady, chaplain of the college, presented the candidates for degrees, which His Excellency, the Most Reverend Urban J. Vehr, conferred upon Claire Irene Dunphy, Margaret Mary Dunphy, Mary Kathleen Fitzpatrick, Mary Alma Fregeau, Jeannette Gies, Mary Evelyn Kirby, and Lorraine Mary O'Meara, Bachelor of Arts; Agnes Piccoli, Bachelor of Music; Isobel Frances Mahoney, Bachelor of Philosophy.

When the college was renovated and remodeled in the summer of 1930, the library was removed to new quarters in the northeast wing of the main floor. Sister M. Constantia, the librarian, bought the new equipment and furniture: charging desk, reading tables, chairs, periodical racks, bulletin board, the bust of His Holiness, Pope Pius XI, scholar and librarian—practically all furnishings in the present library. Since the initial installment of the furnishings and equipment, other stacks have been added and the lighting system improved. The total cost of the improvements approximated $7,000.

In addition to the accessions secured each year by purchase, the number of books and periodicals has been increased from time to time by generous donations of friends. On December 12, 1930, the Most Reverend J. Henry Tihen, Bishop of Denver from 1917 to 1931, made a gift of 112 books. Many of these books are valuable, rare holdings published by the Arthur H. Clark Company. The greater number of books of the collection were placed on the history and English shelves. His Excellency, when Bishop of Denver, manifested in a number of ways his personal interest in the college. The Sisters of Loretto will always appreciate this last mark of Bishop Tihen's generosity.

The late Right Reverend Monsignor Brady, chaplain for many years at Loretto Heights, willed the greater part of his library, about 2,500 books and periodicals, to the college. Besides these larger donations, many benefactors have contributed fine collections, encyclopedias, and books for general reference.

Gifts deserving special acknowledgment, besides those mentioned above, were received from the Right Reverend W. M. Higgins, the Reverend Wm. J. Mulcahy, the Honorable Lawrence Lewis, the Honorable A. L. Morrison, Mrs. Margaret Aley (French collection), Mrs. H. W. Anderson, Mr. Wm. J. Cox, Misses Claire and Margaret Dunphy, Mrs. Wm. E. Earley (Reddin collection), Mary Elizabeth Hanson, Mr. Timothy J. Hurley (complete file of *Fortune Magazine*), Mr. T. F. Mahoney, Lucille Mannix (Reverend E. J. Mannix collection), Mrs. M. J. O'Fallon, Virginia Seep, Mr. and Mrs. Alwyn Smith, Mrs. M. C. Z. Spence (German classics), and Mr. James Tulley.

Sisters of the college faculty who have contributed fifty or more books: Sister M. Dolorine, Sister M. Edmond, Sister Francis de Sales, and Sister M. Vivian. Sisters of the faculty and other Sisters of Loretto contributing twenty-five or more books: Sister M. Alonza, Sister Ann Francis, Sister Bathildes, Sister Celestine, Sister Felician, Sister Lilliana, Sister Marie Anthony, Sister Marie Clyde, Sister Maura, Sister Miriam, Sister Pancratia, Sister Roberta, Sister Ursula, and Sister William Joseph. Sisters of Loretto contributing fifteen or more: Sister Aloyse, Sister Edwin Mary, Sister Eustachia, Sister Frances de Chantal, Sister Francisca, Sister Georgetta, Sister Marie Lourde, Sister Mary Nerinckx, Sister Rebecca, and Sister Rose Margaret.

Others to whom grateful acknowledgment is made are Margaret and Anna Fallon, Helen Finn, Marie Foley, Mrs. W. A. McCammon, Mrs. P. J. Sullivan, and Mr. Ray Taylor.

Besides the individuals listed above, generous donations were received from the Carnegie Endowment for International Peace, Denver Public Library, Loretto Heights Alumnae (The Reverend Charles J. Carr collection); Sisters of Loretto, Loretto Motherhouse; Sisters of Loretto, St. Mary's Academy, Denver; and Sisters of Loretto, Sterling, Illinois.

Sister Constantia, on becoming librarian, began to reclassify and catalogue the library; Sister M. Pancratia, assistant librarian for several years, took up the work and devoted much of her time to it. Miss Ann Samuels, during her period of service in the library, carried still farther the labor of reclassifying and cataloguing. Miss Alice O'Neill, the present assistant, expects to finish this important work.

After the death of Sister Constantia, October 5, 1933, Sister Rose Margaret was given general charge of the library, a duty which she has performed with meticulous care. Sister Rose Margaret as director of the library has been conservative, practical, a good financier, and wholly devoted to the development of the library service.

Members of the Alumnae Association installed a fine new card case in loving memory of Sister Constantia. The Sisters of Loretto of St. Mary's Academy, Denver, donated busts of Dante, Homer, and Vergil; and Mrs. H. W. Anderson, a fine atlas stand. The latest project for the expansion of library facilities is the opening of the former green social hall as a periodical and reference room, which, according to plans, will connect with the main library by means of a stairway.

The librarians as members of the American Library Association and the Catholic Library Association have attended the meetings and participated in the programs. Sister Pancratia, assistant librarian, attended conferences of both associations in Kansas City, Missouri, in the summer of 1938. In November of the same year Sister Pancratia and Sister Frances Therese participated in the meeting of the Catholic Library Association, at the Benedictine College, Tulsa, Oklahoma. Sister Pancratia presided at the Round Table High School Division, and Sister Frances Therese read a paper on "The Library as an Aid in Character Building."

In October, 1939, Sister Rose Margaret and Miss Ann Samuels were present at the regional meeting of the Catholic Library Association at Marymount College, Salina, Kansas; and in May, 1940, Sister Rose Margaret attended the joint meeting of the American Library Association and the Catholic Library Association which met in Cincinnati, Ohio. Miss Samuels represented the college at the Midwest Unit of the Catholic Library Association at Creighton University, and, in the absence of Reverend E. J. Sandoval, S.J., presided at the Catholic Readers Round Table and read a paper entitled ''The Literary Parade of 1941.'' In April, 1941, Sister Rose Margaret attended the Catholic Library Association which met in New Orleans in connection with the National Catholic Educational Association.

Loretto Heights College was host to the Midwest Unit of the Catholic Library Association which met October 11, 12, 13, 1941. The convention was carried on in a manner different from those of former years. Miss Ann Samuels, assistant librarian of the college, had prepared a program which introduced different phases of the library and its work. The college, high school, elementary school, and hospital sections had representatives, who led discussions in their respective fields. Instead of formal prepared papers, the convention took the form of a ''library clinic,'' where the various problems of librarians were discussed. Each librarian attended the meetings which interested him most and would aid him in his field of work.

Book displays, sponsored by the Denver Public Library, were of interest to those working with library publicity. The display offered by the Dieter Bookbinding Company demonstrated the methods used in this certified library bindery.

A sightseeing trip to Red Rocks and Lookout Mountain, from 12 to 3, Sunday afternoon, enabled guests to view two outstanding points of interest in the Denver Mountain Parks, the new open-air amphitheater and Buffalo Bill's grave.

In the summer of 1935, Sister Mary Edmond was transferred to Webster College as director of the Classical department; Sister Marie Clyde of Webster College became director of the English department at Loretto Heights and Sister Miriam from Webster College replaced Sister M. Edmond in the Classical department. Sister Miriam had been professor of Classics and director of the department at Webster College from its opening in 1916; and, in addition to her teaching schedule, was dean of Webster College from 1932 to 1935.

After the many programs which marked the close of the scholastic year at Loretto Heights—the annual May crowning of Our Lady, the Loretto "Loyalty Girl" ceremony, and Baccalaureate Sunday with its conventional observances—the seniors, Ellen Mary Campbell, Jane Carroll, Eugenie Guindon, Raphael Gwynn, Kathryn Lewis, and Mary J. O'Donnell, who claimed quality if not quantity as their distinctive mark, received degrees at the commencement on June 3, 1936. Eight Sisters of Loretto finished their college course at the close of the summer school, July 31.

From the time Loretto Heights Academy was opened in 1891, the fine arts, drawing and painting, formed one of the most attractive and best patronized of the cultural courses offered by the academy; but when the high school curriculum made increasing demands on the students' time, interest in the art department waned. Finally, the art studio was closed to give place to a much-needed class room.

When requests for art became frequent in the college, Sister Mary Norbert Parsoneault was released in 1933 from regular school duties in order to study art at the Chappell House, the school of art of the Denver University. While pursuing her own studies, she built up an interest in this subject among the students in the two periods she taught weekly and the Saturday morning classes. After receiving the degree of Bachelor of Fine Arts from the Denver University in June, 1935, Sister Mary Norbert became a full-time instructor, and the number of students interested in art increased.

In order to take care of the classes adequately, a second room with a fine northern exposure was opened in 1938. This room and the adjoining first studio afford ample space for lecture and laboratory classes. Through the generous donations of an interested patron, a fine lighting system, studio furniture, casts, statuary, anatomical charts, and colored slides have been provided. The walls of both rooms are specially prepared for exhibits of work. On the south wall of the new studio and the north wall of the first studio hang Sister Mary Norbert's murals, painted in oil and tempera: "Christ Blessing the Mother of a large Christian Family," a mural 7 feet by 5, was painted in oils in 1938; "The Sorrowful Mother and Saint John at the Holy Sepulcher," 5 feet by 3½, was painted in the Fine Arts Center, Colorado Springs, in 1939. A third mural, 15 feet by 6½, showing college students engaged in the art courses offered in the studio, occupies the space in the main hall between the two doors of the art rooms. This mural was the painted thesis required for her Master of Arts degree, which Sister Mary Norbert received from the art department of Colorado College in 1941.

The art courses offered in the department include free hand drawing, design and composition, commercial art, painting, interior decorating, style design, lettering, appreciation of painting, history of art, and methods of teaching.

Nine students were graduated, June 2, 1937. His Excellency, the Most Reverend Bishop Vehr, gave the address for the occasion and conferred the Bachelor of Arts degree upon Joan Catherine Ayers, Lucille Anne Edwards, Jewel Elizabeth McGovern, Gladys Golden O'Farrell, Anne Marie Sullivan, and Agnes Josephine Weber; Bachelor of Science, Marcella Eleanor Colburn; Bachelor of Science in Home Economics, Mary Catherine St. John; Bachelor of Philosophy, Irene Catherine Friel. On July 30, three Sisters of Loretto received the Bachelor of Arts Degree.

In August, 1937, Sister Roberta Hardesty, who had been dean of women from September, 1934, and Sister Ethelbert Owens were transferred to the Modern Language department of Webster College; Sister Isabella Marie Foley went to Webster College as instructor in Latin. Sister Lucy Marie Janes, of Webster College, became instructor in French at Loretto Heights, and Sister Mary Nerinckx Blincoe replaced Sister Isabella Marie as instructor in Latin. Sister Frances Therese was appointed dean of women and Sister Francis de Sales, dean of studies.

Both sisters were well qualified for these appointments. Sister Frances Therese had spent more than two years in graduate study in the field of education at St. Louis University and the University of Colorado. Sister Francis de Sales received her undergraduate degree from Loretto Heights College in 1928; the Master of Arts from the University of Colorado in 1934, and after three years of graduate work at the Catholic University of America, the Doctor of Philosophy in June, 1937, her major field being Spanish, her minor, French and Italian; and her doctoral dissertation, *The Allegorical and Metaphysical Language in the Autos Sacramentales of Calderón.*

About two hundred Sisters of Loretto from Arizona, California, Colorado, Illinois, Kentucky, Missouri, New Mexico, and Texas, delegates to the fifth Educational Conference of the Sisters of Loretto, convened November 26 and 27, 1937, at Loretto Heights College. Mother Ann Francis, president of the college, was the general chairman of the convention, which had for its theme, "Vocational Guidance." The conference opened with the celebration of Mass in the college chapel by the Most Reverend Urban J. Vehr, Bishop of Denver. At the conclusion of Mass, His Excellency addressed the delegates on the true meaning of guidance of Catholic youth.

Distinguished educators in the field of guidance spoke at both the general sessions and the divisional groups. The Very Reverend Raphael McCarthy, S.J., president of Marquette University, discussed the necessity of knowing the psychology of the child and the adolescent as the fundamental principle of all correct guidance, in a paper entitled "The Role of the School in Character Training." The Reverend Hubert Newell, diocesan superintendent of schools in Colorado, gave an interesting account of vocational guidance in the schools under his direction in a paper developing his subject: "The Beginning of the Guidance Program in our Diocesan Schools." Mother Edwarda Ashe, mistress of novices, read an informing paper on "Guidance in Junior Colleges Affiliated to Novitiates of Religious Communities," and Sister Frances Marie Walsh, dean of women of Webster College, discussed "The Technique of Placement." Reports on the status of the personnel program in Webster College and Loretto Heights College were given by Sister Frances Marie and Sister Frances de Chantal, respectively. The Reverend Daniel A. Lord, S.J., addressed the assembly on "The Boy and Girl Problem."

Doctor George F. Donovan, president of Webster College, was chairman of the college division on November 26. By the vote of the delegates Loretto Academy, El Paso, Texas, was the place selected for the sixth Educational Conference in November, 1938.

Accordingly, the next year, 1938, on the two days following Thanksgiving, the sixth annual Educational Conference was held in El Paso, at Loretto Academy. The Sisters of Loretto in that southwestern city had arranged an excellent program, educational and social, which received high commendation from the delegates who attended. The conference the following year met at Webster College under the general supervision of the president, Doctor Donovan.

The eighth consecutive educational meeting was convened, for the second time, at Loretto Heights, November 22 and 23, 1940. About the same number of delegates, representing the same number of states as at the meeting in 1937, assembled for the two-day conclave. Doctor Paul J. Ketrick, president of the college, was the general chairman; he and the committees collaborating planned sessions which were instructive and inspirational. The theme of all papers and discussions was "Catholic Education and the Social Order."

Doctor George F. Donovan gave an able discussion of the conference theme; "Catholic Education in a Democratic Society" was the subject of the paper read by the Reverend Wilfred M. Mallon, S.J., dean of the College of Arts and Sciences, St. Louis University. The Reverend John F. Flanagan, S.J., dean of Regis College, spoke before the division of high schools on "Guiding the High School Graduate to a Catholic College." Sister M. Francisca, director of the general educational program of the Sisters of Loretto, discussed "The Loretto Spirit" in a paper considered so pertinent that it was printed later and distributed to each member of the Society.

At the opening of the fall term of 1937, the Reverend James Stakelum, C.M., Ph.D., replaced the Reverend Charles Convery, C.M., S.T.D., as professor of philosophy; and Miss Grace Virginia Conley, M.Ed., was appointed instructor in physical education.

The year 1937-38 carried a well-balanced schedule—not all work, not all play: Sodality meetings, student radio programs, annual convention of the Association of Catholic School Press Relations, attendance of the faculty at various educational conferences and meetings of learned societies, Catholic action discussions in Vocation Week, musical recitals, senior play, prom, and banquet—these activities kept both faculty and students fully employed. For the first time in the history of the colleges, Regis and Loretto held joint Baccalaureate services in Loyola Church, Denver, Sunday afternoon, May 29, at four o'clock.

Graduating exercises took place in the college auditorium, June 1, at eight o'clock in the evening. The Reverend Daniel A. Lord, S.J., editor of the *Queen's Work* and national director of the Sodality of Our Lady, delivered an address on "Catholic Action." Monsignor Brady presented the candidates for degrees which the Most Reverend Urban J. Vehr conferred upon Margaret Collette Fitzpatrick, Marie Antonia Floyd, Leona Agnes Gallagher, Marjorie Ellen Gray, Mary Clarke Meek, Jane Elizabeth Menten, Mary Adelaide Morrow, Hazel Claire Murphy, Mary Cecilia Pegano, Doris Jane Porter, Anna Marie Wade, Madeline Elizabeth Weber, and Genevieve Catherine Wilson, Bachelor of Arts; Ellen Rita Milan, Maxyne Rogers, and Catherine Teresa Thackrey, Bachelor of Arts in Journalism; Clare Margaret Werle, Bachelor of Science in Home Economics; Clare Loretto Mooney and Kathleen Elizabeth O'Hare, Bachelor of Science in Nursing; Ruth A. Yont, Bachelor of Literature. In August of that year, four Sisters of Loretto received the Bachelor of Arts degree.

The announcement in the summer of 1938 that Doctor Paul J. Ketrick would take over the duties of president of Loretto Heights College aroused general and local interest. This surely was a departure from precedent! Reporters on the various papers sought and obtained interviews from the president-elect as soon as he arrived in Denver. Doctor Ketrick, though still young when he became president of the college, had already attained distinction in many fields. His scholastic record shows that he received the Bachelor of Arts degree at the University of Scranton in 1927; the Master of Arts at the Catholic University of America in 1928 and the Doctor of Philosophy from the same university in 1931. The new President's teaching experience, honors, and literary productions gave evidence of his scholarship and versatility.

His teaching positions: Instructor in English, Catholic University of America, 1927-37; member of Council of Graduate School, *ibid.*, 1934-37; visiting lecturer, Dominican College, San Raphael, California, summer of 1934; visiting lecturer, Loras College, Dubuque, Iowa, summer of 1935; professor of English, St. John's University, 1937-38; professor of English and director of the department, Loretto Heights College, 1938-.

Honors: President, Aquinas Philosophical Society, 1927; Knights of Columbus fellow, 1928-31; honorary member, *Institut Artistique et Littéraire de France*, 1939-; president, Colorado Poetry Fellowship, 1942-.

Publications: *Manual of English Bibliography*, Washington, D. C., 1930; *Relation of Golagros and Gawane to the Old French Perceval;* Washington, D. C., 1931 (Doctoral Dissertation); "Literature and Catholic Education," in *Essays on Catholic Education in the United States*, New York, 1942; Reviews published in *The Writer, The Catholic Educational Review, The Catholic World;* Poems published in *The Magnificat, The Forge, Skyline,* and *Poet Lore.*

Articles: "Reading in Rhetoric One," *Catholic Educational Review*, April, 1930; "The Informal Approach to

Grammar," *Modern Education,* April, 1931; "Divine Apollo," *The Xaverian,* 1934; "On the Use of Authorities," *Catholic University of America Bulletin,* January, 1935; "The Medievalism of Dante Rossetti," *Thought,* March, 1936; "Some Homeric Nods," *The Xaverian,* January, 1937; "Daniel Sargent: Metaphysical Poet and Biographer of a New World," *Catholic World,* March, 1941.

Mother Ann Francis, the superior of Loretto Heights and retiring president of the college, and the administrative officers planned a series of events which introduced Doctor and Mrs. Ketrick to the faculty, to the student officers, and to the friends and patrons of the college. Shortly after arriving in Denver, Doctor and Mrs. Ketrick and their small daughter, Paula, visited the sisters informally and were entertained at dinner; on September 1, Doctor Ketrick entered upon his official duties and met the faculty on September 11 in the first formal assembly.

On Sunday afternoon, December 11, more than three hundred guests greeted the new president at a formal reception in the Gold Room of the college. This room and the spacious tile hall, at the south side of which stood the tea tables, were beautiful with cheery Christmas decorations of evergreens, palms, and poinsettias. The Reverend Harold V. Campbell, pastor of the Blessed Sacrament Church and for many years professor of senior religion in the college, introduced Doctor and Mrs. Ketrick to the guests. The Misses Margaret and Anna Fallon, Mrs. W. H. Anderson, Mrs. Frederick Schmidt, Mrs. M. J. O'Fallon, and Mrs. T. A. Cosgriff, good friends of the Sisters of Loretto and charter members of the Loretto League, were in the receiving line.

On the following evening, December 12, a dinner at the Denver Country Club was the culmination of the inaugural ceremonies. Those present besides Doctor Ketrick were His Excellency, the Most Reverend Urban J. Vehr, twenty-four pastors of the city churches, many doctors, and a number of patrons of the college.

The school year went on as usual under the direction of the new president, who, young, affable, a ready speaker, an inspiring teacher, and an administrator willing to learn, soon made many friends on the campus and in a short time became a leader in Denver's literary and Catholic circles.

Since a knowledge of shorthand and typewriting, especially the latter, is a necessary adjunct to a complete education, even for the student who does not intend to devote herself to this kind of work, courses in these subjects had always been given in the college, but without credit. Within the past few years the demand for business training carrying college credit created the necessity of developing a department of secretarial studies. Accordingly, one of the large rooms which were vacated, when the students became residents of Pancratia Hall in 1934, was fitted with necessary equipment for more adequate business courses. Again in 1936 the scope of the department was enlarged, and specially trained instructors were in charge: Miss Ruth Larsch, M.S., from 1936 to 1938; Sister M. Ursula, S.L., M.S., 1938-40; Miss Anna Marie Connelly, M.S., 1940-41; and Mrs. Bertha A. Bay, M.A., 1942.

During the summer of 1941, the dean, Sister Francis de Sales, supervised the enlargement and equipping of the department of secretarial studies. The adjoining room was added, both rooms were redecorated, floors were sanded and finished, and the most modern business furnishings were installed at a cost of $1,000. The new equipment included bookkeeping tables, an A. B. Dick mimeograph, mimeoscope, Monroe calculator, ditto liquid duplicator, fifteen typewriters, and desks and chairs for instructors.

In addition to the regular commercial subjects, the department offers courses in accounting, business English, office practice, economics, advanced accounting, business law, and a teacher's course. The aim of the college in offering a bachelor of science degree in secretarial studies is to prepare college trained secretaries and efficient teachers of high school commercial subjects.

Ten seniors were graduated June 3, 1939: Bachelor of Arts, Mary Maxine Davis, Martha Ellen Dea, Dorothy Ann Evers, Mary Elizabeth Gallagher, Madelyn Prudence

Nickolds, Teresa Elizabeth Pegano, and Virginia Elizabeth Vollmar; Bachelor of Science, Nancy Gregory Quintana, Patsy Ann Savage, Margaret Irene Toohey.

In August, 1939, Sister Frances de Chantal was transferred to Webster College to direct the chemistry department; Sister Pancratia, assistant librarian for several years, went to St. Mary's High School, Sterling, Illinois; and Mrs. Regina Wachtel, director of dramatics from 1933, accepted a position as instructor in speech at Marycrest, Davenport, Iowa. The new faculty members that fall were Sister Mary Helen Denvir, instructor in biology; Sister Frances Marie, education; Mrs. Mary Halbert, M.A., speech; Miss Ann Samuels, A.B., L.S., assistant librarian; Sister Adella Brocktrup, assistant in home economics and part-time student in the college; and Sister Alonza Smith, director of the chemistry department.

Shortly after the opening of the fall term, Sister Miriam, professor of Greek and Latin, died suddenly, of a heart attack, on October 2. Though death came quickly, it did not come unexpectedly. Sister's whole life from her entrance into religion had been devoted to her profession, the profession of sanctity. Christ's injunction for correct living had been followed unswervingly: ''Seek ye first the kingdom of God and his justice and all these things shall be added unto you.'' Love of God and love of learning combined to make Sister Miriam a remarkable religious and a scholar; in her death the Loretto Society suffered a great loss.

A second and a third time death came that year removing two sisters who had contributed generously to the material and spiritual life of the community. Sister Floscella Keating, so well remembered for her years of faithful service and for the kindliness with which she served, died after some weeks of illness, March 23, 1940. Though Sister's life was pre-eminently one of living for others, yet she frequently found time to go apart from the crowd and rest before the silent Tabernacle. No one has been found to fill adequately the post which Sister Floscella held and to which she gave herself so untiringly.

One week later, Sister Jovita Mills, after seventy-one years in religion, filled with work, prayer, and self-effacement, entered into her reward on March 30. It may be truly said that Sister Jovita's life was hidden with Christ in God.

The closing weeks of school brought the usual events which make the last days memorable for the seniors. In June, 1940, fifteen students received degrees: Frances Ann Childers, Veronica Gegan, Gladys Givan, Geraldine Mc-Cauley, Margaret Mahoney, Ann Elizabeth Monaghan, Eva Sydney Monaghan, Margaret Anna Mullen, and Dorothy Starbuck, Bachelor of Arts; Rosalie Lawrenson, Natalie Rosemary Elliott, Helen Kelley, Mercedes Riordan, Natalie Swan, and Gertrude Waters, Bachelor of Science. Seven Sisters of Loretto received degrees at the close of the summer school, August 2, 1940.

On Sunday evening, June 17, just a few days before the opening of the summer session, great commotion existed for some hours at Loretto Heights when the message was flashed through the building that the laundry was on fire. The engineer had banked the fire about one o'clock in the afternoon and had left the premises at eight o'clock. Many of the sisters during the evening recreation crossed and recrossed the campus, enjoying the calm and peace of the beautiful scene which seemed a fairyland in the silvery moonlight.

Sister Conrad Hardesty, when retiring about 9:30, glancing in the direction of the laundry, noticed that light was streaming from the windows of the building. At first she thought that it was simply the reflection of the moonlight which caused the brightness, but when she heard the windows and doors forced outward, she knew that the laundry was on fire. Hurrying to the west porch of the main floor, Sister rang, long and violently, the old historic St. Mary's bell. The alarm having been turned in to the neighboring fire departments, firemen from three Denver, two

Englewood, and the Garden Home Volunteer companies were soon at the scene; but finding that the two-story laundry building was enveloped in flames, they attached fire pumpers to the two artesian wells near the laundry, which furnished sufficient water to keep the flames from spreading.

The fire was visible from Morrison, Lookout Mountain, and from nearly all parts of Denver and surrounding areas. Automobiles hurrying from all directions jammed Federal Boulevard from West Alameda Avenue to the college. Not only were the laundry building and equipment destroyed and the near-by carpenter shop, storage, and tea rooms damaged, but all the accumulation of material—valuable antiques and otherwise—which had been stored through the years on the second floor of the laundry, even from the time of "the founding sisters," was lost. The insurance covered only part of the cost of rebuilding.

Not long after this catastrophe, Mother Ann Francis went to the Motherhouse to attend the general chapter of which she was a member in virtue of her office. At the elections on July 16, Mother Edwarda Ashe, superior of Webster College, was chosen Superior General by the votes of the delegates, the highest office the sisters can confer on one of their members.

After the chapter, Mother Ann Francis was made superior and regent of Webster College, and Sister Frances Marie Walsh was appointed to the same offices at Loretto Heights College. The duties which Sister Frances Marie had performed for many years at Webster College had brought experiences which were of service to her in her new position; besides being director of the department of education, Sister had been dean of women and moderator of the Loretto Foundation, an active organization which has sponsored many of Webster's worth-while projects.

At the close of the annual retreat, August 15, Sister Lucy Marie, director of the French department, was appointed assistant mistress of novices; and Sister Francetta Barberis, who had just received her Master's degree at the

University of Notre Dame, became the director of the French department at Loretto Heights. Sister Mary Nerinckx, after two years of graduate study at St. Louis University, returned to take over the classics, Greek and Latin, and finish her doctoral dissertation; Miss Anna Marie Connelly was appointed instructor in secretarial studies, and Doctor Anna Joyce Reardon, assistant in mathematics and physics.

Before the opening of the scholastic year, several necessary improvements were made on the first floor of the main building; the kitchen was remodeled and refurnished—a new range and other much needed labor-saving devices were installed; both dining rooms were redecorated, and the guests' dining room was fittingly furnished.

The president, dean, registrar, and faculty members attended professional meetings occurring at intervals within the year; the students showed their versatility in the various activities and benefits which they sponsored successfully; the seniors, besides leading in all extra-curricular events, found time to prepare seriously for the comprehensive examinations which the faculty had inaugurated as a further means of developing their study habits and securing sound scholarship.

All the traditional exercises were carried out toward the close of the year 1940-41. On Sunday evening, May 25, the entire student body participated in the spiritual graduation, a chapel ceremony, and renewed their promises of fidelity to Mary, their Mother. Baccalaureate services began Thursday morning, May 29, with a Solemn High Mass; this was followed by the time-honored custom of planting the ivy on the campus. The Reverend Joseph F. Higgins, pastor of St. Patrick's church, Pueblo, delivered the address to the graduates at the commencement exercises, June 1. The Most Reverend Urban J. Vehr conferred degrees upon twenty-two candidates: Marie Anastasia C de Baca, Pauline Marie Guindon, Virginia Mary Hornig, Adelaide Benita Lackowsky, Rose Marie Lucy, Merylmarie McAvoy, Mary Irene McMahon, Helen Mary Nieters,

Mary Catherine O'Byrne, Leah Ann Pape, Mary Margaret
Qualkenbush, Barbara Katherine Sparn, Ferne Vivian
Tooke, Dorothy Jane Vogel, Marguerite Amelia Wathen,
and Elizabeth Germaine Woodman; Bachelor of Science in
Home Economics, Dorothy Anna Cudmore, Elizabeth Emma
Kelley, Flora Louise Meek; Bachelor of Science, Margaret
Rose See, Margaret Zook; Bachelor of Science in Nursing,
Mary Ellen Green.

That same June, Sister Mary Nerinckx received the
Doctor of Philosophy degree in classics at St. Louis Uni-
versity. Her dissertation was *The Use of the Exemplum in
Cicero's Philosophical Works.*

Sister Consilia Brown, who had just completed her
work for the Master of Arts degree at Notre Dame University, was transferred in August, 1941, to Webster College. Sister Alice Carlene Roach was appointed assistant
in the journalism department; Sister Mary Florence Wolff,
instructor in history; Sister Cecille Reddin, instructor in
mathematics; Sister Francis Aloys Hunleth, assistant instructor in chemistry; and Sister Catherine Patrice, assistant instructor in music. Mrs. Bertha Bay from New York
replaced Miss Anna Marie Connelly as instructor in secretarial studies; Miss Rosalind Longfield from Madison,
Wisconsin, became instructor in physical education; and
Miss Alice O'Neill of St. Paul, Minnesota, assistant librarian.

At the opening of the school year, President Ketrick
when welcoming the students, new and old, urged the correct use of time and suggested that a college education was
the best means to prepare for national defense:

The year's work which you have chosen for yourself
is one which will surely have its reward in a bonus of individual happiness. Ask yourself why you are in college!
Remind yourself now of the deeply fixed reasons which led
you to be a part of an institution of higher education. For
a Catholic youth there is only one kind of college that represents traditional culture and valid education. You are in
such a college, and there is no reason why you should not
enjoy a splendid and successful year.

Perennially, the question may spring up in your minds concerning what you will achieve tomorrow and what you will become. Some of your high school classmates, barred from your advantages, have already circumscribed their opportunities in a way from which they may never free themselves. You, however, are still free to choose gloriously, to bend every effort for leadership, to press every hour toward enlightenment, to devote every thought and effort to striving toward whatever is good and true. For you, college life may mean a coming and going through noisy halls, chatting with friends, and a routine procession of classroom displays. Or it may mean a climbing toward power, and seizing of opportunities for personal and civic leadership.

All this is why, throughout the country, girls have returned to college in greater numbers than ever before. They know that plans have scarcely been formulated as far as the place of women in National Defense is concerned. They know that when the time comes, college-trained women will enjoy priorities of the type now being gained by college-educated young men. If only a miracle can prevent the use of force within the months to come, intelligent service must be the watchword which the college girls of 1941-1942 must keep in mind. In peace or in war, you must rate Class A for this test.

Getting settled was an interesting experience when the students returned to school in the fall of 1941. Since 1934, the college girls had occupied the third and fourth floors of the south wing of Pancratia Hall; but now that the high school was closed, the whole building, with the exception of a few class rooms, was taken over as a residence hall. The Home Economics department was transferred to Pancratia Hall in order to give more space in the administration building. The kitchen and dining room of this department are on the first floor; the clothing room, on the main or second floor; and the practice house, which for some years was located in the cottage on the south campus, now occupies the former music suite.

A cafeteria and student union room have been opened on the first floor. On the main floor, the dean of women may be found in what used to be the office of the principal

of the high school. One of the class rooms on this floor has
been redecorated and furnished as a parlor. The former
high school study hall is now the college assembly; here
are held activities which formerly took place in the auditorium. On the third floor is an inviting student lounge,
artistically furnished with the wicker sets from the green
social hall in the main building.

The form of student government adopted when the
college was still young has remained in force with the exception of some few changes in addition to those which
were deemed necessary to take care of the different living
conditions. While the dean of women has general supervision of the discipline of the residence building, the students are directly responsible for order on the different
floors. The government of Pancratia Hall is in charge of
a president, a secretary, and a resident council. This latter
is composed of all the seniors who live in the hall and a
representative from the junior, sophomore, and freshman
classes. The duties of the governing board are to preserve
quiet during study periods, to grant minor permissions, to
make regulations for the government of the residence hall,
with the approval of the student council and the dean of
women, and to plan for harmonious living, particularly
through the development of the spiritual life of the resident students. The purpose of the system is to train the
student to responsibility and respect for authority. The
plan finally adopted for student government became more
effective through the following modifications: increasing
the number of members in the student council by admitting
the prefect of the sodality, the president of the missions,
and the president of the resident council; banking the student fund, and budgeting this fund by the student council.

That organization, co-operation, loyalty, and a Catholic
spirit do exist among the students was demonstrated by
their efficiency and devotedness to alma mater during the
golden jubilee year, 1941-1942. The Sisters of Loretto from
schools out of the state, the members of other religious
orders, and visitors who attended the jubilee celebrations

remarked on the fine *esprit du corps* of the students of Loretto Heights.

In the first social event of the year, 1941-42, the freshmen, in keeping with the golden jubilee theme, presented their Halloween party in true frontier style. Gay cartoons and clever invitations informed the guests that the entertainment would show life around "The Old Corral." Rude living conditions, the "medicine man," and the Indians gave the local setting of fifty years back.

The golden jubilee was formally inaugurated by religious ceremonies in the first week of November; a Solemn High Mass of thanksgiving was the peak of the celebration. Many of the student activities of the year were centered around the jubilee; but the grand finale was the sacred concert, Pergolese's Oratorio, *Stabat Mater,* presented in the college auditorium, on the afternoon of April 19 by the Dolora choir of fifty voices, trained in the College Voice department and directed by Monsignor Bosetti.

During the illness of the late Monsignor Richard Brady, chaplain for many years at Loretto, the Reverend James W. Stakelum, C.M., of St. Thomas Seminary, served as chaplain. On June 15, 1940, the Reverend William J. Mulcahy, assistant at the Blessed Sacrament Church, in Denver, took over the duties of chaplain at the college and pastor of St. Patrick's Church at Logan town; some weeks later he was appointed Catholic chaplain at Fort Logan with the privilege of offering three Masses on Sunday. The duties at the Fort became so interesting and engrossing that no one was surprised when Father Mulcahy volunteered on December 8, 1939, feast of the Immaculate Conception, as a full-time army chaplain.

On February 27, 1942, Father Mulcahy received the official notice of his appointment as chaplain and instructor in aeronautics at Mather Field, in the vicinity of San Francisco. As a special privilege to the seniors at the Heights, Father gave them his farewell blessing in the chapel of Our Lady of Loretto before he departed, March 17, for his new assignment in the army.

After the departure of Father Mulcahy, Father Stakelum filled the chaplaincy for some months. On June 13,
the Archbishop, the Most Reverend Urban J. Vehr, appointed the Reverend Anthony Weinzapfel, assistant at St.
Francis de Sales Church, chaplain at Loretto Heights and
pastor of St. Patrick's Church near Fort Logan. Father
Weinzapfel performed his first official duties at Loretto
and St. Patrick's on Sunday, June 21, 1942.

The seniors of 1942 considered themselves a privileged
class. They had the honor of representing the student body
at many of the functions commemorating the golden jubilee,
the chief event of the year; and at the close of their college
life they had the double distinction of having the Most Reverend Joseph Corrigan, Rector of the Catholic University
of America, deliver the commencement address, and the
Archbishop of Denver confer their hoods and diplomas.

On June 3 at 4:30 in the afternoon, Doctor Paul J.
Ketrick, president of the college, presented the candidates
to the Archbishop, the Most Reverend Urban J. Vehr, who
conferred the degrees upon Emma Romano, Bachelor of
Science in Music; Isabel King and Dorothy Popish, Bach-
elors of Science in Home Economics; Rita Abegg, Katherine
Glore, Bachelor of Science; Virginia Bailey, Katherine
Blodgett, Mary Elizabeth Eisenman, Angela Eisenman,
Laura Mae Givan, Helen Haddican, Mary Kathryn Hagerty,
Helen Mahoney, Patricia Ann McLaughlin, Margaret Nie-
ters, Catherine O'Donnell, Betty Schroll, Adelaide Sem-
melmann, Kathleen Shiel, Jean Singer, and Josephine
Walsh, Bachelor of Arts.

With the close of the scholastic year 1942-43, Loretto
Heights College will have completed its first twenty-five
years as an institution of higher education. Twenty-five
years—a short period of time, but long enough to establish
customs and traditions. This, Loretto Heights has done.
The students of today at Loretto are carrying on customs
which have been followed since the opening of the school.
Customs and traditions have an intangible influence on the
life of the student and make for disciplines in later life.

A college is more than a place for dispensing knowledge. Its values do not depend upon the magnificence of its halls or the completeness of its equipment; rather upon the subtle influences which pass from soul to soul and remain as enduring possessions. What Loretto Heights College has done for its students during these twenty-five years cannot be told here. Each Loretto girl has had her own experience; each one knows what colors and textures she has woven into her life's tapestry because of her years at Loretto Heights. Each alumna must be her own biographer.

Chapter XXII

MONSIGNOR RICHARD BRADY

The history of *Loretto in the Rockies* would be incomplete if it did not include one who was so closely connected with the life of the institution, during the greater part of the period preceding its golden jubilee year. Monsignor Richard Brady was chaplain at Loretto Heights for forty-four of those fifty years. The place was home to him. He identified himself with it, sharing its joys and sorrows, its successes and defeats. No figure stood out more clearly on the campus; no personage was more graphically etched on the minds of the pupils of the academy and of the collegians of the earlier years than "Monsignor."

Who that ever lived at the Heights does not remember Monsignor Brady as he took his daily exercise, morning and afternoon and evening—now apparently free from care, again in reflective mood, but always accompanied by his faithful dog, Jack, padding along by his side and suiting its demeanor to that of its master? Again and again the circuit of the building was made by the tall, erect *soggarth aroon,* who took these walks to keep himself "in good form" and, perhaps, to exercise his dog.

Richard Brady was born in County Cavan, Ireland, April 4, 1867, and received his early education in the National Schools of his native land. While still a seminarian, he was adopted in 1886 into the Archdiocese of St. Louis and for the next two years studied the classics and higher mathematics under the direction of the Franciscan Fathers, at St. Joseph's College, Teutopolis, Illinois. An exercise book in Geometry, a memento of his student days at that college, was found among his keepsakes. The book, written in his neat, characteristic penmanship, contains, apparently, some special assignments, for the dates show that the problems were not daily lessons: *Pensum* I was performed January, 1887; *Pensum* II, February 17, 1887, and so through the

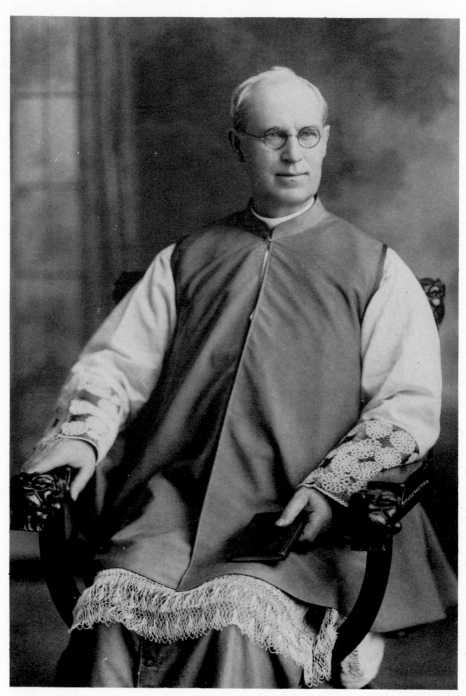

Monsignor Richard Brady

Mother Eustachia

Mother Ann Francis

Sister Dolorine

Sister Vivian

months. Farther on in the book is this notation: May 30, '87, Final *Pensum* for the year '86-'87. Another treasured relic of his student days at St. Joseph's College is a small pocket notebook, which contains outlines of all the Sunday sermons preached by the Rector of the college during the year 1887. These are not careless jottings, but well-written notes, divided into topics and sub-topics, showing the same exactness which is found in all Monsignor Brady's later writings.

After returning to Ireland for his philosophy and theology, the young student must have contemplated entering the American College at Rome. The following letter which he received from the Rector of that college, in reply to an inquiry, was preserved through all the succeeding years:

American College, Rome.
Apr. 27, 1891.

My dear Sir:

Yours of the 22d inst has just come to hand, and I beg to say in reply that the lectures begin about the commencement of Nov. but the students are expected to present themselves at the College about the middle of Oct. to enable them to have their outfits and some knowledge of Italian and of the ways of the College before the lectures begin, to lose no time afterwards.

The first year of Theology in Rome is devoted to the study of *"Loci Theologici"* and the knowledge of this tract must be perfect. Besides there are Canon Law, Liturgy, and History.

If you have never been in the United States, a dispensation from the Pope will be required for your admission.

With best wishes for your success, I remain

Yours sincerely in Xto
D. J. O'Connell
Rector.

Mr. Richard Brady
Carlow.

His plans for studying at the American College in Rome were not carried out. After completing his studies for the priesthood at St. Patrick's College, Carlow, Richard Brady was ordained June 11, 1893, in Carlow Cathedral, by the

Right Reverend Michael Comerford, Bishop of Kildare and Leghlin.

The Most Reverend Peter Richard Kenrick, Archbishop of St. Louis, appointed Father Brady, in August, 1893, assistant at the Cathedral of St. Louis IX, on Second and Walnut Streets, now known as the "Old Cathedral." Since in those days the chaplaincy of Loretto Academy on Pine Street, St. Louis, was in charge of the rector of the cathedral, Father Brady, the assistant, served as chaplain at the academy. The sisters, interested in the timid young cleric, newly ordained and taking up his duties in a strange land, gave him many an encouraging word which helped and cheered him during the first months when he was adjusting himself to his surroundings. This was Father Brady's introduction to the Sisters of Loretto and the beginning of a friendship which continued through the remaining years of his life.

In 1894 the young priest came to Colorado seeking to build up his health which had been impaired, no doubt, by close application to his studies in preparation for ordination. For two years, Father Brady served as chaplain at Glockner Sanatorium and St. Francis' Hospital, Colorado Springs, also at St. Mary's Hospital, Pueblo. Then, in August, 1896, the Most Reverend Nicholas C. Matz, Bishop of Denver, appointed him chaplain at Loretto Heights Academy and pastor of St. Patrick's Church near Fort Logan. A few years later, in September, 1900, he received another assignment, the pastorate of the mission at Littleton. There he organized a flourishing congregation and in 1901 built St. Mary's Church.

Living quarters were prepared for the young chaplain at the Heights on the main floor of the academy building— the two rooms on the left of the main entrance, now the council room and the president's office. These rooms Father Brady occupied until the bungalow was built shortly after the completion of the chapel in 1911. It is difficult to visualize how Father Brady fitted into these two rooms with all his books and periodicals which accumulated so readily around him; but here he lived for seventeen years, performing punctiliously his duties as chaplain, pastor of St. Patrick's Church near Fort Logan and St. Mary's at Littleton, and instructor in the religion classes of the academy.

Besides these responsibilities, Father Brady held many offices of honor and trust under His Excellency, Bishop Matz, who soon recognized the superior knowledge and efficiency of the chaplain at Loretto Heights. At the time of his elevation to the rank of Monsignor, he had been diocesan consultor for a period of four terms or twelve years; synodal examiner for fifteen years; and acting secretary to Bishop Matz for nineteen years. As secretary of the Fourth Diocesan Synod, held July 15, 1904, he prepared the statutes pertaining to the diocese, and as Diocesan *Officialis* from May 13, 1898, he brought the affairs of the diocese into systematic form. In addition to these official duties, he was diocesan *procurator fiscalis* for many years. The Reverend John P. Moran, pastor of St. John's Church, Denver, wrote of him (*Denver Register,* April 16, 1942): "My earliest recollections of Monsignor Brady are of a man learned and energetic on whom Bishop Matz placed great reliance and to whom he constantly referred all matters pertaining to canon law."

These diocesan duties required many trips to and from Denver. As those were still the "horse and buggy days," he went back and forth with his good horse, "Doc," and his faithful dog, "Jack." One can easily picture the scene on a winter day: an open buggy, a desolate countryside, the piercing wind and snow of those early days, and Father Brady, faithful to his tasks and solicitous about his horse, braving all kinds of weather.

Besides the above duties, Father Brady prepared for many years—fourteen and more—the diocesan statistics for the *Catholic Directory.* The publishing firm often congratulated him warmly on the fact that the book had never been once delayed in receiving data from the Denver diocese.

In the summer of 1909, Father Brady was one of a group who toured Italy, France, and Ireland. A card con-

taining the names of all who made the trip as members of
"McCrane's Pilgrimage Party of July 8, 1909" was found
among Monsignor Brady's souvenirs. He, the Reverend F.
J. Jones, and the Misses M. A. and Mary Jones, St. Louis
friends, formed a group within the group; together they
visited and enjoyed the historic places included in the itinerary. Kodak pictures taken en route tell the story of their
trip.

Here they are in Rome, in regulation formal attire,
ready for an audience with the Holy Father, Pius X. In another picture, bearing the caption, "Noble Romans," Father
Brady and Father Jones are dressed as Roman priests,
wearing the soutane and clerical hat. Again, the party of
four are shown, seated in a sort of landau, near the "Campo
Santo," in Milan. Next they are in Padua; and now in Venice, surrounded by the pigeons in St. Mark's Square. A
resident at the Heights on seeing this last picture would in-
voluntarily say: "Father Brady did not have to go to Venice
in order to appear in a picture, surrounded with pigeons,
for these frequent every available place at the Heights—but
pigeons at the Heights are not held in favor."

The friends continued their journey. Pictures show
them at Capri, Versailles, and Naples. In Ireland they are
at Blarney Castle; in a second picture they are seen pressing
on with the crowd, hastening to kiss the Blarney Stone. Another Irish scene shows three of the friends perched on an
Irish jaunting car; in a second picture, the four are in one
of the historic vehicles, somewhat crowded but happy, surely,
since they are in Ireland and are being transported in true
Irish fashion. The final picture, "The last glimpse of Ireland," showing Queenstown harbor, must have brought a
feeling of nostalgia, especially to a priest leaving his mother.

Father Brady and the Reverend Percy A. Phillips, chancellor of the diocese and rector of the Cathedral of the Immaculate Conception, received official notice, February 28,
1913, that His Holiness, Pope Pius X, had conferred on them
the title of domestic prelate. Although the appointment was
received rather early in the year, he deferred the investiture

until June 11, the twentieth anniversary of his ordination to the priesthood. When in accordance with the wish of the chaplain it was decided that the ceremony should take place in the chapel of Our Lady of Loretto, the Sisters of the Community felt that it was fitting that Father Brady's investiture should be the first great ceremony, after its dedication, to take place in the recently completed chapel.

The investiture of the two clergymen was an important affair not only for Loretto Heights but for the city of Denver since prior to this there had been but one other priest of the diocese upon whom the dignity had been conferred, the Right Reverend Monsignor Henry Robinson, pastor of the Church of the Annunciation and Vicar General of the diocese, who had died May 3, 1913. *The Denver News, Denver Republican,* and *Denver Post* gave great publicity to the event.

The Western Catholic of Quincy, Illinois, June 13, 1913, had this news article:

Wednesday, June 11, 1913, will go down in history as a great day for Loretto Academy and the Denver Diocese at large. On that day two of Denver's best and most learned priests were clothed in purple by command of the saintly pontiff, Pius X; in this instance it was a case of honor and dignity seeking the men and priests who have done well and deserved well at the hands of their superior. On that day Monsignor Richard Brady and Monsignor P. A. Phillips were invested in purple and received the title of Domestic Prelate to His Holiness in the Academy Chapel of Loretto Heights, Colo.

A brief address was delivered by the eloquent Father O'Ryan. The assistant priest, Reverend David T. O'Dwyer, read the pontifical briefs in Latin and also in English. Deacons of honor to the Right Reverend Bishop Matz were Very Reverend J. J. Brown, S. J., president of Sacred Heart College, and Very Reverend J. J. Cronin, C. M., president of St. Thomas Theological Seminary.

The Right Reverend Bishop blessed the rochets and placed them over the heads of the Monsignors, after which he put the mantellettas over their shoulders. The ceremony was concluded by Solemn Benediction of the Blessed Sacrament—celebrant, Very Reverend G. Raber, P. R., Colorado Springs; deacon, Reverend C. J. Carr of Denver; subdeacon, Reverend Edward Barry, S. J.; master of ceremonies, Reverend J. M. Walsh; thurifer, Reverend J. J. Murphy.

Following the services of the investiture a congratulatory dinner—a gift of the Colorado clergymen—was served to the Monsignori and their many friends among the clergy and laymen. At the banquet table, Bishop Matz announced that Monsignor Brady would succeed the late Right Reverend Monsignor Henry Robinson as pastor of the Annunciation Church and Vicar General of the Diocese. But after taking over the duties of the large Denver parish of the Annunciation, he soon found that the work taxed his physical strength and left him little or no time for his other diocesan duties. For this reason he returned in May, 1914, to Loretto Heights, and in December, 1914, he resigned as pastor of the Annunciation but retained the office of Vicar General until December, 1917.

On June 11, 1918, twenty-five years had passed since he had been pronounced a priest forever by the powers which his Bishop in his native land had conferred upon him. Twenty-two of those twenty-five years Monsignor Brady had spent at Loretto Heights. The celebration of the event was a memorable occasion. About forty clergymen representing many parts of the diocese were present at the Jubilee Mass which Monsignor offered in the chapel of Our Lady of Loretto. His Excellency, the Most Reverend J. Henry Tihen, Bishop of Denver, and the Right Reverend P. A. Phillips, Chancellor of the diocese, were in the sanctuary. The Reverend William O'Ryan, devoted friend of the jubiliarian, preached the sermon, a eulogy commemorating the contributions which Monsignor Brady, during his years of service, had made to the diocese. In concluding the Reverend Speaker said:

We are here primarily to honor the great Priest, Christ. But here also is one of his ministering priests, an humble priest, a self-sacrificing priest, an imitator of Him who was holy, undefiled, innocent, separated from sinners, and made higher than the earth. We thank God for him and his rich years. We pray many years of blessings and fruitfulness, the long evening, the sacred and peaceful Indian summer of life.

Your Bishop is here, Father Brady, to feel joy with you; many priests who have known you for many years are here to thank God for you; the noble sisterhoods of the Church are represented here today; many of your laymen friends are assembled; and best of all, the little children of this academy who are your first care and love; and their mothers and older sisters, your care of other years, are here to wish you well. You should be happy! God keep you holy!

One should recall Monsignor Brady as he was on that silver jubilee day and for many years later, in the full flower of his powers of mind and body, not as he was when age and illness had made their heavy toll. He was a scholar, an Irish scholar. Precise and accurate, devoted to truth and facts, he could brook no mental slovenliness in anyone who laid claim to learning. Generous in dispensing his knowledge, he gave freely to all who called upon him—bishops, priests, religious, students, and laity; and as judge for years of the matrimonial court of the diocese, his influence extended beyond the confines of the state.

While Monsignor could give offhand the information sought, he was never satisfied to let the questioner depend simply upon his word. "Just wait a minute," he would say, "and I'll show you that on page 201 of volume V of——." And, then, several days later, if you happened to meet him, he would add: "If you come over to the house, I will show you a further statement on that matter." Often the sisters, when discussing a particular topic with the students, would remark; "Why don't you consult Monsignor who is an authority on that subject?" "Yes, Sister," the reply would be, "but if you ever ask him anything, he never lets the matter rest; every time you meet him, he keeps adding more and more information."

Monsignor Brady was so tireless in his investigations and so accurate in his findings that many thought he had missed his avocation. Had he ever devoted himself to professional research, he would have satisfied the most exacting university president who considers that the research worker is the *sine qua non* of an educational institution.

Those who went to Monsignor Brady for assistance, in any matter which required accurate scholarship, always felt that they had received reliable information. Many instances of this could be cited, but the following example must suffice. Elizabeth C. Lynch, one of Monsignor's correspondents, in a letter dated March 20, 1934, refers to Mr. Philip O'Connell's forthcoming book, *History and Antiquities of Kilmore,* and quotes what Mr. O'Connell had written her about the help received from Monsignor Brady:

Regarding my *History and Antiquities of the Diocese of Kilmore,* I am glad to be able to inform you that the printers are busy at it. From several American sources I have received much help and encouragement. My good friend, Right Reverend Msgr. Brady of Loretto, Colorado, has been a tower of strength.

Mr. Philip O'Connell, the author of this erudite work, *The Diocese of Kilmore Its History and Antiquities,* which was published in 1937, acknowledges in the introduction, the aid which he had received from Monsignor Brady:

I am very deeply indebted to my valued friend, Right Rev. Msgr. Richard Brady, Doctor of Canon Law, Loretto Heights College, Colorado, U.S.A., for many useful extracts and for his kind assistance in the revision of the proof sheets. Monsignor Brady, who was born in the parish of Drumgoon, has had a very distinguished career, is one of the Pope's Domestic Prelates and Judge of the Ecclesiastical Court of the Diocese of Denver. Amid all the arduous duties of his exalted office he has found time to abstract for me from the reports of the American Historical Association and from State records, a very considerable number of original documents and letters relating to the labors and activities of Kilmore priests in America during the eighteenth and early nineteenth centuries. He has also procured for me copies of the *Austin Papers,* a voluminous collection of documents preserved in the Rosenberg Library, Galveston, Texas, containing, *inter alia,* the correspondence of Irish priests in Texas in the period of 1830-1840. During some of his vacation visits to his native parish I had the great pleasure of accompanying Monsignor Brady on some tours to places of historic interest in Breiffine and elsewhere.

For several years after Loretto Heights College was opened in 1918, Monsignor taught religion and church history. He drew lavishly upon his store of knowledge and poured out facts and important data upon the members of his class. Exact himself, he tried to inculcate that quality in those whom he taught. In grading examination papers, he paid little attention to the amount of matter covered; it was rather the thoroughness with which one single topic was treated which merited a good mark. After teaching for a number of years, Monsignor was quite willing for younger priests on the faculty to take over his college classes.

There was another side to the chaplain's character, kindly and human, which those who knew him well love to recall. He was loyal and devoted to his friends, enjoying nothing more than to entertain at his table his priest associaates or to meet them at "Clarke's" for an hour's pleasant conversation. As these beloved friends began to depart, one by one, from this life, he was deeply affected. A Sister of Loretto who knew Monsignor Brady well has given this insight into his character:

Monsignor's was a gentle, sympathetic, retiring nature. Often did he brush aside the falling tears as he offered the holy sacrifice of the Mass for a departed friend as the angel of death took its toll of the pioneer associates. Each departure seemed to affect him more deeply—his own much-loved mother, Father Carr, Monsignor O'Ryan, Sisters Paschal, Columba, Bartholomew, Mother Pancratia, Sisters Flora, Dominic, Jovita, kindly Sister Floscella, and other faithful friends of years. A scene familiar to many of us was Monsignor paying his farewell, on the evening before the burial of one of the Sisters. He would kneel for a short time beside the casket, then rising gaze intently on the Sister and, before he turned away, rest his hand upon hers as though releasing her from this life with his blessing.

Monsignor Brady was fond of all animals but particularly of birds and dogs. In the winter months, the birds which did not migrate were his care. Every morning after breakfast, he paid a visit to the kitchen to procure food for his dependents. One would meet him proceeding on his way, his hands filled with bread which he took great delight in scattering to his feathered friends as they flocked around for their quota—with him there was no parsimonious rationing of food. After taking care of his out-of-door neighbors, Monsignor turned to the duties of the day. But the dogs which, in a long line of succession, formed so important a part of his household, were his special companions. When there was a question of dogs, Monsignor Brady was not "choosey." He preferred, of course, fine collies, and from time to time, owned them. A whole dynasty of "Jacks"—not, however, lineal descendants—held his affection, some for a longer, others for a shorter period. The founder of the dynasty, Jack I, was a beautiful, big collie, the finest and noblest of them all, not only in appearance but in deportment, loyalty, and affection for his master. His immediate successor was a pretty pup, a little, round fluffy ball, when some friends brought him, unwisely—as later events proved—as a gift to Monsignor. As Jack II grew and waxed strong, he developed untoward traits which made him obnoxious to all except to his owner. This dog came to an untimely and unregretted end.

Jack II, during his strenuous life, was the main actor in many a bit of drama. One morning after scampering over the wet lawn, he bounded up several flights of stairs and pushed his way into the little girls' dormitory. Sister Mary Luke had charge of this large room and kept it in beautiful order. The small beds, perfect in every detail, were adorned with spotless counterpanes and pretty shams. The children were taught to have great regard for their dormitory. But no place was sacrosanct to Jack II. As soon as he entered the large room, he recognized its possibilities as a playhouse. Springing up on one of the beds, he leaped in great glee from one to the other, leaving the imprint of his four wet, muddy paws on each immaculate spread. Sister Mary Luke, becoming aware of the unwonted thudding noise, hastened to the scene of action and found the dog hugely interested in his new sport. After driving him with great difficulty from the dormitory, she betook herself in righteous indignation to her superior, Mother Mary Linus, to report this latest exploit. With telling words she related the affair, expecting an understanding sympathy from her superior and a suggestion of some punitive measures for the dog. But Mother Mary Linus, on hearing the recital, burst into peals of laughter. In utter amazement, Sister Mary Luke looked incredulously at her superior, who, recognizing the suspicion which had entered the mind of the irate sister, exclaimed: "O, Sister Mary Luke, let me laugh first and then I will get angry!"

Monsignor Brady was devoted to his mother, relatives, and to the land of his birth. Regularly, during his long years at the Heights, every second or third summer, he visited his friends in Ireland and the boyhood haunts which always remained dear. The time spent there was not all idled in simply vacationing; he returned from each visit with an added store of knowledge, garnered from the sacred and historical places visited in his native land. Monsignor gave a worth-while account of his last memorable trip to his homeland, in 1930, in an interview to one of the young editors of *The Pancratian.*

I had the pleasure of visiting or revisiting many sacred shrines and other places of great historical and antiquarian interest. Trinity College and the National Museum, Dublin, are rich in ancient Irish manuscripts, in metal work, and in shrines of books and bells. In Trinity College I saw (for the third time) the famous *Book of Kells,* the *Book of Durrow,* and the *Book of Dimma,* all attributed to the sixth or seventh century. The *Book of Kells* is a treasure of which Ireland may justly be proud. It is a copy of the Four Gospels, magnificently illuminated and decorated with initial letters of surpassing beauty. Professor J. O. Westwood of Oxford, in his ecclesiastical work, *Paleographica Sacra,* states: "This copy of the Gospels is unquestionably the most elaborately executed manuscript of early art now in existence." It has been stated by other competent authorities: "No description can give an adequate idea of the *Book of Kells*—it must be seen and studied to be duly appreciated." It is truly a marvel of ancient Irish art. On examining another of these ancient masterpieces, Giraldus Cambrensis exclaimed in astonishment that it was a work not of men but of angels.

Visiting the ancient town of Kells, I inspected St. Columkille's House where the *Book of Kells* was written and preserved for many centuries. There are also a famous Round Tower and an ancient Celtic Cross in this historic town, besides many other objects of interest.

In the town of Donegal, the chief object of attraction to the tourist is the magnificent old castle, the ancient seat of the O'Donnels, Lords of Tirconnell. This ruin, compared with others in Ireland, is in good state of preservation and from present indications must have been a splendid mansion, worthy of the rank of those powerful chieftains. The once famous Franciscan Monastery of Donegal, in which many remarkable works were collected in the first half of the seventeenth century, is now a complete ruin. It was there that the monumental work, *The Annals of the Four Masters*, was begun and completed between 1632 and 1636.

There are many other places of great interest which I visited, e.g., Sligo Abbey, Loch Cé, Boyle Abbey, etc. The last mentioned was built by O'Connor, King of Connaught, in 1257. But, like many other buildings of its kind, it was attacked during the Elizabethan wars of the sixteenth century and left roofless. Its imposing ruins today clearly indicate its former splendor and magnificence.

When Monsignor Brady returned from his visits to Ireland, he always received a cordial welcome from faculty and students. After one of his homecomings, when a student asked what scene impressed him most on his trip, Monsignor replied: "The most impressive scene I witnessed for years was that on the lawn (of Loretto Heights) when the students sang a classical home-made song of welcome to greet the wanderer on his return. My good friend 'Jack,' " continued Monsignor, "wished to present his greetings to the poet for the honorable mention accorded him in the song At the same time 'Jack' considers that in the receiving line he demonstrated conclusively that he could speak for himself in a very simple and impressive language, far superior to any dog Latin."

That Monsignor Brady's return from Ireland was an affair of local interest Elizabeth O'Meara, '32, shows in her story in the *Heightsonian*, November, 1930:

Friday morning, October 31, Right Reverend Monsignor Brady returned from his vacation in Ireland. That all were glad to have Monsignor back was evidenced by the way he was greeted upon his arrival at the College. All the Sisters welcomed him. The college girls marched down the steps singing a parody composed especially for the occasion. They were followed by the girls from Pancratia Hall, who also sang a parody. If they were glad to have Monsignor back with them, he was just as glad to be back. He greeted everyone happily, and even yet he may be seen about the college shaking hands with someone that wasn't lucky enough to be present when he arrived.

Another friend of Monsignor's who is glad to have him back is Jack. Shortly after his arrival, Monsignor whistled, and Jack, who heard him, immediately left the old shoe he had been guarding for the past few months and broke all speed records to reach his master. He jumped up to Monsignor's face and licked it, and, as if to show his happiness, kept racing back and forth, emitting sharp, joyful barks. Since Monsignor's return a wonderful change has come over Jack. He walks with a much lighter step, and if you look close enough you may see the corner of his mouth turned up.

This devoted collie, which showed his joy and demonstrated in such a spectacular manner his appreciation of the reception accorded Monsignor Brady at his return from Ireland, disappeared a few years later from the campus and was seen no more. One of the Denver dailies commented on the loss:

Jack, a beautiful collie whose reputation for devotion to his master extends far beyond the environs of Denver, is missing. Jack was the pet and constant companion of Monsignor Richard Brady, chaplain of Loretto Heights College. Whether he was stolen or met a worse fate, Chaplain Brady does not know, but he is certain that the dog did not go away of his own free will. He would return, his master feels sure, if set free and able to run or crawl.

He disappeared ten days ago and after widespread search has not been found. He is of good stock, but his master declares it would be impossible to put a value on him. Jack's devotion to the chaplain started back in 1927, when as a young dog he replaced "old Jack," former pet which died and was buried under the elms at the college.

Jack's most spectacular demonstration of devotion occurred in 1930, when his master left him in Denver while on a summer visit to Ireland. The dog was miserable for weeks. Only with difficulty could those with whom he was left persuade the dog to eat. Then a box of old clothing for the poor was set outside a door. Jack dived in, scattered the contents, and emerged with an old shoe—Monsignor Brady's. After that he seemed reconciled to his lonely wait for his master's return. Everywhere, night and day, he carried the shoe with him.

One of the college students, in an article which appeared in the *Heightsonian,* December, 1933, voiced the regret of all on the campus at Jack's disappearance:

Jack, the loved collie, the mascot of the college, the faithful guard of Monsignor Brady, barked his farewell to the collegians the day before Thanksgiving. Their holiday suggestions to him of "Enjoy your turkey bones, Jack," were in vain, for Jack 'got lost' before his turkey-day feast.

Jack seemed a trifle unconcerned that last day. Perhaps he sensed the vacation spirit pervading the halls and was a little lenient when the students ran past him. Usually such behavior on their part would call forth loud protests from him. But Jack merely snuggled his nose closer to the floor and kept his guard.

He had numerous friends, including alumnae, visitors to Monsignor, to the faculty, and the students. Few ever returned to the college without an inquiry concerning him. Jack had no respect for honored speakers, climaxes of plays, or tense moments. This at-home-ness made him more appealing to those who heard that amiable pattering down the aisle of the auditorium to his master, in the midst of a serious performance. He knew his position and appreciated it.

Monsignor Brady, though devoted to the land of his adoption, never lost any of his ardent love for his native land. An enthusiastic student of Irish history, he was well versed in its literature and folklore; but his special hobby was Irish genealogy.

One day when conversing with Sister M. Vivian, the director of the history department, on the early settlement of Maryland, Monsignor remarked with finality: "But Lord Baltimore was Irish; he came from Ballymore." "Why, Monsignor Brady," rejoined Sister Vivian, "according to you, Adam and Eve must have come from Ireland!" An amused crinkle played around Monsignor's mouth, but he made no reply to Sister's retort. The next morning, at the earliest possible moment, he went to the main floor seeking the professor of history. When Sister Vivian saw Monsignor standing at the door of her class room, she felt that some important matter had brought him at that unusual hour. But he, handing her a newspaper clipping, said laconically: "Read that." Taking the proffered clipping and wondering what news item Monsignor was bringing, Sister read: "It has been proved, without a doubt, that Gaelic was the language spoken in the Garden of Eden."

For several years after his return from his native land in 1930, Monsignor Brady was in usual health, performing all his duties as chaplain and teaching religion in Pancratia Hall, the high school department. Then gradually his health began to fail. In the summer of 1939, he made a last visit to friends in St. Louis and other cities. These were saddened to see the great change in Monsignor and realized that the end was close at hand.

As one loved friend after another, among the priests of the Denver diocese, answered the roll call with their *adsum,* Monsignor Brady was more and more aware that the shadows were lengthening and that his own time was not far away. While still in good health he went to Mount Olivet cemetery and selected the place where he would be laid after death among his fellow priests.

His health continuing to fail, he was sent in July, 1940, to St. Vincent's Sanatorium, St. Louis, where after a short time, he died on July 20 at the age of 73. His remains were brought back to Denver for burial. The Sisters of Loretto at Loretto Heights College, whom he had served faithfully and well for about forty-four years, arranged to have the body brought to the college on the afternoon of July 25.

All that was mortal of that once magnificent physique lay in state before the altar of the college chapel where as chaplain Monsignor Brady had celebrated daily the Holy Sacrifice for the community; where he had been invested with the purple of a monsignor; where he had celebrated the silver jubilee of his ordination to the priesthood. The sisters of the community and of the summer school, in great numbers, kept guards of honor, all through the night, until the Reverend William Mulcahy, chaplain, celebrated a Requiem High Mass at 6:15; immediately after the community Mass, the Most Reverend Christopher E. Byrne, Bishop of Galveston and friend of the deceased, who had come from his see in the Southwest to assist at the funeral rites, offered a requiem Mass.

Later in the morning of Friday, July 26, His Excellency, the Most Reverend Urban J. Vehr, Bishop of Denver, celebrated a Solemn Pontifical Mass at 9:30 in the Cathedral of the Immaculate Conception. Three Bishops, one hundred eighteen priests, hundreds of sisters, and members of the laity attended the services of Holy Mother Church for Monsignor Richard Brady. The Most Reverend Patrick A. McGovern, Bishop of Cheyenne; the Most Reverend Christopher E. Byrne, Bishop of Galveston; the Right Reverend Matthew Smith; the Right Reverend Hugh L. McMenamin, and the Very Reverend John J. Mulroy were present in the sanctuary. The Reverend Joseph P. O'Heron, close personal friend of the deceased prelate and administrator of his estate, preached the sermon. After reminding his audience that "All things grow old and as a garment are changed, but God alone remains the selfsame and forever," Father O'Heron recalled the sacred ties which bound old and young to Monsignor Brady:

Monsignor Brady was not a prominent figure in public life. This may have been owing to a natural timidity which he never overcame. But there were many who loved him. Among these were bishops and priests, sisters, students, laymen and women. His scholarly attainments attracted all. From his point of vantage at the Heights, he had a clear view of many of the clouded issues of the day. He was well informed in Church affairs and in matters pertaining to the history of the Church. Particularly was this true with regard to his adopted land and to his native Ireland which he loved so well. Whether it was the humble layman or the scholar who came to his door, all were welcome to share the fund of knowledge which was his.

Coming down from this shrine of learning at the Heights, we see this shepherd of souls tending his flock in Fort Logan, Littleton, and the surrounding country territory. The love of the people is evidenced even today by their reference to him as "good Father Brady." They have not forgotten the days when things were far different from what they are now and how he ministered to their families. We priests, who serve in the same territory, realize that if it were not for his ministrations, many of these families might not be Catholic. He has sown the good seed where we today reap the harvest.

Monsignor Brady bequeathed his valuable library of 2,500 volumes to the college. These were his treasured friends, not chosen at random, but selected with care and discrimination. The annotations and comments, written in his neat, characteristic penmanship, which have been found in many of the volumes, testify to the scholarly use which he made of his library. Sister Mary Norbert of the college Art Department has made an appropriate bookplate which represents Monsignor standing in his library, holding a volume in his hands. This *ex libris* plate will mark the books as the "Brady Collection."

Chapter XXIII

LORETTO HEIGHTS ALUMNAE

With the alumnae forming one of those intangible but nevertheless necessary parts of a college or school, if the school is to be successful, it follows that alma mater, alumnae, and student body, all three, through the gift of understanding, supported by counsel and fortitude, form a united and constructive organization.

Each school, each college, has its objective, a *raison d'etre* which justifies its existence. Its course of study is planned according to this objective; its customs, even its traditions have their source in it. The success of the school is evaluated according to the conformity of the alumnae, the finished product, to the pattern outlined by the aims and purposes of the school.

In the trinity of interrelationships, the alumnae are dependent upon student body and alma mater. They watch eagerly the activities of the school, contributing happily to its growth, in divers ways, but particularly by their interest which manifests itself by that thing which all women are said to indulge in, the art of talking—talking about their school or college, the best in the land.

The "old grads" have not forgotten the store of knowledge they garnered from instructors and professors, knowledge which they could never have gleaned from books. They have an abiding love for their alma mater, more deeply rooted and lasting than that which any number of "Colleys" could have felt for their revered teacher as they whispered their last farewell to him: "Good-by, Mr. Chips!"

Loretto alumnae return from time to time to the old school to rest their souls again in the convent chapel and relive the dreams and aspirations which were theirs as they knelt there, in days now gone, when the whole world seemed young and promising. Once more they traverse the spacious

corridors, which teem with happy memories of the days
when they rushed pell-mell with an armful of books to make
the next class before the second bell; they visit again classroom after classroom, pointing out the very chairs where
they sat, recalling even how the patches of sunshine used to
slant across the floor, and wondering whether the students
of the present generation really appreciate the opportunities
which surround them. As they make the rounds of the old
haunts, they realize that, since the institution still holds to
its traditions and high standards, they must co-operate and
remain worthy of their teachers and school.

Loretto Heights has always stressed the cultural
courses. These, strengthened by the refining influence of
religion which permeates life at Loretto, have made the
alumnae different from the rank and file of other women.
The chief aims of the faculty have been to cultivate the
intellect and elevate the taste, to make the students God-
fearing, intelligent, capable, active members of society.

It would be difficult to follow the graduates through
the years which have elapsed since they left Loretto Heights
and give correct reports on their occupations and way of
life. Excerpts from letters written recently to the faculty
present a fair cross section of the alumnae. The girls give
impressions of school and college which have remained and
show what Loretto Heights has enabled them to do for themselves and others in the life and vocation they have chosen
to follow.

The first two graduates of the class of 1891-92 write
letters of interest to all who have been students in the same
school. Sister Menodora Casey, S. L., of Loretto Academy,
Las Cruces, New Mexico, writes:

When we were in the third year of high school at dear
old St. Mary's, Denver, our class, about twelve in number,
were all excited about the new academy going up on one of
the most beautiful sites southwest of Denver. After much
thought and deliberation, Ollie Fort and I, two of the twelve
graduates, decided to go for the last year of our academic
work to the new academy. I have often wondered what became of Ollie; she was a very sweet girl. I would surely love

to see her again. I was almost sure I would see her at the golden jubilee celebration of Loretto Heights. We may meet, perhaps, at some other time.

Loretto Heights College—it was Loretto Heights Academy when I had the privilege of attending school there— means a remembrance of all that is solid and enduring, of skillful planning and noble striving, of deep religious hope and convictions. Yet I am not expressing what Loretto Heights really means to me, for it is all these and more— it means the highest, the purest, the best of everything intellectual, religious, and sacred.

As I stated above, it was my great privilege to have been one of the first year's graduates of my dear Heights, and from the classroom, I might say, I entered the sacred halls of the religious life. Anyone who has embraced that holy state does not need me nor anyone else to tell what as a religious I am doing. The greatest part of my religious life has been spent in the classroom. What I have accomplished there only the Master in whose service I enlisted almost fifty years ago shall say. All I may say is I have tried to work for Him.

This letter is characteristic of the humility of Sister Menodora who has spent her life in the classroom, instructing others unto justice, and has by her daily example given edification to all among whom she has lived and worked.

It was with deep satisfaction that the sisters received a message recently from Mrs. O. F. January, Ollie Fort, the other member of that first class, who wrote greetings from her home, 3234 Abell Avenue, Baltimore, Maryland:

I was in the first class graduating from Loretto—there were two of us, Kate Casey, the other member—fifty years ago. It is a long time as I look back, but as I lived those years, they passed quickly. They have been active years filled with rearing a family, keeping a home, and trying to be both mother and father to two half-orphaned babies. Some of you dear sisters may remember that my husband was a lawyer; I have missed him very much since he died. My love of study caused me to spend much of my leisure time in pursuit of knowledge. My greatest ambition, after leaving Loretto, was to attend college, but circumstances prevented. While disappointed myself I always held this goal in my heart for my children.

I moved here to Baltimore with that thought in mind, but my son not being a student did not wish to continue beyond high school. My daughter went through Goucher College and the New York School of Social Work and is now working in her chosen field in that city.

Now with my family gone, I am living the last years alone in quiet and contentment but with my longings and ambitions waning with the years.

Mrs. Georgy W. Cohn, 1414 Marion St., Denver, wrote, November 26, 1942. The appended excerpt shows the pride which Mrs. Cohn takes in Regina, her only living child:

I do want to tell you how very much I enjoyed being at the first Alumnae meeting of this year. To attend Mass, have breakfast, meet many of the new sisters and girls, and, best of all, to have a chance, even if it were for such a short time, to visit with the older sisters with whom it is always a joy to recall fond memories—all these will remain in my mind for a long time.

I was certainly happy to learn that you had heard from Ollie Fort. How nice to know something about her and her family. I do think it most interesting that her daughter, too, should have gone in for social service. Thanks so much for having told me about her. I hope to write to her very soon.

My daughter, Regina, is, since August, 1939, a psychiatric social worker in the Department of Psychiatry in the University of Louisville. This is in connection with a Commonwealth Fund Grant for experimentation with undergraduate teaching of psychiatry. Her duties are concerned with administrative responsibility for out-patient psychiatric clinic in the Louisville City Hospital. She also supervises work done by medical students and other social workers in the department.

The writer of the next excerpt is Mrs. J. A. DeBouzek of 108 Virginia Street, Salt Lake City, the former Minnanne McDonald, '96, sister of Sister Mary Jane, superior and directress of the School for Girls, conducted by the Sisters of Loretto in Shanghai, China. Minnanne writes:

All my school years were passed under the precious guidance of Loretto Sisters, and my period at Loretto Heights, a most enlightening experience, still stands out among my most happy memories. My field in life has been just mother and homemaker, a career not the least unusual but most worth-while. I am sorry to have missed your fine jubilee celebration, but at that time it was impossible to attend. Dear Mother Linus wrote me a lovely letter telling me all about it. Greetings to all the dear sisters at Loretto Heights!

Mamie Mackin, '05, of 420 North 38th Avenue, Omaha, Nebraska, writes lovingly of her school and teachers:

When I pause to consider what Loretto Heights as a school means to me, I conclude that it means mostly happy memories. Memories of dear Mother Pancratia, Sisters Mary Linus, Mary Edith, Dolorine Morrison, Bernadette Farhe, and Mary Luke Barrett, who showed us by word and example how we might live in accordance with the motto of Loretto Heights, *Fides, Mores, Cultura.* I consider myself fortunate in having been taught by the Sisters of Loretto, during four happy years, how to think and live.

From a member of the class of 1912, the centenary year of the Sisters of Loretto, comes a recent and interesting letter. Sister Agnes Dolores, Sister of Charity of Cincinnati, formerly Agnes Neuer of Colorado Springs, writes from the Cathedral School, Denver, that there are many reasons for remembering Loretto Heights, all good and filled with poignantly happy memories:

First and foremost, I count my spiritual benefits—the beauty in the lives of the religious strengthened by good common sense; the lasting impressions received during my years in the grade and high schools are the finest and most important factors in my life. I am proud of my scholastic training there, for I know the best was the rule. If I had been more appreciative as a student, I would have profited more from those years. I began my vocal work at the Heights, where I received good instruction, encouragement, and opportunities of public performance. After finishing at the Heights, I continued to study voice.

I studied for over four years in New York and sang professionally during that time. I received some very fine training at Colorado College, Colorado Springs. Then suddenly the crucial moment arrived when I realized that I could best serve God in religion by devoting the talent He had given me to His greater honor and glory, teaching His children to lift their voices to Him in song. In May, 1921, I entered the Order of the Sisters of Charity. I had always thought that a Sister's life was beautiful, but never realized that life could be so brimming over with happiness until I became a Sister of Charity.

Very often it is the busiest person who finds time to follow the desire to send a message to alma mater. Mrs. N. J. O'Dea, Lucille Mannix, '18, in the academy and '23 in the college, living now at 4740 West 30th, Denver, a busy mother and teacher, writes:

To me Loretto symbolizes all that is good. It has inspired me to live a better life that I might reflect credit on the Heights. One of the biggest thrills of my life was my graduation from college; then the next year I was appointed to teach in the Denver School System. I was particularly happy because I was the first Loretto Heights girl to receive such an assignment.

My first teaching was in the country, at a little place called Bovina, fourteen miles from the railroad. During those lonely months, I recalled my years at Loretto that I might derive courage and fortitude to remain and endure the awful living conditions and hardships. I felt, too, if I were to leave, I would be called a "quitter." This, I knew, would hurt the sisters who had been so interested in me; so I remained.

I owe a great debt to the Sisters of Loretto, one I shall never be able to repay. In dealing with my own little girl, Therese, who is four, I find that I try to guide and train her as the dear Lorettines tried to teach me. My earnest hope is that I shall be able to send my daughter to Loretto so that she may receive the correct influence, guidance, and teaching.

In the following excerpt from a letter written by Ursula Fagan, Loretto Heights Academy, '24, is a frank statement of her views on education:

Loretto Heights is to me an outstanding Catholic institution, a monument devoted to education and high ideals. Living in Omaha, I took my college degree from Creighton University, and have done some graduate work at two state universities. The impression I have received from these last two universities is that secular schools lack the very spirit of education.

I have devoted several years to social work. During four of those years I was County Director of Geary County, Kansas. Since August, 1942, I have been associated with the American Red Cross as Home Service Correspondent in the Midwestern Area Office, St. Louis, Missouri.

Sister Miriam Jerome, Mary Margaret Stout, college '24, is now located at Loretto Academy, Santa Fe, New

Mexico. Sister Miriam Jerome would send all girls ready for college to Loretto Heights:

I, one of the first graduates of Loretto Heights College, think that Loretto is *the* school of the West. I feel that if the girls and their parents realized the advantages to be derived from an education in such a college, there would be several additions in the form of science halls and dormitories on Loretto campus. I would build science halls, of course, as it is my good fortune to be privileged to teach science and mathematics.

Another nun, who as a girl radiated brightness and fun around her for four years at Loretto Heights, writes:

To tell what Loretto has meant to me as a college is not a hard task for so frequently—I may say almost daily—there has been the constant practical application of theories learned and ideals nurtured at the Heights. This is true of spiritual as well as my educational experiences.

A love of all that is true and beautiful, refinement, culture—terms synonymous with my teachers, the Sisters of Loretto—coupled with a desire to reach the highest ideal of womanhood as represented by them, this is what L. H. C. means to me.

I am in the music department at the College of Mount Saint Joseph-on-the-Ohio, "fiddling my time away," or delving peacefully into intricacies of modern harmony with all its discord. One paragraph with one sentence suffices for my account of self. The S. C. after my name, Sister Bernadette Marie, tells the remainder of my story.

Many readers have recognized the writer of the above excerpt. Of course, it is Bernice McGroarty of the class of '24. The Sisters of Loretto of Loretto Heights College are grateful for the many one-time students who have chosen the better part.

Margaret Sullivan of the same college class, '24, crowds into one paragraph a summary account of the many activities which have occupied her since finishing her college course:

It is eighteen years since I was graduated from Loretto. During this time I have done many different things: a year at St. Mary's Academy, Denver, teaching dramatics; three years in Montana public schools, teaching Latin and English; eighteen months traveling; a year at Columbia University, New York, where I received the Master of Arts degree; three years clinic work in my own speech school; and seven years as speech clinician in the Minneapolis schools. I have taught clinical speech at Denver University one summer and at the University of Colorado four summers. This year I have received a leave of absence for further study.

It is difficult to point out what preparation my years at Loretto gave me, for the training of the sisters there has become so much a part of me. Without it I surely would have been a different person.

Objectivity is more easy about other people than about oneself. It is when considering Loretto graduates among my friends that I realize what education at Loretto means. The Loretto Heights Alumnae are conspicuous everywhere, I think, for their painstaking thoroughness in their respective fields and especially for their willing and unselfish service to the underprivileged. Theirs is such a sane, thoroughly Catholic point of view that it makes me proud to call Loretto Heights my alma mater.

Students follow the same courses, the same lectures, the same routine during their years in school. Vivacious and interested, each one shows her individual response—there is no reducing to a common level or common appreciation. After school days, the same thing happens. Each graduate finds herself following a path quite different from the route -chosen by other members of her class. Versatility and variety characterize the alumnae of Loretto Heights.

The college days of Surilda Wilson, '24, the first editor of *The Heightsonian* during the year 1923-24, gave no indication that she would enter political life. A recent letter from the former editor, now Mrs. Surilda McClaskey, democratic state vice-chairman, with headquarters at Calhan, Colorado, shows her interests and employment:

At present I am back in the teaching field as superintendent of the Calhan Union High School. The past few years I had been active only as substitute teacher. I have been very busy during those years as a farmer's wife and mother of three children.

I am serving my second term as Democratic State Vice-chairman in which capacity I contact the democratic women in the 63 counties of the state, doing organization work, encouraging study clubs, and directing study of national policies, government, and international relations.

I think that the training I received at Loretto has made it possible for me to meet easily the many people from all over the nation that come to Colorado for political reasons. Certainly my practice teaching under the direction of the sisters at the Heights has stood me in good stead. Loretto Heights means to me the true foundation for a worth-while, satisfying adult life.

After fifteen years away from her alma mater, Mary Ann Taylor, now Mrs. F. Dwyer Smith, writes in her own honest way of Loretto Heights and its meaning to her:

Every time I think of Loretto, I think how honored I was to have had the opportunity of attending the college which has influenced my life so much during all these years I have been away. I married three weeks after my graduation in June, 1927. My married life has been very happy, filled with joy, contentment, and simple living. We have had four children, but one of these is in heaven. My boy is thirteen, my girls are eleven and eight.

At present I am taking an active part in our community defense setup, doing some welfare work and trying to make our home a happy one. As I look back upon my life at Loretto, I think it was perfect.

The religious training and the beautiful philosophy of living taught at Loretto have made an imprint upon my life that will always enable me to face the future with complete trust in the will of God. The type of education given at the Heights fits a girl for any walk of life. It gives her many choice patterns, and as she follows the design she has selected, experiences and lessons learned while at college help her to solve the problems that constantly flash upon the horizon of her chosen field.

Loretto Heights is preserving the fine traditions of the past, which Mary Ann Taylor and other mothers among the alumnae have helped to make, for the "granddaughters" who will be the college students of tomorrow.

The following excerpt shows the busy life of a teacher. Sister Charles Ellen (Dorothy Lonskey, '28) writes from St. Mary's Convent, Cincinnati, Ohio:

I know that I can never write here what Loretto means to me. Loyalties are almost like a religion with me, and Loretto is one of my warmest. First of all, a scholarship was a glorious surprise on my graduation day from high school. It made possible what I had no right to hope for, with illness at home and four younger children. My four years at the college were happy ones.

Excellent teachers gave me a preparation for my teaching which I know is solid and for which I shall ever be most grateful. During my thirteen years as a Sister of Charity and the one year I taught in Colorado after graduating, I have been chiefly a teacher of languages. Latin was my major with Sister Edmond. I still feel her strong influence in every Cicero and Vergil class that I have the privilege to instruct. French has been my principal field for eleven years, with my graduate work in that language. This year I have two Spanish classes. Sister William Joseph gave me my start in both these modern tongues, bless her! Sister was very good to me in the long ago. I wonder where she is now located. Sister Vivian and Sister Dolorine will always live in my memory as strong forces for good both in and out of class.

There is one other happiness, the great happiness of my life, my religious vocation which I realized fully as my privileged destiny during my freshman year. I shall always believe that it was God's special providence which kept me in the protective atmosphere of the Heights, during the years of enforced delay, that kept His call alive.

Another interest which was fostered at school and in which I still delight, was activity in the missions. I have had the joy for some time of directing our Crusade Unit at St. Mary's. I remember how we used to read and talk about Crusade Castle in Cincinnati. Every time I visit the Castle now, I love to stand before the shield erected by Loretto Heights College and bearing her coat of arms. I feel as if I am saluting my dear alma mater and all the good friends of former days. In the *Register*, which I read eagerly each week, I notice that you are doing much for the Church and for social work.

My prayer as a loyal alumna of Loretto is that the college will grow steadily in numbers and in the fine quality of her Catholic spirit. Although I have been away from Denver for thirteen years, and so many are gone, including Monsignor Brady and most of my teachers, I look forward to a vist sometime to my school on Federal Boulevard. I never forget the Sisters of Loretto and my debt of gratitude to them. May I hope for a little place in your prayers. God's blessing on your work under the care of His sweet Mother.

Society expects the college graduate to go far on the road of opportunity because of the educational advantages which have been hers. But what of the college graduate deprived of the sense of hearing? Is she out of the sphere of progress? Not if she is anything like Mary K. Reardon, '29, of 1321 Milwaukee, Denver, who despite her handicap is making quite a name for herself through her free-lance writing. Her articles and stories have appeared in *America, The Catholic World, Extension, Poise,* and several other worth-while magazines. Mary writes:

What has Loretto Heights College meant to me? Those four years in pursuit of a Liberal Arts degree gave lustre to my life and a keen awareness of the beauty and power of Catholic philosophy as interpreted in the college motto, *Fides, Mores, Cultura.*

Considered pertinently, they were the years of my apprenticeship to a chosen avocation—free-lance writing. For mentor and guide there was dear Sister Dolorine, a great teacher and a true lover of literature. Hers was the talent of awakening in the minds of her students a deep and enduring appreciation of literature. Her courses were sheer delight. In the charmed atmosphere of her classroom, Dante, Shakespeare, Browning—all the immortals of the literary world—became glowing personalities. The fairies of her own beloved Erin pranked in every corner, and all things Irish took on a beauty and significance to those who shared her heritage.

And hers was the power to inspire creative writing. I remember that, instead of giving us dull and definite assignments, she would say: "Tell me what you see . . . what you think . . ." With exquisite psychology she taught me to be grateful for the gifts of sight and observation and gave me the courage to measure life's incompleteness because of a hearing handicap with God's infinite love. I shall hold forever in my heart the vision of the gracious welcome reflected in lovely Irish eyes whenever I entered the room. In those personal chats with her, she set small sparks of writing talent flaming, and in her constructive criticisms of my initial efforts gave me all the encouragement of a generous heart. One day Sister Dolorine showed me a notebook which she had tried to keep in some fashion since she was a girl, dreaming always of some day becoming a great writer:

"The designs of God," she said, "called me to serve Him by teaching others to write. I still yearn to write but my life is so full and so busy that I can only pass the torch on to my students." And then with magnificent confidence in me, she added, "You will go far . . . Read, read, read—everything of the best and beautiful in literature. It will give you a rich background that will compensate you for the words you cannot hear, and some day you will find yourself expressing thought in terms of beauty."

Is it then surprising that in the years since achieving a coveted Bachelor of Arts degree I have followed the apostolate of the pen? And always the truest reward for my work is the little loving note of congratulation that has come to me from Sister Dolorine whenever I score a victory.

Another member of the class of '29, Rosalie Buchmann, now Mrs. Morton L. Newhoff, sends her version of what Loretto means to her, far removed as she is from the school she loved. Rosalie writes from 1595 East Mendocino Street, Altadena, California:

To say what Loretto has meant to me would be so difficult—it is deep in my heart and so dear that words are quite inadequate to express my feelings. However, one of the greatest contributions that Loretto has given to me is the motto on which we have built our family life. Each Sister there had repeated so often "To be happy, you must bring happiness to others." We have proved the truth of this in our living. My husband and I have shared and served, everywhere possible, and have been and are blessed with unusual happiness.

Loretto Heights is proud of what Rosalie Newhoff has accomplished by her deeds of kindness. The Newhoffs have been favored with two gifted daughters who are particularly talented in music.

From St. Mary's Community High School, Sterling, Illinois, comes a community letter, containing the sentiments of five Loretto Heights College graduates—Sister Gerald Farrell, Sister Maura Campbell, Sister Aloysia Honey, Sister Rose Patricia Doyle, and Sister Marie Claire Dunphy:

Our alma mater equips the young woman with a clear cut, unified, practical set of Christian principles so that she is able to take a definite Catholic stand and hold her footing in the vortex of the tumultuous slashing of opinions rampant in our bewildered modern world. She introduces the student to Jesus Christ as the central figure of all history. In the light and wisdom of His love, she learns to see Him in others, in the home, in the classroom, in the office, or in the active service of her country's defense. That in part has been the goal of Loretto Heights College; and she has admirably achieved her purpose.

In retrospect our minds wander back to the Heights that we knew and loved as girls: the familiar surroundings of the administration building, the bells, and classes with their happy, happy activity. Days sped by then on wings of song, and the weeks and months slipped by unnoticed into years. We were learning all the while deep, eternal lessons, which were beyond the actual courses studied. Lessons in humility and Christ-like charity, lessons in courage, in loyalty, and in prayerful living; lessons from a faculty of great-hearted teachers who taught more powerfully by their compelling spiritual, interior lives than by their vast knowledge in the humanities and sciences.

There was for us all a spiritual growth amid an atmosphere of culture and friendship, of goodness, and clean fun. Vaudeville and music, proms and dramatics are mingled with so much we remember; but through them all runs the rare privilege of daily Mass, Holy Communion, and hurried, extra visits between classes to Our Lady in the chapel.

In this Golden Jubilee year, when the Heights finds herself facing the challenging problems of our war-torn and inexpressibly sad world, she may truly look back on a harvest rich and gratifying. Hundreds of students bear her beloved name, students who because of Loretto training, and culture, and discipline are now prepared to bear the burden of responsibility and leadership in every walk of life; students who have learned to live out the mystical body of Christ, and, fired by eternal values, have no room in their hearts for one single doubt, or fear, or modern hate.

Long ago these students heard in Loretto halls, "I am with you all days," and "I thirst for souls." To us, as to so many other girls who have studied at the Heights, those words have become more and more insistent. And now, after these privileged years of work among young souls, teaching beautiful minds and learning so many poignant lessons from generous laughing hearts, we turn back to the Heights with tender gratitude for the religious vocations she fostered there. Under an infinite loving God and after the life-long dynamic example of our "soldier" mothers, it is to Loretto in the Rockies that we owe our greatest debt.

We extend to the Heights in her jubilee year our congratulations and prayers. May God grant you, our alma mater, length of golden days. May your traditions grow brighter as the years go on, and, at life's eventide, may Our Lady bring every student, dear to Loretto, safely home.

The next message brings to light a three-in-one combination, wife, mother, and social worker. Mrs. T. Burnite, Alvena Leversedge, '31, writes from the Bureau of Public Welfare, Department of Health and Charity, Denver:

Uppermost in my mind are the splendid religious teachings which have been important to me as wife, mother, and social worker. The air of culture and refinement which permeates the halls of the Heights will remain with me as a precious jewel. As you see from the above, my life is a three-cornered arrangement at this time, and no doubt will continue to be for the duration of the war, as long as women's help is needed by our country.

This year I have placed my two older children under the guidance of the Lorettines. Mary Claire is at St. Mary's Academy, Denver, in pre-school, and John Thomas is in the first grade at St. John's. The baby, Judy, at the ripe age of two is very unhappy that she is not attending school so that she may be able to talk about her "Sister" with the rest of the family.

My present duties, Sisters, are centered on the Aid to the Blind program. We have in our department the preventive service, which includes surgery and treatment for the improvement of faulty vision. In addition to a definite case load, I have a group work program including the Colorado School for Deaf and Blind, the Industrial Work Shop for the Blind, the Adult Blind Home, and one Convalescent Home for the Aged and Chronically Ill. In group work we are conducting classes in which the participants are making cards for the American Red Cross. These cards are placed in the packages given to the soldiers leaving our shores. In order that I may keep out of mischief, because of idleness, I have numerous committee affiliations including the Defense Council and Professional Groups.

So you see, Sisters, again I am carrying out the advice so often proffered in the good old college days, "Be useful rather than ornamental.'' However, my husband is pretty proud of our home and maintains that its good taste is due to my ornamental and musical tendencies.

The next letter comes from Mrs. James W. Close, Jane Winburn, '31, 9329 Sudbury Road, Silver Spring, Maryland, where she is an active and loyal collegian of Loretto Heights. Jane says that it has always been comforting to feel that alma mater has such a keen interest in her alumnae though they may be many miles away. In a recent letter Jane writes:

On my three trips back to Loretto since I have been married, I have never failed to get the same thrill and inspiration which I experienced the first time I crossed its threshold as a timid freshman in 1927. At each visit I felt more and more deeply what the noble inscription, *Fides, Mores, Cultura,* should signify to the young women who pass daily under the arch on which is engraved in stone this Loretto motto.

During these trying times of world distress when we all need something good and solid to grasp, I pray to God that my young son may be a better man and my three little girls better women because I went to a college where the best scholastically and religiously were taught us so well and graciously.

My husband keeps very busy as counsel to President Roosevelt. As he is still a young man, I consider this quite an achievement. His training at Regis College, Denver, gave him a splendid foundation. When two people who have the same principles of philosophy and religion, permeating their lives ever since they were born, work side by side to rear a family, don't you think that life should be happy and successful?

Jane Winburn Close, always eager to do something for her alma mater, is organizing a circle of Loretto Alumnae, located in and around Washington.

From Mary Leslie, another member of the class of '31, now Mrs. Tom Brady, 605 West Rollins, Columbia, Missouri, comes an interesting letter. Mary attributes her unusual happiness to the religious training received at Loretto Heights College:

As you know, my husband is a professor of history at Missouri University and is a non-Catholic. Consequently most of our friends are from the University and are non-Catholic also. Private evening parties in this circle usually develop into friendly arguments. I am proud of my husband when by logical reasoning he pins the arguments down to first principles and is all the while on the firm ground of Catholic philosophy. I rarely take an active part in these discussions, yet I follow and enjoy them because of my training and study at Loretto Heights.

My family has grown since I was last in Denver, two years ago. We have a new little girl, born last May. She is named Sarah and called Sally. Susan, our eldest child, is now seven and is in the second grade at Sacred Heart school, here in Columbia. Our second child, Tommy, named for his daddy, is almost five. The three of them keep Tom and me busy and happy.

Columbia is situated in heavily wooded, rolling hills—the beginning of the Ozarks. There is a quiet beauty here which I have come to love. Missourians are kind, friendly people with much warmth and sincerity—a good people to be among:

From 1413 Old Shell Road, Mobile, Alabama, Sister Naomi, Elizabeth O'Meara, '32, writes:

Near the top of the list of blessings for which I daily thank God is my Catholic college education. It was at the Heights that I saw the principles of Christian living exemplified in the lives of those who were my teachers there. Since my novitiate days, I have been missioned in Mobile, at Bishop Toolen High School, an ideal place for applying the lessons learned at L. H. C.

Another letter from a member of the class of '32, the woman orator at Loretto that year, Lucille Riede, now Mrs. H. Montgomery, gives her appreciation of the instruction received and the use she later made, in the world of commerce, of the training:

Loretto as a school means you Sisters to me. It means a drilling into me of the "K's" and other rules from *Smart's Handbook of Freshman English;* it means polishing off the roughness of my poor offerings in theme work; it means struggling through the masterpieces of Greek literature for a background in Literary Criticism; and, finally, it means the Sisters giving generously hours and hours of time, inspiring me with ambition, and encouraging me in any achievement I made along the arduous path of acquiring a college education.

All this has flashed through my mind many times while I was working in the commercial world as private stenographer of the government divisions in Washington, D. C., and other places in the United States. The courses in the English Language department gave me confidence in holding positions not only as stenographer but as office manager where training in English, especially grammar and sentence structure, is so important.

My state of life was abruptly changed with my marriage; my chosen field up to the time of my marriage was to be a capable secretary in the service of my government; now it is to be an inspiring partner to my husband. Sister Vivian once said, "The hand that rocks the cradle rules the world." With a college education the cradle should be rocked the straighter. On December 16, 1942, God sent us a son, a treasure from heaven, surely. We are, indeed, doubly happy!

Marie J. Trenchak, '32, a member of Kappa Gamma Pi, national honor society for graduates of Catholic women's colleges, writes of the life of a social service worker in New Jersey. After finishing college, Marie received her Master's degree in social service studies at the Catholic University and has held responsible positions in the field of her chosen work:

It is about a year ago that my mother and I paid a visit to Colorado. Loretto Heights, of course, was on our itinerary. I recall our welcome which was just as warm and sincere as though I had not left you over ten years ago.

Loretto Heights has the brightest spot in my memories. As I look back I am again enmeshed in the glorious activities, both scholastic and extra-curricular, of my four very happy college years. Even my final examinations each year held a sort of fascination for me. My association with Sister Vivian as her assistant registrar was a rare privilege. I think of her every time I visit the National Shrine of St. Joseph—she was so devoted to that great saint and she invariably passed on that devotion to her students.

I shall never forget the grand time we had during those busy weeks preparing for the Irish Operetta, *The Wishing Well;* I was selected to sing the part of "Lady

Mary,'' opposite Helen McGraw, ''Terence O'More.'' I
can still see the six fairies, all Irish colleens, rising mys-
teriously from the depths of the wishing well. Margaret
Reddin taught us the dancing for the Operetta. We received many compliments from a crowded house in the
Little Theater, remember?

My chosen field is in Social Service Work. I am supervisor of casework in the Morris County Children's Home
here in New Jersey. We are a foster home and adoption
service agency. We have under our care 309 children who
are in foster homes; five caseworkers supervise them, and
I direct the case workers. I am called upon to interpret in
Court and in other social agencies because I speak
Bohemian, Russian, and Polish.

I am secretary of the New Jersey Chapter of the
American Association of Social Workers and Publicity
Chairman in the American Association of University
Women. I still have no romantic interests, so I think I'm
destined to be an old mail social worker; but of this I
solemnly assure you, I shall never wear low heels.

The next excerpt comes from another veteran in the
Social Service Field, Marie Stillhammer, class of '32, living
at 315 South Sherman Street, Denver:

Since leaving the Heights in 1932, I attended the Social
Service School at the Catholic University for one year and
have been employed by the Denver Catholic Charities for
nine years. I have had the splendid opportunity of working in a variety of capacities with the Catholic Charities,
especially in the fields of Family and Child Welfare. I
am now serving as Intake Secretary for the Central Office
of the Catholic Charities. This type of work involves acceptance of applications for any type of service, which our
agency includes in its program, and determining whether
these applications should be accepted as a responsibility
or on a co-operative basis with other agencies. These de-
cisions whether accepted or rejected are subjected to the
approval of our Diocesan Director and Case Supervisor.

The foundation which I received at Loretto through the
Liberal Arts convinced me that I was adapted for social
service. As my four years of college came to a close, I
determined that under the Catholic Charities' auspices I
would really accomplish many things for the comfort and
uplifting of Christ's poor. Sisters, it gives me a contentment, which I had thought was not possible for me to have

in this world, in coping with the multitude of problems which arise. Of course I could never have this personal satisfaction if I did not know there was spiritual help and guidance at hand.

Sister Agnes Regina, also of the class of '33, then known as Regina Montgomery, writes from Loretto Academy, El Paso, Texas:

Spiritually, intellectually, and culturally, my heritage is greatly dependent on those four important years at Loretto Heights College. Inspiration derived from words heard there and actions performed still pervades my life. My daily prayer is for continued success and happiness for my alma mater.

Patricia Lucy, '34, after finishing at the Heights, took graduate work in social service at the Catholic University, received the Master of Arts degree in this field, and returned to her home town, Denver, where she has done efficient work in behalf of the poor and neglected. So outstanding has Patricia's work been in Denver and the surrounding counties that the Red Cross is sponsoring a fellowship for Miss Lucy at the St. Louis University School of Social Service where she will work for her doctorate.

Sister Pauline Marie, a Sister of Loretto, known to her classmates of '33 as Pauline Smith, writes from Immaculate Conception High School, Las Vegas, New Mexico:

My attendance at the Heights ranks as one of the most important phases of my life. To it, I firmly believe, I owe my vocation and my present happiness. If it were in my power, I would open the doors of the Heights to all those girls who know her not. It is not only the knowledge which she imparts which makes her worth—any college can instruct people—it is the ideals also which she implants and the inspiration emanating from her teachers which place Loretto Heights above the class of ordinary colleges.

Phoebe Pulver, '33, now Mrs. Andrew Dickson, greatly interested in writing while in college, has continued to cultivate her gift, even as a busy mother and homemaker. She writes of her children: "I have two little boys, Andrew John, 5½, and Steve, just 3; on October 5, God sent me a little girl, the most perfect thing that ever happened to me.'' In reminiscent mood Mrs. Dickson recalls the days at college:

The experiences, associations, and incidents which came my way for four of Loretto's golden years are very dear to me. In those days our chicken and turkey dinners were supplied by home-grown fowl. One night the chicken house burned down while three fire engines fought the flames, but every freshie, including me, slept undisturbed through all the excitement. I remember, too, the time Gerry Grey brought a piece of wedding cake to the dorm and we all took turns sleeping on it to see if we could dream of future husbands. Many were the delightful dinners at Lafalot; picnics at the club house; taking part in Sister Dolorine's Shakespearian productions; cutting classes all day to work on the *Heightsonian,* and finally getting the last bit of copy in the mail in the wee, small hours—that was when we had the publications in the little room on the third floor—remember?

But, seriously—to me Loretto stands firm as always against her background of eternal hills. I know she lives just that way in the hearts of the old ''grads,'' a symbol of peace and security in these troubled times.

Sister, even though I have a busy life taking care of my wonderful family, I have tried to keep on writing and have sold several articles and stories. I belong to the Writer's Club and was, for two years, publicity chairman of the Woman's Club. For a time I had the privilege of being editor of the Woman's page in the *Boulder Daily Camera.*

Another writer who has made the magazines, especially with her poetry, is a member of this gifted class of '33. Margie Cannon, now Mrs. Frederick Murphy, 26 Williams Lane, Chevy Chase, Maryland. Her volume of poetry, *Blue Shadows and Other Poems* has been aptly summarized:

A friendly voice speaks simply and directly here of shared human experience, speaks conjointly of the human and the Divine in the matter-of-course (but not matter-of-fact!) confidence that makes true Catholic poetry a delight. Simplicity shadowing into depths, the familiar irradiated by the Divine—here are poems that meet the master prescription of a ''record of life's best and happiest moments.''

Margie Cannon Murphy, first editor of *T'Akra,* the college literary magazine, is sister to Helen Cannon, an outstanding social worker of the class of '27. In a recent letter to the Heights, Margie wrote:

Bishop Corrigan, in speaking to the women of Catholic Universities and Colleges, impressed this great reality upon them, that they were living tabernacles of the living Christ and that their success or failure was finally measured by the way in which they lived that "perfection" dwelling within them.

Loretto was and is the spiritual mother helping us to be worthy physically, spiritually, and mentally of that exalted position. This is being done surely through the example of the teachers, the subject matter of the courses studied, and the abundant graces issuing from the chapel.

The influence of Loretto enters daily into my vocation as wife and mother. The inspirations of spiritual and human friendships formed, the discipline of the course of study, and the memory of its peace and beauty—each one of these in turn learned at Loretto is applied on a smaller scale to one's home and family.

Greetings to all the Sisters. Love from Frederick, 4½, and from John Christopher, 2½.

Elizabeth Cullen Saya, 2710 Fillmore, Denver, class of '34, who believes it is fun to clean house, wash dishes, sew, and teach her fourteen-months-old daughter to walk, talk, and refrain from household activities, writes of her daily life:

My "doings" at present couldn't be written even by Shakespeare and have literary value while Mary Agnes, my fourteen month old daughter, is leading me a merry chase as I try to keep her out of the intricacies of grown-up accomplishments such as running up and down the stairs, making a pie for daddy's dinner, and helping with the laundry. She talks to herself in a language that only a fourteen month old baby could understand.

I'm spending my hours, days, and minutes trying to make a happy home, trying to forget that war may cause a temporary, maybe a permanent, break in our home. I'm proud of being a graduate of Loretto Heights. I think because of my training there I can face more squarely conditions brought about by this awful war. I know that I am a better wife and mother because of my four years when I was learning sound Catholic philosophy for which Loretto is noted. Seeing the result of such an education work out in my own life, I want my daughter, also, to have the advantage of a college course at Loretto. To me Loretto presents the heights in education, background, and, in fact, everything which tends to make a happy life. I plan that Mary Agnes will be a graduate of the class of 1963. This looks like long years ahead, but they will pass quickly—so, keep a place for us, please.

Mary Elizabeth Hanson, '34, during the last year of college, was all aflame to consecrate her life to God as a missionary in the field afar. In the fall of 1934, she went with high heart to that distant mission, St. Francis Convent, Honolulu, to devote her life to the lepers, if her superiors assigned her to that work. From colorful Hawaii, from the very heart of the war zone in the southern Pacific, Sister Bonaventure, O. S. F., writes:

I firmly believe that it was through the prayers of my people coupled with the influence of Loretto Heights that I received the spiritual outlook and character training that were to serve as a foundation for my future life as a religious. My present life is a complete fulfillment of all my hopes, though in a manner I could not have foreseen. Do you remember you asked me whether it was not the adventure of the thing that was calling me to Hawaii? I was highly indignant, I recall, but I know now what you meant. My life was not to be spent, as I chose, among the lepers, but in teaching, as God chose. I have learned to love this work as I never thought I would.

This is my fifth year teaching high school here at St. Francis Convent. I have charge of the freshman class, the science department, and the music students. A teaching sister is called upon to do a variety of things; life has no chance to become monotonous. Our teaching problems are about the same as are found in any mainland school, the level of intelligence being, in most cases, about average. However, there are some problems which, I believe, are peculiar to the Islands, including the lack of education and appreciation on the part of the parents, the lack of suitableness and family life, and the extremely careless use of English. These difficulties make our work different from that of our fellow Sisters in the States.

Perhaps the most interesting phase of our teaching lies in the variety of racial origins representing our students. In my classes alone there are Spanish, Portuguese, Hawaiian, Japanese, Chinese, Negro, Irish, Filipino, and even American Indian. We find in general that the girls of pure blood are more intelligent, though certain mixtures seem to bring better results than others. There is no friction on account of these racial differences, even since the war. In fact close friendships exist between girls whose nations are at war, for example, Japanese and Filipino.

God has been good to us in preserving us from danger since the war started. Though we are definitely in the war zone, we have lived in comparative safety and comfort. We lack no necessity and few luxuries. We live in intimate companionship with our gas masks, and we have learned to navigate remarkably well in the dark; otherwise our ways are not far from normal. Since school began in September we have been able to return to our regular class schedule, to receive a larger enrollment than last year, and to have a house full of boarding students.

I believe the war has brought to all in the Islands a fuller and deeper realization of our dependence on Divine Providence. We open school each morning with an assembly of all students; we pray for peace and sing patriotic songs. It is inspiring to see so many students of different nations united in prayer for their loved ones. There is a remarkable and most welcome lack of hatred and ill will among the pupils.

We Sisters make a daily holy hour in community before the Blessed Sacrament for peace and protection for our nation, our fighting men, and our community and its works. Even in our little household, there is scarcely a member who has not some loved one in the services. We often meet men from the States who visit us, hungry for the company and conversation of the Sisters and who are quick and proud to claim some relative or friend in the community "back home." It is rather tragic, yet wonderful, to meet such men, knowing that they may at any time be called upon to make the supreme sacrifice, but knowing, too, that they are spiritually prepared.

From the heart of the war zone in the Southern Pacific to Santa Fe, New Mexico, in the peaceful land of America, is quite a detour. Regina Coll, who married, immediately after her graduation from Loretto Heights College, Louis C. de Baca, writes in her Christmas letter:

My loyalty to the Heights is deep-rooted, and the friends I made and the pleasant memories I have, shall always be cherished as a treasure that no money can buy.

Loretto gave me a perspective on life that has been of great value to me. Although I was not inclined in the direction of "student," as the term is actually meant, I nevertheless feel that I learned principles which have been a bulwark and shield to the temptations of every day living.

I feel that I can present arguments that are sound and true against the prevalent ideas of a large group whose philosophy of life throws discretion in all directions. These people live by what they think is right rather than by what is right. I do not profess to be prudish and narrow-minded, yet I do say that I am guided by principles which are the result of Loretto training. I am prepared to present arguments that tear aside the "isms" and false doctrines permeating so many of our luke-warm Catholics, who are Catholics in name only.

Loretto is my second home. I always look forward to visiting the "Heights" during my brief stays in Denver. My major professor was a beacon light whose good advice and sound judgment I have reflected upon many times since graduation. The wisdom of her remarks has served as a "stop light" when I was on the point of being impulsive and impractical in matters which might have proved detrimental to my soul and body. To her I owe a debt of gratitude. My love and prayers will follow her always. God bless her!

My eldest little girl, Mary Lou, is in the second grade and is taking lessons on the violin. Gracie is in the first grade. Both go to Guadalupe school conducted by the Dominican Sisters. Jay is going on four and is into everything. He is more difficult to take care of than a dozen girls. Little Corrine was two years old, November 30. She is beginning to say everything; she and her daddy certainly enjoy each other.

In closing this letter, my thoughts go back to graduation day when I poured my heart into the refrain, "Loretto sing we." I hope my girls will have the opportunity of going to Loretto and that God will spare their dad and me to be present on their graduation day when I will join them in the college song, "Forward, Loretto."

Margaret Mary Dunphy Lowry, '35, writes of the school which she proudly claims as her alma mater:

My alma mater is not just another beautiful college in which I spent a few rollicking years. No, it is truly my foster mother. My sister Claire and I were left completely alone in the midst of our college years. The tender solicitude and gentle mothering which you sisters showered on us at that time are never forgotten. I am now married and have a two-year-old boy trotting and chattering around the house; yet, even now, when troubles tower and seem too big, or when special joys and blessings come, instinctively I fly to Loretto to share with the sisters, who have been my dearest friends and closest confidantes, the shadows and the sunshine which pattern my life.

When I recall the faces of my friends and classmates, I think fondly of "Izzy," and smile when remembering the hilarious pranks we engineered together, and with the memory I feel nostalgia creep over me.

I remember other times when I felt the restraining hand of discipline and sipped the bitter cup of disappointment. I know now that therein lay the strengthening that has taught me to accept the thorns which prick as we gather roses along life's highway; to hide beneath a smile and ease by doing little duties the greater sorrows and frustrations which all must meet.

I have not said half the things I could or would, but words are so inadequate. I must so live my life that it may say to all the dear and lovely things which Loretto means to me.

The following excerpt from Gladys Golden O'Farrell, '37, shows a former student devoting herself magnanimously to the betterment of others, a noble work performed nobly:

When Loretto is in my thoughts, I think of Colorado; and when I think of Colorado, I think of home. From this you may see, Sisters, that I love Loretto as home. My professional interest has always been concerned with the delinquent boy and the problems which are his. The splendid background of Loretto ethics and teacher training have helped me to perform this work for which I have a special attraction.

I am at present the principal of the academic section of the State Industrial School for Boys at Golden. There are two hundred boys attending the school, each one is to be rehabilitated to a better way of living. It is a tremendous task but quite worth-while. I am convinced that the thorough training which I received all through my school life from the sisters who taught me has helped me to pass the civil service examination and thus secure my present position.

From Salt Lake City comes a letter from Lucille Edwards (Mrs. Fred Kirk), '37, just in time for a few excerpts to be included in *Loretto in the Rockies*. Lucille wrote last December 26:

After I was graduated from Loretto Heights College, I taught for one year at St. John's parochial school in Denver, continuing, in this way, my happy association of eight years with the Sisters of Loretto. Then I went to work as secretary to Mr. John F. McGuire, investment banker, and formed with him one of the finest friendships I have ever had.

Mr. McGuire once told me, Sister, that he had met hundreds of girls in his lifetime, socially and in business, but that he had never met a finer group of girls that those from Loretto. He followed Loretto activities faithfully through the *Denver Catholic Register*.

I was working for Mr. McGuire on that most happy day, the day I met Fred. We were married one year and a half later and will shortly celebrate our third anniversary, with our little boy, who was a year and a half old on Christmas day. This brings us to the immediate present, Sister, here in Salt Lake City which we like as much as we could any place that isn't Denver. We consider ourselves fortunate to be still together in these terrible days of war.

A few excerpts from letters of the more recent graduates are included in this section devoted to the alumnae. Though time has not yet tested the principles of living learned at Loretto, yet they feel that they, too, are succeeding because of their college education. Gladys Givan, '40, writes a characteristic message:

Of course I am just as full as ever of "ego" and believe that you would like to know what this teacher is doing. Strange to say Laura Mae is still enjoying her teaching. This year I am teaching seventh and eight grade geography and history and have complete charge of the art department —this includes the junior and senior high school art here at Windsor, Colorado. Charcoal drawing, pastel, water color, and oil painting, all enter into the daily routine of the work I like so much. It is fortunate that I have the privilege of teaching my major subject at Loretto. I express here my deep gratitude to Sister Mary Norbert, who, besides being a very fine art instructor, was my dear friend. Loretto Heights College means three things to me—a way of life, a practical preparation for making a living, and an appreciation of all that is good and beautiful.

Dorothy Vogel, '41, writes:

Loretto has made it possible for me to join the ranks of the teaching profession. It is and always will be to me an example of a truly fine college. The time that I spent under its guidance is priceless—four years filled with valuable spiritual and intellectual training.

Mary Kaye Hagerty, '42, president of the Press Club for two consecutive years, chairman of the Association of Catholic School Press Relations for the same two years, and editor of *Loretana* (1941), the college yearbook, winner of a loving cup for Press services, writes that she is doing secretarial work at one of the business firms in Denver. She finds that he major in journalism is helping greatly to assemble data, make contacts, and meet dead lines.

Foremost in my mind when I think of what Loretto has done for me is the fact that my contacts there strengthened my faith. In the business world in which I find myself now, people speak a different language. Without the background from Loretto, I might be tempted to be swayed toward their point of view. Then, again, Loretto means friendships which have been formed, friendships with faculty and students. With a feeling of real pride I point to Loretto and say "That is my school." I realize more fully every day that I have received the best possible education which a Catholic girl could wish to have. Loretto trained me to be honest, truthful, reliable, and sincere toward my employer.

The summer of '42 witnessed two Catholic weddings when Patty Ann McLaughlin and Kaye Blodgett, both of the class of '42, became the brides of William Gossett and William Bishop, respectively. Patty Ann wrote recently:

Will you believe me, Sister, when I say that Loretto means everything to me: my dearest friends I found there, and, strange to say, I met my husband at a Press Club dance. So, you see, my present happiness is closely connected with Loretto. Please do not think that I have forgotten about my writing future—right now I am revising a short story about the Military Police. Sister, I can hear you say: "Patty Ann, be careful about your data on this subject. Government material, you know, may not be tampered with loosely." All right, Sister, I shall watch out for this and promise not to become too ambitious.

Kaye Blodgett, editor of *T'Akra* in '41, and secretary of the Press Club in '41 and '42, writes:

In my own foolish way I thought that once the sheepskin was in my hands I could cheerfully say good-bye, but, as a matter of fact, I never felt so lonely and forgotten in my life as on registration day in September, 1942. I had to struggle to keep the tears back. It seemed so unnatural not to be going back to the library and the journalism room, and seeing all the sisters again.

Do you know, Sister, that the important thing Loretto did for me was to take the green off: it brought me safe out of the adolescent stage and helped me to accept womanhood gracefully. In other words, Loretto has molded me into a woman who can face almost anything instead of being frightened at the world and everything in it. When friends say that college is foolish, especially now that the war is so much more important, I do not agree. What Loretto offers to the young woman of today are the things we'll need to make intelligent and alert citizens in the post-war era. The philosophy, the religious training, and the cultural foundation the Sisters of Loretto give their students supply the stamina we need to face the world. The technical training we receive is useful, of course, but in my opinion it is secondary to these other cultures.

Meanwhile I'll be going along being an army wife with a tiny longing for my old college days tucked down inside me. My husband is advancing in promotions right along. He ranks now as a commissioned sergeant. I'm really proud of him.

These messages from former students who are now serving God, home, and country, in various parts of the world, show the influence which Loretto Heights is still exercising over their adult lives.

Seven hundred thirty-eight students have been graduated from academy and college since that first class in June, 1892; three hundred seventy in the academy from its opening until it was closed in June, 1941; three hundred sixty-eight from the college within its first twenty-five years.

The alumnae, for the most part, are engaged in gainful occupations. Five are executives in business or teaching; eight are employed in newspaper or magazine fields; five in library work; thirty-two as secretaries; twenty-five in social service; twenty as music teachers; ten as nurses; five in dramatic art; two in art; one hundred seventy-two are teachers—several of these are teaching in China and the Philippines; seventy-five have continued their higher education and have received either the Master of Arts or the Doctor of Philosophy degrees; several have died; over seventy have consecrated their lives to God in the religious life; some have remained single; the greater number of the girls have married.

In World War I, many of the alumnae of the academy were generous in devoting time to Red Cross service and other war activities; in this second and more destructive world war, the younger generation of graduates are following the traditions established twenty-five years ago by the older alumnae. Loretto is represented in Red Cross and Social Service; the students are buying and selling war bonds; they are secretaries and workers in munitions plants and are in actual service as commissioned officers, holding the rank of first and second lieutenants as nurses and WAACs. Dorothy Starbuck, '40' holds the rank of lieutenant in the WAACs. She was the third person chosen from Denver for the honor of entering officers' training, and, after completing her course at Fort Des Moines, was selected out of 700 candidates as one of the officers. The Woman's Auxiliary Army Corps, not a part of the regular army, is a unit which works with the army. The greatest demand for WAACs is for motor transport drivers, clerical workers, signal communications personnel—including telephone and telegraph operators—cooks, and bakers. Lieutenant Starbuck's official work is drilling new members when they enter Fort Des Moines for training.

Winifred Espy, '33, after giving distinguished service for some months at Fort Des Moines as recreational director, went to Washington, D. C., November 21, 1942, where she reported for training for foreign service with the American Red Cross. After receiving the Bachelor of Arts degree from Loretto Heights, Winifred did graduate work at the University of Chicago and the University of Utah.

Sister Menodora Casey—First Graduate of Academy

Main Corridor, Tile Hall

Student Body of '21—Mary Hayden, center, only Graduate

Several of the girls after finishing at Loretto Heights College became medical technologists in various cities: Martha Ellen Dea, '39, Glockner Sanatarium, Colorado Springs, Colorado; Mercedes Riordan, '40, Hotel Dieu, New Orleans, Louisana; Margaret Anna Mullen, '40, Red Cross medical social work, Fitzsimons General Hospital, Denver; Peggy See, '41, office of Dr. L. A. Conway, Denver; Peggy Zook, '41, Hospital, Alton, Illinois; Rita Abegg and Kathryn Glore, '42, fellowships, St. Mary's Hospital, Kansas City Missouri.

Other alumnae have found enjoyable and lucrative positions in the work which interested them while in college. The following are engaged in some form of dietetics and are at the same time giving valuable service to their country: Mary Catherine St. John (Mrs. Joseph Krebs), '37, Desloge Hospital, Nutrition Clinic, St. Louis, Missouri; Clara Werle, '38, Instructor Cathedral High School, Denver; Helen Kelley, '39, St. Mary's Hospital, St. Louis, Missouri; Nancy Gregory, '39, instructor, public high school, Puerto Rico; Natalie Swan, '40, Walter Reed Hospital, Army Medical, Washington, D. C.; Rosalie Lawrenson, '40, Mount Vernon Hospital, New York City; Flora Meek, '40, Food Demonstrator, General Electric, St. Louis, Missouri; Gertrude Waters, '40, Home Demonstration Agent, Farm Security Administration, Trinidad, Colorado.

A number of graduates have entered the field of social service and are holding responsible positions: Helen Irene Cannon, '27, consultant for crippled children in Public Health Department, Denver, has been employed in this work ever since she finished her studies in the School of Social Service at the Catholic University of America and is considered one of the most efficient and best informed women in the field. Regina Call, '34, Mrs Louis C. de Baca, is engaged in social service in Santa Fe, New Mexico. Ellen Mary Campbell, '36; Joan Ayres, '37, and Ellen Milan, '38, are devoting themselves to this work. Recent graduates, Mary Qualkenbusch and Helen Nieters, '41, and Peggy Nieters, '42, are studying at the Graduate School of Social Service at the Catholic University.

These messages from a cross section of the alumnae and the brief account of their various activities and employment give a fair idea of the useful lives of those women who claim Loretto Heights as their alma mater. Many of the former students, feeling the responsibility which present world conditions bring, are giving generous aid in the national crisis. This chapter dedicated to the Alumnae of Loretto Heights shows that an education whose central theme is God keeps the mind and heart of the graduates courageous in carrying on their chosen work.

Chapter XXIV

GOLDEN JUBILEE OF LORETTO HEIGHTS

As the decades in the life at Loretto Heights began to be told off—ten, twenty, thirty, forty years—the sisters of the community often said to one another: "Keep in mind that 1941 will be the golden jubilee year." But as they recalled the date it always seemed remote; therefore, they thought, there was no need for immediate planning. Then with the opening of school in September, 1941, the day which would complete the fifty years was almost upon them. "Fifty years," they said, "impossible!" But almost fifty years had passed since that memorable November day on which the faculty and girls had left old St. Mary's, had boarded the Circle train, which took them the greater part of the journey, had walked the remaining distance and finished the trip up the steep hill to the great, magnificent building, standing in the midst of a field of cactus and soap weed, where they were to begin a new venture in education.

The appropriate celebration of this important historic event was of concern to all the sisters, for they were mindful of the Lord's injunction to Moses: "And thou shalt sanctify the fiftieth year . . . for it is a year of jubilee; it shall be holy unto you." The recently appointed superior, Sister Frances Marie, with the help of the faculty, planned a program which would commemorate with fitting observances the achievements of the pioneer sisters at Loretto Heights, who had begun so courageously the work of Catholic education out on Loretto hill, fifty years ago, and that of their successors, who had followed so closely their example of cheerful and generous service.

Those first Lorettines who, with the daring of the hardy settlers on the edge of civilization, met and overcame the difficulties confronting them in this foundation, bequeathed their spirit which still lives at Loretto Heights —a spirit of self-forgetfulness, humility, charity, and zeal.

In the golden jubilee year the prayer of the Lorettine who recalls the life and times of the founders of the Heights, who sowed, in the midst of toil and abnegation, the seed which continues to bring in a harvest of golden sheaves, might well be: "Lord God of Hosts, be with us yet, lest we forget, lest we forget." As members of the alumnae are considered successful in so far as they reproduce the spirit of their school, so a Sister of Loretto is a success in the measure in which she keeps close to the early standards of her religious Society.

The ceremonies of the jubilee year began with a Solemn High Mass in the college chapel, November 5, 1941. The officers of the Mass were the Reverend William J. Mulcahy, celebrant; the Reverend James W. Stakelum, C. M., of St. Thomas Seminary, deacon; and the Reverend Joseph O'Heron, pastor of St. Louis Church, sub-deacon. The Very Reverend William H. Higgins, pastor of St. Philomena's Church, spoke in praise of the lives of the sisters of the community during the cycle of fifty years:

The work accomplished by the Sisters of Loretto here at the Heights is beyond calculation — precious results brought about by the grace of God. These humble women have dramatized for us the supernatural. Sister Helena who has spent forty-five consecutive years at the Heights is an example of what I mean by the supernatural. Through her humility she has supernaturalized her work and brought blessings upon the institution.

In their days of formal prayer before the Blessed Sacrament, these Sisters have spent over two and one half million hours; each sister has assisted at over 18,500 Masses, thereby helping to bring the blessings of God on all in Colorado.

Down in the little cemetery, not far away, lie the saintly remains of those who have died in the discharge of their duties. God has lavished supernatural life upon these sisters and their students. He lifts them into another world by His grace.

This opening ceremony of the year's celebrations was honored by the presence of the Reverend William A. Forstall, S.J., of Regis College, the only one present who had attended the ceremony of laying the cornerstone of Loretto

Heights Academy, September 21, 1890. Father Forstall, a link with the past, had helped to seal the great granite block by applying the cement fifty years ago.

Since the students of the college felt that they should be participants in the activities of the golden jubilee year, they set aside December 11, 1941, as Student Dedication Day. Mass was celebrated at 8:30 by the Reverend Daniel A. Lord, S.J. Later that morning, the Reverend William J. Mulcahy, college chaplain, received the aspirants into the Sodality of Our Lady. In the afternoon there was a rally at which several officers of the Student Government Council and class presidents gave enthusiastic talks on participation in the jubilee celebrations. At that assembly, the student body dedicated itself formally to the support of the year's activities.

Their most important project was the drive to raise sufficent money to establish a scholarship and publicity fund as a student memorial golden jubilee gift. Margaret Anne Madden, general chairman, assisted by her sister, Mary Catherine, began definite work before the Christmas holidays by appointing committees and publicizing their plans. On February 5, 1942, the Mothers' Club took an active part in promoting the drive; the mothers joined their daughters in raising funds by means of a Patriotic Card Party. Mrs. Earl Bell was general chairman of the affair which closed the students' project with gratifying financial results.

Of great importance to the Catholic Church in the West and of special gratification to Loretto in its jubilee year was the ceremony which took place in the Cathedral of the Immaculate Conception on the morning of January 6, 1942. His Holiness, Pope Pius XII, through his personal representative, the Most Reverend Ameleto Giovanni Cicognani, Apostolic Delegate to the United States, elevated Bishop Vehr to the archiepiscopal rank, established the ecclesiastical Province of Denver, and erected the Diocese of Pueblo.

Splendor unprecedented in all the Rocky Mountain region was witnessed that morning in the Cathedral where, more than ten years before, Bishop Vehr had been installed as fourth Bishop of Denver. Seven archbishops, forty-one bishops, fifty monsignori, more than two hundred priests, hundreds of religious women, and many of the laity gathered to witness the impressive ceremony.

The sermon on that memorable occasion was preached by the Metropolitan of Cincinnati, Archbishop John T. Mc-Nicholas, personal friend of the new Archbishop. When responding to this address, Archbishop Vehr pledged himself to work for the extension of God's kingdom and the good of souls and, in concluding, said: "We pledge anew our loyalty and devotion to our country. We love it and its institutions. May God bless it in these days of trial, and may He smile favorably upon all with His favors and benedictions."

Loretto Heights College, its faculty, and students were honored on January 7 when Archbishop Vehr brought the Apostolic Delegate to visit the college. His Excellency, when addressing the sisters and students, the latter in cap and gown, expressed his satisfaction in visiting the college in its golden jubilee year and congratulated the Sisters of Loretto on their cultural and educational work. "Loretto Heights," Archbishop Cicognani said, "makes higher culture available to young women. Culture marked with spirituality is beautiful; culture without spirituality is as nothing. In this college moral and religious treasures are gained."

The Apostolic Delegate concluded his informal talk with the wish that Loretto students may be noble influences in their individual homes, a consolation to their families, to the Sisters of Loretto, and to their Archbishop. After bestowing the apostolic blessing on the assembly, His Excellency granted a holiday to the students and generous privileges to the sisters.

Hanging in a prominent place in the college library is a large picture of the Apostolic Delegate, Archbishop Cicognani, which he gave to the faculty and students, autographed with these lines: To the Faculty and Students of Loretto Heights College in happy memory of my visit with every blessing. A. G. Cicognani, Archbishop of Laodicea, Apost. Delegate, Denver, January 7, 1942.

A special feature was added to the jubilee program on March 19, when the college girls paid tribute to their fathers by entertaining them on the feast of St. Joseph, patron of Christian families. A father-daughter spaghetti dinner, served in the students' dining room, was the means of bringing together a large group of men, widely known in Colorado and surrounding states—stockmen, judges, merchants, business men of all kinds, the fathers of many of the students.

On the evening of March 22, Miss Emma Romano, a major in music, appeared in a senior recital which was marked by distinction and originality. Besides interpreting with finesse selections from famous composers, Miss Romano played her own composition, "Impromptu," a number which was received with enthusiastic appreciation. This student, prior to matriculation in college, had no musical training. Toward the close of her four-year course, she presented the following program: Sonato Op. 27, No. 1, Beethoven—Andante, Allegro molto e vivace, Adagio, Allegro vivace; Praeludium, MacDowell; March Wind, MacDowell; Etude Op. 10, No. 12, Chopin; Prelude Op. 28, No. 15, Chopin; Impromptu, Emma Romano; From the Spanish Suite Andalucia, Lecuona—Cordova, Gitanerias, Andalucia; Capriccio B Minor, Dohnanyi.

The music department of Loretto Heights has always maintained a high degree of efficiency. Sister Teresa Marie Hentzen, director of the department since the fall of 1926, a finished musician and a capable and inspiring instructor, has not only preserved the former standards but has made a rich contribution to the cultural life of the students by educating them to recognize and appreciate good music.

As one would expect, Home Day or Loretto Sisters Day was one of the high points of the year's celebration. The day reserved to honor the Sisters at the Heights was March 27, Friday in Passion Week, which is set aside by the Church for commemorating the Seven Dolors of Our Lady, the patronal feast of the Sisters of Loretto. The Reverend Maurice J. Singleton, C. M., of St. Thomas Seminary, celebrated at 6:30 a High Mass for the community. The beautiful floral decorations on the altar were the gift of the resident students. The officers of the Student Government, the presidents of the classes, in fact, all the collegians took special pride in sponsoring the banquet for the sisters of the community, which was served at five o'clock in the guests' dining room. The tables were beautifully decorated with flowers, which the students had placed with loving hands to honor their Sisters on their special feast day. The alumnae had provided individual floral gifts for each Lorettine.

The happiness of this Home Day for the Community was made complete by the presence of several members of the General Council: Mother M. Edwarda, Superior General; Sister Mary Linus, Vicaress General; Sister Mary Urban and Sister Kathleen Marie, Assistants General.

Fittingly reminiscent were the speeches following the banquet. Sister Mary Linus, who had been a member of the faculty that first year, took the community back fifty years, to live the scenes she described vividly in her touching recollections. Sister Celestine added another early chapter when she narrated the events of opening day at the Heights, November 2, 1891. Sister Rose Margaret paid a well-merited tribute to the late Monsignor Brady, chaplain at Loretto Heights for so many years. Sister Marie Clyde recalled incidents which occurred twenty-five years ago, when the institution celebrated its silver jubilee. Sister Mary Vivian gave personal recollections of the opening of the college in September, 1918, presenting a picture altogether new to many of the younger religious, who naturally had thought that conditions were always as they knew them. Sister Mary Vivian could speak with authority for she was one of the trio who opened the college about twenty-five years before. During that long span she has been registrar and director of the history department. A capable teacher, an alert and well-informed administrator, she has given invaluable service to the college, its faculty, and students whom she has served so well.

Sister M. Cecille gave an interesting talk on the opening of the new high school building, Pancratia Hall, in 1930. Sister Frances Marie spoke appreciatively on the Community of Loretto Heights. Mother M. Edwarda, Superior

General, gave an inspiring account of the work in education which the Sisters of Loretto in various places are accomplishing. The day was one of thanksgiving and praise— thanksgiving to God for His provident care through the years; praise and appreciation of those sisters who, in the days of struggle and privation, had practiced the self-denial which had assured the life of the institution.

Shortly after the home celebration, Sisters Religious Day was observed on Easter Monday, April 6. Two hundred twenty-five sisters of the archdiocese gathered at the historic college to participate in a day of prayer, thanksgiving, and rejoicing. Reverend Gregory Smith, pastor of St. Francis de Sales Church, was the celebrant of the High Mass in the college chapel at 10:30 a. m. At the noon hour, the various sister friends were guests at luncheon and at 2:30 at an entertainment in the auditorium.

Representatives from all the religious orders of women in Denver and other cities in Colorado attended Religious Day at the Heights: Sisters of Charity of Leavenworth; Sisters of Charity of Cincinnati; Sisters of Charity of the Blessed Virgin Mary; Dominican Sisters; Franciscan Sisters; Sisters of Mercy; Sisters of St. Joseph; Servite Sisters; Missionary Sisters of the Sacred Heart; Sisters of the Precious Blood; and Sisters of Loretto from their schools in the city and state.

The alumnae were mindful of their alma mater during the year of jubilee. Duly appreciative of the honors coming to their school, they, too, assembled around her to congratulate and rejoice. Former students were present at many of the public functions of the jubilee, but, on April 18, they gathered in happy reunion into the corridors and classrooms, greeting friends old and new among the faculty. At seven o'clock in the evening, hundreds of graduates from Loretto Heights Academy, Pancratia Hall, and the College joined in happy reminiscences around the banquet tables. The "good old days" and days not so old united all on that festive occasion.

Sister Mary Linus, former superior and president of the college, and Sister Mary Dolorine, for many years dean,

were guests at the banquet; also Sister M. Genoveva, superior for nine years at St. Mary's Academy, Denver, and
Sister M. Anastasia, a former teacher of music; Sister M.
Menodora of the class of '92, first graduate of the academy,
was alumna guest of honor. Mrs. J. F. Prinzing, president
of the Alumnae Association and toastmaster, had arranged
a program of interesting after-dinner speakers: the Reverend H. R. McCabe, former pastor at Idaho Springs and
good friend of the Sisters of Loretto in Colorado, recalled
events of historic value which took place at the time-honored
institution; Very Reverend John J. Flanagan, S.J., president of Regis College; Very Reverend Harold V. Campbell,
and Reverend James Stakelum, C.M., professors of the college, gave clever and timely sketches of more recent happenings; Doctor Paul J. Ketrick, president, toasted the college
of today, its faculty, and students; Sister Mary Linus, going
back over the long route of fifty years, outlined the story of
the first Lorettines, who built so broad and sure on a foundation of faith and hope; Sister Frances Marie, superior and
regent, gave her impressions of Loretto as it is today; Sister
Mary Dolorine spoke enthusiastically of Loretto Heights and
the dear familiar scenes of past years; Sister M. Menodora
gave the local color of the school from the student's point
of view, fifty years back. Mrs. Ella Mullen Weckbaugh
recalled manners and customs of the early days at Loretto
Heights, which, when compared with the modern way of
living, seemed primitive. But there was nothing primitive about the teaching, Mrs. Weckbaugh declared; it
was always of a high order. Mrs. J. H. Prinzing, in closing
the program, pictured the cultured yet homey life which as
a student in more recent years she had lived at Loretto.

The sacred concert, directed by the Right Reverend
Monsignor Joseph Bosetti, Vicar General of the archdiocese,
was the special student contribution to the golden jubilee.
At three o'clock, on the afternoon of April 12, Pergolese's
Oratorio, *Stabat Mater,* was presented to a capacity house
in the auditorium. The Oratorio carried a chorus of fifty
college students, under the immediate training of Sister
Peter Joseph, voice instructor. The soloists were Mrs.

Anne O'Neil Sullivan and Mrs. Katherine Perenyi, accomplished singers in Denver musical circles. A string ensemble of twelve members of the Denver Symphony Orchestra accompanied the Oratorio.

Duets by college students included Virginia Bailey, Francis Wilson, Martha Norris, Barbara Murphy, and Virginia Duggan, sopranos; Eileen Evert, Jeanette Esponda, and Betty Dikitolia, altos.

The Sisters of Loretto of Loretto Heights College received many congratulatory letters and telegrams on the occasion of the golden jubilee celebration. From the metropolitan of Denver, His Excellency, Archbishop Urban J. Vehr, came a letter which will be treasured in the archives of the institution. The Most Reverend John J. Glennon, Archbishop of St. Louis, sent cordial jubilee greetings; so also the Most Reverend John J. Cantwell, Archbishop of Los Angeles; the Most Reverend R. A. Gerken, Archbishop of Santa Fe; and the Most Reverend Samuel A. Stritch, Archbishop of Chicago. The following bishops sent congratulations: Henry Althoff, Bishop of Belleville; C. E. Byrne, Bishop of Galveston; Joseph Corrigan, Rector of the Catholic University; George J. Donnelly, Auxiliary Bishop of St. Louis; Bernard T. Espelage, O.S.M., Bishop of Gallup; Francis C. Kelley, Bishop of Oklahoma City and Tulsa; S. M. Metzger, Co-adjutor Bishop of El Paso; P. A. McGovern, Bishop of Cheyenne; Anthony J. Schuler, S.J., Bishop of El Paso; T. J. Toolen, Bishop of Mobile; Joseph C. Willging, Bishop of Pueblo.

Congratulations were received from United States officials and others: the President of the United States, Franklin D. Roosevelt; United States senators and representatives from Colorado; the Governor of Colorado, Ralph L. Carr; the Mayor of Denver, Ben F. Stapleton; university and college presidents; the Loretto Heights Alumnae Association; many Sisters of Loretto, including former students of both high school and college at Loretto Heights; and many good patrons and friends.

Tribute to Loretto Heights College and to the Sisters of Loretto for the achievements made on behalf of Christian education in the past fifty years was paid in a congratulatory message by the Most Reverend Urban J. Vehr, Archbishop of Denver, in the following letter:

> Archbishop's House
> 777 Pearl
> Denver, Colorado
> March 26, 1942

Sisters of Loretto
Loretto Heights College
Loretto, Colorado

The Sisters of Loretto pioneered in Catholic education in our Rocky Mountain area. Almost eighty years ago, when Denver was a mere sprawling hamlet, the Sisters of Loretto braved the dangers and hardships of the barren eastern plains and the lurking Indians in the fabled covered wagons, to bring the blessings of Christian culture and education to our west land. From humble beginnings have grown St. Mary Academy and Loretto Heights College whose golden jubilee we celebrate this year.

The hundreds of graduates of Loretto bless her for the Christian training in moral principles, in real culture, and godly ideals which they in turn have transmitted to succeeding generations.

We are particularly proud of Loretto Heights College because it is the only four year college exclusively for young ladies in our Rocky Mountain region and because it has given such noble graduates to State and Church these many years. The college represents the initiative, the self-sacrifice, and toil of devoted Sisters who have labored under difficult conditions to give to our region the means of higher Christian culture.

As an accredited college of recognized standing, Loretto should have a special attraction to our Catholic young women who are privileged with the opportunity of higher education.

We commend the noble achievements of fifty years of Christian education and hope that this golden jubilee will elicit from our Catholic people, particularly, continued and increasing support and patronage for our only Catholic college for women in the Rocky Mountain area.

✠ Urban J. Vehr,
Archbishop of Denver.

The first graduate of Loretto Heights College, Mary Hayden, '21, became a Carmelite nun. From her monastery, Hawley Boulevard, San Diego, California, Sister Céline of the Trinity wrote to her alma mater, February 27, 1942:

My dearest Sisters of Loretto:

The thought of a Golden Jubilee at the Heights starts vibrating the dominant note of joy in my heart, for from the beginning our beloved Lorettines mastered the art of making learning attractive. Solid classes in Greek, mathematics, and science were followed by happy hours with brush and quill, the sweep of drama, and lyric melody. Thus sped our college years, filled with lessons profitable for the future. As I part the silver mist that veils the past, I see the May crowning, the floral tributes at Our Blessed Lady's feet, the rose-festival; I am again in the procession on Cap and Gown Sunday, or with a radiant group rambling over Colorado hills.

Fides, Mores, Cultura! This inscription, indelibly engraved on the minds of dawning youth for half a century in that hallowed spot in the Rockies, where the richest pigments are blended on Nature's palette, has followed Loretto students into ever-varying careers and has remained their guiding motto in many a testing moment.

The Silver has been minted into Gold. May the gold be set with diamonds rare, and may there be jubilee in heaven in unison with the jubilee on earth in a great wave of thanksgiving for the graces of these fifty years, in petition for the faculty and their loyal pupils, in intercession for our cherished Alma Mater!

Congratulations! Loving wishes! God's blessing on this Aureate Year! The one gift from Carmel by the Western Sea can be an augmentation of fervor in choiring song for Loretto Heights College and all that the name implies. It is offered at every canonical hour of every day.

A few months later this first college graduate, Sister Céline of the Trinity, sent the following golden jubilee greeting:

> Gold is your heart, a monstrance bright,
> Pulsing with God's own life and light,
> To which souls myriad may trace
> Alchemy of gleaming grace.
> Arife with bells the vibrant air,
> For half a century of prayer
> Forms a golden, columned spire
> From Heights we know to heights still higher.

'Agape' at dawn unites
Far-flung Alumnae of the Heights
Partaking of the Grail of Gold
Offered by knight royal-stoled.

Precious the silver crown of years,
Cherished the gold which now appears,
Though rich, 'tis but the setting of a gem
For diamond feast and diadem.
Your fifty golden years at last!
When half as many more have passed
We shall intone the happy strain,
A glad *Te Deum* sing again.
Loretto Heights, no twilight mist
Will veil the radiant sunset tryst;
Of heaven's beams the angels now
Prepare a nimbus for each brow.

The climax of the religious observance of the golden jubilee year came on April 25, known among the Lorettines as Foundation Day, since on that date in 1812 the first three postulants were clad in a simple religious garb, by their holy founder, the Reverend Charles Nerinckx, in St. Charles Church, Marion County, Kentucky.

Solemn Pontifical High Mass was offered in the Cathedral of the Immaculate Conception, at 10 a.m., in thanksgiving to God for the blessings bestowed on Loretto Heights during its fifty years and for the kindness and generosity of friends who had made possible its apostolate of Catholic education. The officers of the Mass were His Excellency, the Most Reverend Urban J. Vehr, Archbishop of Denver, celebrant; the Very Reverend Thomas D. Coyne, C.M., president of St. Thomas Seminary, assistant priest; the Very Reverend John J. Flanagan, S.J., and the Very Reverend William H. Higgins, deacons of honor; the Very Reverend Charles H. Hagus, deacon; the Very Reverend Harold V. Campbell, sub-deacon; the Reverend Bernard Cullen, master of ceremonies; and the Reverend Elmer Kolka, assistant master of ceremonies.

Present in the sanctuary at the Golden Jubilee Solemn Pontifical Mass were the Most Reverend Joseph C. Willging, Bishop of Pueblo; the Most Reverend Patrick A. McGovern,

A Favorite Beauty Spot on Loretto Heights College Campus

Daylight to Dark at Loretto Heights College

Bishop of Cheyenne; the Right Reverend Matthew Smith, editor of the *Denver Register;* and the Very Reverend Monsignor John R. Mulroy, head of the archdiocesan Catholic charities. St. Thomas Seminary choir, under the direction of the Reverend T. J. Barrett, C.M., sang the Mass. More than fifty priests from the parishes of the archdiocese, of the secular clergy and religious orders, were in attendance at the Jubilee Mass.

The Very Reverend Martin J. O'Malley, C.M., president of Kenrick Seminary, Webster Groves, Missouri, preached the jubilee sermon. In developing his text: "Not by might, nor by power, but by my spirit, saith the Lord of Hosts," Doctor O'Malley gave a masterful panegyric on the early work of the Lorettines, who, blazing the path out on the edge of civilization, began the work of education in Colorado in June, 1864. The introduction to his sermon made articulate the feelings in the heart of every Sister of Loretto who was present in the Cathedral. Only passages of that tribute are quoted here:

Our hearts are singing this glad morning as we come to God's altar to humbly say our thanks for the blessings showered by the Divine Hand upon Loretto Heights during the fifty years of its glorious life. During the months that have recently passed, Loretto's friends have been commemorating with joyous memory the achievements of Loretto's golden years. This morning led by the Reverend Shepherd of the flock, we come to the Source of all Loretto's blessings, humbly to speak at the Eucharistic Altar of Thanksgiving in this blessed temple of the living God our gratitude to the Giver of all good gifts.

Not by might was Loretto set upon its imposing eminence a half century ago. Rather by the spirit of the blessed Christ, the spirit of sacrifice. Pioneers the founders were, the Sisters of Loretto at the Foot of the Cross. Did they not belong to a Community with a living tradition of sacrifice . . . ? Out from Kentucky went those trail blazers of the spirit into the great Empire of the Southwest. Out they went as traveled the Apostles from the upper room of far away Judea, not questioning the bulk of the mountains, not tracing the course of the rivers; out they went to a crude, raw, sprawling civilization, bearing to it what it needed most, purity of heart, gentleness of manners, loyalty to Church, consecration of life to the spread of the message of the Prince of Peace. Their benison fell upon Denver as early as 1864, bringing to the young ambitious village of civil war days convent education and all that it connotes: superior education, rare refinement, genuine culture, a development of all that is best in womanhood.

Heaven-sent they came, and with heaven-fixed aim did they build at a later date, by the spirit of truth and love, Loretto Heights. What a monument—those lofty convent heights above the Colorado plains and beneath the eternal Rockies! A monument of what Loretto zeal will dare and do to make the institutions of the Church the noblest of the land! A symbol, too, they stand of Loretto's holy work whose purpose it has always been to raise all things upward from the earth nearer to heaven, close to God—the purest of aims, the sublimest of works, the loftiest motives of life. By my spirit, saith the Lord of Hosts.

Loretto Heights is young as colleges reckon their years. It is not young in the great, historic culture it continues. It is not young in the eternal principles it teaches and demonstrates. Within its realm, religion is a genial and gracious thing. Morality there has sanity and poise. Social life has warmth and color, though restrained by refined and gentle manners. The saint here is king and sainthood royal; but the philosopher and the scientist, the poet and the artist are held in high regard. Things of the mind and heart find at the Heights congenial clime.

Who can measure the contribution which Loretto has made to this mountain community? Who can weigh the accomplishments of these fifty years? The Divine Teacher it was who said: "By their fruits you shall know them." And by her fruits shall men know the work of Loretto Heights College; by her Alumnae here in Denver and throughout the country—five thousand have passed through her portals—cultured Christian women, making distinctive contributions to their communities by their active enlightened and understanding faith, their sound education, and their deep devotion to Mother Country and all the good for which she stands.

Dear Sisters of Loretto at the Foot of the Cross, your Golden Crown of Jubilee is not hammered out by verbal word-smiths. It is not fashioned by mere verbals. May I remind you? Your crown is promised by Him who said: "They who instruct others unto Justice shall shine for all eternity."

At the conclusion of the Solemn Pontifical Mass, Archbishop Vehr ascended the pulpit and read the official message from His Excellency, the Apostolic Delegate, the Most Reverend A. G. Cicognani, conferring the Apostolic blessing of His Holiness, Pope Pius XII, upon the Sisters of Loretto in the Archdiocese of Denver, their faculty, students, and friends, and his own felicitations:

Apostolic Delegation
3339 Massachusetts Ave.,
Washington, D. C.
April 25, 1942.

The Most Reverend Urban J. Vehr, D.D.
Archbishop of Denver
777 Pearl Street
Denver, Colorado.
Your Excellency:

I am very happy to inform Your Excellency that His Holiness, Pope Pius XII, has most graciously deigned to confer his paternal Apostolic blessing upon Loretto Heights College and the Sisters of Loretto in the Archdiocese of Denver for the golden jubilee of the founding of this institution, a token of appreciation for these 50 years of faithful service in the cause of Christ and an augury of continued benedictions. The Sovereign Pontiff has desired also that this papal benediction be extended to the president of the college, to the members of the faculty, and to the student body, as also to the benefactors of the college and to all those who take part in the religious observance of the anniversary. For myself I desire to participate in the benign kindness of the Sovereign Pontiff, offering heartfelt congratulations on the achievements of these five decades and most earnest felicitations for the many years which lie ahead. I am particularly pleased to be the bearer of this message from the Vatican and to present my good wishes, because it was my privilege to visit Loretto Heights College recently and see for myself the splendid good being accomplished. I pray that the blessing of the Vicar of Christ may be an earnest of heavenly favor and a lasting assurance of graces from on high.

Sincerely yours in Christ,
✠ A. G. Cicognani
Archbishop of Laodicea
Apostolic Delegate.

After the ceremonies in the Cathedral, Archbishop Vehr, Bishop McGovern, Bishop Willging, and about thirty-five priests were guests of the Sisters of Loretto Heights at a noon-day luncheon at St. Mary's Academy on Pennsylvania Avenue.

The golden jubilee banquet, beginning at 7 p. m., took place June 2, at the Denver Country Club. The toastmaster, the Honorable Judge J. J. Walsh, introduced His Excellency, Archbishop Urban J. Vehr, who in turn presented the guest speaker of the evening, the Most Reverend Joseph Corrigan, rector of the Catholic University of America. Other guests at the speakers' table, in addition to Archbishop Vehr and Bishop Corrigan, were the Honorable J. C. Vivian, Lieutenant-Governor of the State of Colorado, and the Honorable B. F. Stapleton, Mayor of Denver. The official program of the evening included a toast to "Loretto" by the Very Reverend Dr. William M. Higgins, pastor of St. Philomena's Church; music by a string trio; talks by Dr. Paul J. Ketrick, president of Loretto Heights College, Mayor Stapleton, Archbishop Vehr, and, finally, the address of the evening, "Jubilees and Epochs," was given by Bishop Corrigan.

Although the main subject of the address was the golden jubilee year which was being celebrated, the speaker showed the seriousness even of the celebration since its background was not peace but war:

The golden jubilee which has come to this Catholic college for women and the diamond jubilee of Catholic education in this whole region are glad reasons why in happy pride these years should be acclaimed. They could never have a deeper significance than they have here tonight, a significance which comes from the work accomplished but now necessarily viewed through that heavy shadow lying so gravely on our native land. The lives and work both of the Sisters and their graduates must be weighed here to establish the value of their contribution to America's dire need in the war of today and in her still more vital needs in the peace which shall come after.

After showing that patriotism and religion are but the dual fulfillment of one duty, Bishop Corrigan emphasized the need of leadership since multiplied are the paths of influence open to Catholic women who will accept leadership of the millions who are inarticulate:

Let us hold, then, that it is a glorious commission of Catholic Americans, men and women, to stand forth fearlessly in war and in peace for the things of Christ; that the faithful fulfillment of this glorious commission will keep the American heart right with the heart of God, and in that blessed work of faith the power of our Catholic women will furnish leadership to which will rally not only the Catholic phalanxes of women but every woman citizen still trusting to the justice and love of the one Father of us all.

At the Commencement Exercises on the afternoon of June 3, the special scholastic event of the Golden Jubilee Year was the conferring of the honorary degree, Doctor of Literature, on three Denver women who had distinguished themselves in the civic and cultural life of Colorado: Mrs. Martin J. O'Fallon, Mrs. Ella Mullen Weckbaugh, and Mrs. Helen Bonfils Somnes. Mrs. O'Fallon has been for years a pre-eminent leader in Catholic women's activities in Colorado; Mrs. Weckbaugh has contributed munificently to St. Joseph's Hospital in erecting the Catherine Mullen Memorial Home for nurses and in improving other departments in the hospital; Mrs. Somnes through the *Bonfils Foundation,* established by her father, the late Frederic G. Bonfils of the *Denver Post,* has contributed to Catholic education in Colorado and has given generous benefactions to the Holy Ghost Church, the Annunciation School, and other deserving organizations in Denver.

His Excellency, the Most Reverend Joseph Corrigan, Rector of the Catholic University of America, had come from Washington, D. C., to participate in the academic program commemorating the golden jubilee exercises. The Bishop in his address to the graduates urged the necessity of realizing their spiritual responsibilities as they entered upon their duties in the world and left with them two challenging questions: "What do you think of yourselves and what does God think of you?" As a means of realizing what they should think of themselves, Bishop Corrigan exhorted the graduates to consider the element of cost which had entered into their education—values which cannot be reckoned in gold or silver and yet are far more precious: the sheltered home, the care and solicitude of God-fearing parents, the protecting atmosphere of education sanctified by religion, and the glorious endowment of consecrated lives which had made possible religious education in the United States:

What the Sisters think of you can best be measured by the completeness of their sacrifice. Every Sister who has cared for you, however her personality may have impressed you, was nevertheless supplying a very real portion of the values which go to make up this day of days. In the light of these life sacrifices, what do you think of yourselves? Will the years carry with them for you a growing sense, as life values become more clear to you, of what you have had from every Sister whose life has touched yours?

In answering the question, "What does God think of you?" Bishop Corrigan recalled Calvary as the proof of God's great love, where from the Cross He bequeathed to us His mother:

She is ours, therefore, by the last will and testament of Jesus Christ, and if ever a heritage gained solemnity and eternal sanction from the manner and circumstances of the giving, it was that legacy, bequeathed by a dying God to His sinful creatures, of His well-loved sinless mother. The beautiful light of day is born of dark, dark night; the snow white lily will grow in the common clay of earth, and that seed of benediction and glory, we must not forget, blossomed into flower for us her children in the blood-moist soil of Calvary in the very shadow of that tree which bore redemption.

The banquet on the evening of June 2 was the last social event of the jubilee year. The commencement exercises on the afternoon of June 3 brought to a close the commemorative celebrations of the year—a fitting complement to those of the preceding fifty years.

Did Mother Pancratia and her devoted companions ever envision, in their plans and dreams for a greater and wider educational field, the scene which marked that commencement of June, 1942? They have gathered here—the highest Church dignitary of the archdiocese, the Most Reverend Urban J. Vehr, in his colorful robes; the Rector of the Catholic University, the Most Reverend Joseph Corrigan, representative of the greatest Catholic educational center in the United States; the college president, professors, and instructors in historic caps, gowns, and hoods; the student body filled with laudable school pride; the candidates upon whom the president and faculty were to confer honorary degrees as part of the commemorative jubilee anniversary; and, finally, the seniors of the year, who rejoiced in the distinction of receiving their diplomas on such an auspicious day.

As the academic procession wound its way over the campus, beneath arches of magnificent trees, deciduous and evergreen, which threw long shadows over the velvety lawns, one naturally, if in retrospective mood, went back five decades, and even fewer, to the rough, arid fields, covered with cactus and sagebrush, over which the sisters and their students stumbled as they made their way through the grounds surrounding the building. The picturesque campus, bathed in the western sun, hastening to lose itself shortly behind those mountains, upon which Sister Bartholomew had gazed with appreciation that March day when the Sisters of Loretto had first visited this site and visualized its possibilities, was the result of the dreams they dreamed and the labor they placed upon themselves that their dreams might become a reality.

The program of the jubilee year, beginning November 5, 1941 and ending June 3, 1942, was planned to give honor where honor was due, namely, to the glorious achievements of the revered Mother Pancratia Bonfils, founder of Loretto Heights Academy, and the Sisters of Loretto, who began the sowing fifty years ago; also to those other sisters, who, looking at the furrows which their immediate predecessors had made, continued, even while reaping the fruits of those earlier labors, working in the same self-forgetful way.

To those most deeply concerned, the students, the alumnae, and the sisters, the jubilee year brought satisfaction.

To the students and alumnae it meant a deeper realization of the rich background of their alma mater. They were proud to be able to say, "This is my school!" But for the sisters of the community, the commencement exercises were not the end of the program. The jubilee is still in their hearts; the thanksgivings continue each day; and prayers, too, for the success of the on-coming cycle.

Realizing that a great heritage is theirs, that high standards have been entrusted to their keeping, those who have fallen heir to the history of fifty years of Catholic education pray that, while striving for future growth and development, they may always recognize what is true growth and true progress; that they may carry on the work of their institute in such a manner that the last exhortation of their holy founder, Father Nerinckx, may be fulfilled: O Loretto Sisters, let Loretto be Loretto forever! Loretto houses, Loretto labors, Loretto hardships, Loretto food, Loretto furniture, Loretto sisters, Loretto scholars!

APPENDICES

HONORARY DEGREES CONFERRED

Doctor of Letters
June 3, 1942

Mrs. Martin J. O'Fallon

Mrs. Ellen Mullen Weckbaugh

Mrs. Helen Bonfils Somnes

DEGREES WITH DISTINCTION

Summa cum laude

1927
Mary Genevieve Fuite
Mary Ann Taylor

1929
Mary Ida Petros

1930
Mary Elizabeth Donnelley
Olive Mary Horner
Madeleine Cecilia Milan
Mary Agnes O'Connor

1931
Margaret Ann O'Connor

1934
Helen Elizabeth Collins

1936
Elizabeth Eugenie Guindon

1938
Margaret Coletta Fitzpatrick

1942
Mary Kathryn Glore

Magna cum laude

1921
Mary Catherine Hayden

1924
Helen Marie Doyle

1925
Mary Margaret Carraher
Mary Madeleine Gibbons
Margaret Elizabeth Vinton

1926
Clare Frances Biglin
Bernadine Elma Hagan
Iverne Cecilia Hickey
Mary Ellen Mitchell
Mary Cecilia Sullivan
Ida Ann Uerling

1927
Eileen Joanna Barry
Helen Irene Cannon
Mary Margaret Kelly

1928
Winifred Francis Corcoran

1929
Hazel Ann Lindstrom

1930
Rose Agnes Clinton
Norma Dearhamer
Margaret Mary Keaney
Mary Evelynne Ryan

1932
Lucille Margaret Riede

1933
Mary Magdalene Klausner
Regina Miriam Montgomery

1934
Catherine Agnes Floyd
Patricia Jane Lucy

1935
Mary Kathleen Fitzpatrick
Jeanette Mary Gies
Agnes Piccoli

1937
Lucille Anne Edwards

1938
Mary Adelaide Morrow
Anna Marie Wade
Catherine Genevieve Wilson

1941
Adelaide Benita Lachowsky

Cum laude

1922
Monica Elizabeth Hayden

1924
Marie Shane Eaches
Helen Cecilia Hyland
Berenice Catherine McGroarty
Mary Agnes Shovlin
Margaret Josephine Sullivan

1925
Ethel Catherine Doss
Margaret Lucille Lucy

1926
Margaret Madonna Campbell

1927
Mary Evelyn Campbell
Loretto Agnes McGrath
Eileen Frances Solis

1928
Nellie Mae Hunt
Loretto Rose Kirk
Dorothy Marie Lonskey
Helen Elizabeth McDonald

1929
Regina Helen Black
Marie Kathryne Coffee
Loretta Ann Cook
Rose Mary Agnes Dolan
Bessie Driver
Trinidad Garcia
Elizabeth Frances Haas
Julia Ward Wooldridge

1930
Mary Louise Black
Muriel Eileen Fuite

1931
Mary Elizabeth Leslie

1932
Regina Louise Bessler
Mary Cecilia Collins
Charlotte Mae Hamburger

1932
Elizabeth Loretto O'Meara
Marie Julitta Trenchak

1935
Mary Alma Fregeau

1936
Raphael Gwynn

1937
Jewel Elizabeth McGovern
Gladys Golden O'Farrell
Ann Marie Sullivan

1938
Leone Agnes Gallagher
Jane Elizabeth Menten

1939
Mary Elizabeth Gallagher

1940
Rose Mary Cecilia Elliott
Mary Natalie Swan

1941
Pauline Marie Guindon
Mary Irene McMahon
Dorothy Jane Vogel

1942
Mary Elizabeth Eisenman

MEMBERS OF KAPPA GAMMA PI
National Catholic Honor Society

1927

Eileen Barry (Mrs. Willis D. Nutting)
Marie Fuite (Sister Mary Philibert,
S.L.)
Loretto Academy
Santa Fe, New Mexico
Mary Ann Taylor (Mrs. Dwyer F.
Smith)
104 W. 2nd Ave.
Cheyenne, Wyo.

1928

Winifred Corcoran (deceased)
Route 4
Grand Junction, Colorado
Nellie Mae Hunt (Mrs. William Kelty)
1944 Logan
Denver, Colorado
Loretto Kirk
2745 W. 37th Avenue
Denver, Colorado

1929

Bessie Driver (Mrs. Francis G. Tracey)
Carlsbad, New Mexico
Hazel Lindstrom (Mrs. John Meek)
3346 Josephine Street
Denver, Colorado
Mary Petros (deceased)
1507 Wabash
Pueblo, Colorado

1930

Mary Donnelly (Mrs. Mary Campbell)
El Paso, Texas
Mary O'Connor
635 Beech
Casper, Wyo.

1931

Mary Leslie (Mrs. Thomas Brady)
Columbia, Missouri
Margaret O'Connor
635 Beech
Casper, Wyo.

1932

Charlotte Hamburger (Mrs. James
Kelly)
4384 Winona Court
Denver, Colorado
Marie Trenchak
375 Kemble Ave.
Morristown, N. J.

1933

Regina Montgomery (Sister Agnes
Regina)
Loretto Academy
El Paso, Texas

1934

Helen Collins (Sister M. Michaela)
Loretto Academy
St. Louis, Mo.

Catherine Floyd (Mrs. George Kelly)
Patricia Lucy
2971 Grove
Denver, Colorado

1935

Mary Fitzpatrick (Mrs. L. D. Nelan)
815 Madison
Denver, Colorado
Jeanette Gies
3185 W. Denver Place
Denver, Colorado

1936

Eugenie Guindon
Fort Lupton, Colorado
Raphael Gwynn (Mrs. Anthony
Campbell)

1937

Lucille Edwards (Mrs. Fred Kirk)
Jewel McGovern
5200 Adams
Denver, Colorado

1938

Margaret Fitzpatrick (Sister Mary
Martin, C.S.J.)
St. Louis, Missouri
Adelaide Morrow (Mrs. John Merkl)
3775 Irving St.
Denver, Colorado
Anna Marie Wade (Mrs. Frank Gold)
2925 Vine
Denver, Colorado

1939

Mary Elizabeth Gallagher
Raton, New Mexico

1940

Rosemary Elliott
2520 Dahlia
Denver, Colorado
Natalie Swan
Walter Reed Memorial Hospital
Washington, D. C.

1941

Adelaide Lachowsky
2315 West Colorado Ave.
Colorado Springs, Colo.
Mary Irene McMahon
1665 Grant
Denver, Colorado
Dorothy Vogel
3529 Elizabeth
Denver, Colorado

1942

Mary Elizabeth Eisenman
1406 Monroe
Denver, Colorado
Mary Kathryn Glore
618 Lowell Blvd.
Denver, Colorado

NAMES OF SISTERS WHO HAVE LIVED AT LORETTO HEIGHTS

1891-1943

A

Mother Mary Ann Joseph Mattingly
Sister Mary Adelbert Conway
Sister Mary Adella Brocktrup
Sister Mary Agatha Wall
Sister Mary Agnes Flynn
Sister Mary Agnes Cecelia Seifert
Sister Mary Aimee Hynes
Sister Mary Alban McDonnell
Sister Mary Albert Kohn
Sister Mary Aldegonde Mitchell
Sister Mary Alexander Marie Barthel
Sister Mary Alice Carlene Roach
Sister Mary Alice Eugene Tighe
Sister Mary Alonza Smith
Sister Mary Aloyse Ellingson
Sister Aloysia Marie Blincoe
Sister Mary Alphonsine Hentzen
Sister Mary Althea Daurn
Sister Mary Amabilis Miles
Sister Mary Ambrosia Rahm
Sister Mary Amelia Therese Hultman
Sister Mary Anastasia Maloney
Sister Mary Ann Dolores Moll
Sister Mary Ann Elizabeth Butz
Sister Mary Annette Thomas
Sister Mary Ann Francis McArdle
Sister Mary Antoinette Logsdon
Sister Mary Antonina Ryan
Sister Mary Aquinas Byrne
Sister Mary Arsenia Cooper
Sister Mary Assumpta McIntosh
Sister Mary Augusta Russell
Sister Mary Aurelia Archambault

B

Sister Mary Bartholomew Nooning
Sister Mary Bathildes Skees
Sister Mary Bernice Cromwell
Sister Mary Bernadette Farhe
Sister Mary Bernadita Baukman
Sister Mary Boniface Campbell
Sister Mary Borromeo Hynes
Sister Mary Brendan Barrett
Sister Mary Brigid Fern

C

Mother Mary Clarasine Walsh
Mother Mary Consuelo Baumer
Sister Mary Cajetan Ortiz
Sister Mary Candida Cecil
Sister Mary Carmelita Mahoney
Sister Mary Carmela Ammel
Sister Mary Carmel Bohr
Sister Mary Carmelita Hodapp
Sister Mary Cassilda White
Sister Mary Catherine Patrice Laden
Sister Mary Cecille Reddin
Sister Mary Celestine Casey
Sister Christine Marie Stewart
Sister Mary Chrysostom Sullivan
Sister Mary Columba Higgins
Sister Mary Columba Gallavan
Sister Mary Conrad Hardesty
Sister Mary Consilia Brown
Sister Mary Constantia Schaub
Sister Mary Cornelia Withington
Sister Mary Cornelius Hayden
Sister Mary Corona Griesbach
Sister Mary Crispina Doyle

D

Sister Mary Davina Dunn
Sister Mary De Lourdes Le Houllier
Sister Mary De Sales Hynes
Sister Mary Dolores Faulke
Sister Doloretta Marie O'Connor
Sister Mary Dolorine Morrison
Sister Mary Doloretta Kelleher
Sister Mary Dominic Early

E

Mother Mary Evangelista Bindewald
Mother Mary Eustachia Elder
Mother Mary Edith Loughran
Sister Mary Edgar McCall
Sister Mary Edmond Fern
Sister Edwin Mary McBride
Sister Eileen Marie Heckman
Sister Elizabeth Mary Farrell
Sister Mary Elvadine Dames
Sister Mary Elzear Hall
Sister Mary Emmanuel Buckler
Sister Mary Erasmus Tharp
Sister Mary Ethelbert Owens
Sister Mary Eudocia Chacon
Sister Mary Eudocia O'Brian
Sister Mary Eulalia McFarland
Sister Mary Euphemia Maloy
Sister Mary Eutropia Toolen
Sister Mary Evodia Valdez

F

Mother Mary Francisca Lamy
Sister Mary Faber Wheat
Sister Mary Fara Peak
Sister Mary Felicia Corrigan
Sister Mary Felician Goebel
Sister Mary Fides De Lisle
Sister Mary Flaget Waller
Sister Mary Flavian Hagan
Sister Mary Flora McCauley
Sister Florence Marie Colclazier
Sister Mary Florence Wolff
Sister Mary Florian Duffy
Sister Mary Florita Thomas
Sister Mary Flosella Keating
Sister Mary Frances Aloys Hunleth
Sister Mary Frances DeChantal Mc-
  Leese
Sister Mary Frances Jane O'Toole
Sister Mary Frances Loretto Keefe
Sister Francis Marie Walsh
Sister Mary Frances Slattery
Sister Mary Frances Therese Halloran
Sister Mary Francetta Barberis
Sister Mary Francis de Sales McGarry
Sister Mary Francisca Engles

G

Sister Mary Genoveva Anson
Sister Mary Georgetta Hoermann
Sister Mary Godfrey Payne
Sister Mary Gregoria McLaughlin
Sister Mary Guadalupe Dyer
Sister Mary Joseph Scherer

H

Sister Mary Harriet Moore
Sister Mary Helena Cambron
Sister Mary Helen Charles Nolan

Sister Mary Helen Clare Fitzsimmons
Sister Mary Helen Denvir
Sister Mary Hildaberta Hayden
Sister Mary Hortensia Kruip

I

Sister Mary Ignacia Tobin
Sister Mary Ignacita Mulrennan
Sister Mary Inez Madigan
Sister Mary Innocentia Nestor
Sister Mary Irma Michelle Quinn
Sister Isabella Marie Foley

J

Sister Mary James Dowd
Sister James Marie Murphy
Sister Mary Jean Owings
Sister Josephine Marie Barrett
Sister Mary Josephine Romero
Sister Joseph Mary Hickox
Sister Mary Jovita Mills
Sister Julia Marie Van Leeuwen
Sister Mary Juliene Schaefer

K

Sister Katherine Mary Thro
Sister Mary Katherine Therese Kohl
Sister Mary Kathleen Burke
Sister Mary Kevin Coffey

L

Mother Mary Louis O'Connor
Sister Mary Lavialle Daly
Sister Mary Leocadia Dougherty
Sister Mary Ligouri Mulvihill
Sister Mary Linus Maier
Sister Mary Loretto Daugherty
Sister Mary Loretto McAuliffe
Sister Mary Louise Wise
Sister Mary Lua Kelleher
Sister Mary Lucille McMindes
Sister Lucina Marie Dunn
Sister Mary Lucretia Jager
Sister Lucy Marie Janes
Sister Mary Ludimilla Lehritter
Sister Mary Ludovica Malone
Sister Mary Luisa Romero
Sister Mary Luke Barrett

M

Sister Mary Macarius LeMaster
Sister Mary Madeleine Alexander
Sister Mary Magdalen Dietz
Sister Mary Manuela Fernandez
Sister Marie Claire Dunphy
Sister Marie Clyde Murphy
Sister Marie Lourde Conboy
Sister Mary Martina Sanchez
Sister Mary Martina Thompson
Sister Mary Martin Camp
Sister Mary John Baar
Sister Mary Menodora Wynn
Sister Mary Michael Walsh
Sister Mary Mildred Clare Grinsell
Sister Mary Miniata Robinson
Sister Miriam Judd
Sister Mary Modwena Doyle

N

Sister Mary Nerinckx Blincoe
Sister Mary Nicholas Egging
Sister Mary Norbert Parsoneault

O

Sister Mary Ositha Coming

P

Mother Mary Pancratia Bonfils
Mother Mary Praxedes Carty
Sister Mary Pancratia Madarasz
Sister Mary Pancratius Redmond

Sister Mary Paschal Doyle
Sister Mary Paula Gorman
Sister Mary Paul Glynn
Sister Mary Patrick Keating
Sister Mary Peter Joseph Lyons
Sister Mary Petra Sota

R

Sister Mary Rafaela Baca
Sister Mary Raphael McArdle
Sister Mary Raymond Gubernator
Sister Mary Rebecca Burke
Sister Mary Roberta Jarboe
Sister Mary Roberta Hardesty
Sister Romana Marie Roberts
Sister Mary Romula Dea
Sister Mary Romualda Baca
Sister Mary Romana
Sister Mary Rosann Elair
Sister Mary Rosaline Hutchins
Sister Mary Rosalie Wirthman
Sister Mary Rosaria Ortiz
Sister Mary Rose Margaret Cook
Sister Mary Rose Gertrude McAndrew
Sister Rose Miriam O'Donnell
Sister Mary Rosetta Clemens
Sister Mary Ruth Mattingly

S

Sister Mary Sergia Doyle
Sister Mary Severian Coomes
Sister Mary Sidonia McCauley
Sister Sophie Marie Hunleth
Sister Mary Stephana Courtney

T

Sister Mary Telesfora Jaromillo
Sister Mary Teresa Augusta Owings
Sister Mary Theresa Augusta Hagney
Sister Mary Teresa Joseph Cummings
Sister Mary Thecla Freid
Sister Mary Theodore Droney
Sister Theresa Marie Hentzen
Sister Thomas Marie Farris

U

Sister Mary Urban McFarland
Sister Mary Urbana Murray
Sister Mary Ursula Griffin

V

Sister Mary Valena Eppler
Sister Mary Valentina Duro
Sister Mary Valentina Garcia
Sister Mary Vicenta Gonzales
Sister Mary Victorine Gorman
Sister Mary Vida Jackson
Sister Mary Vida Gruber
Sister Mary Vincent de Paul Carr
Sister Mary Vincent Hicky
Sister Vincent Marie Bohnsack
Sister Mary Virginia Boden
Sister Mary Vitalis Forshee
Sister Mary Vivian Edelen

W

Sister Mary Walburga O'Sullivan
Sister Mary Wenceslaus Stanton
Sister Mary Wilhelmina Thonmen
Sister Mary William Ann Edelen
Sister Mary William Hogan
Sister Mary William Joseph Garcia
Sister Mary Winifred Leahy

X

Sister Mary Xavier Cunningham
Sister Mary Xavier Worland

Z

Sister Mary Zilda Hammond

SUPERIORS OF LORETTO HEIGHTS
1891-1943

Mother M. Pancratia Bonfils...November, 1891 to March, 1892
Mother Ann Joseph Mattingly...March, 1892 to June 25, 1894
Mother M. Praxedes Carty.................June 25, 1894 to Seven Sorrows, March 27, 1896
Mother M. Francisca Lamy.....................Seven Sorrows, March 27, 1896 to June, 1896
Mother M. Evangelista Bindewald..1896—1898
Mother M. Louis O'Connor...1898—1903
Mother M. Pancratia Bonfils..1903—1910
Mother Mary Edith Loughran..1910—1913
Mother M. Pancratia Bonfils..1913—1915
Mother M. Harriet Moore (Acting Superior)..1915—1916
Mother M. Clarasine Walsh...1916—1922
Mother Mary Linus Maier...1922—1925
Mother M. Eustachia Elder...1925—1329
Mother M. Consuelo Baumer...1929—1934
Mother Ann Francis McArdle...1934—1940
Sister Frances Marie Walsh...August 15, 1940

DIRECTRESSES OF LORETTO HEIGHTS ACADEMY AND PANCRATIA HALL

Sister M. Winifred Leahy (one month)...November, 1891
Sister M. Walburga O'Sullivan......................November, 1891—March, 1892
Sister Mary Kevin Coffey..1892—1893
Sister M. Roberta Jarboe..1893—1894
Sister Mary Xavier Cunningham ....1894—1895
Sister Mary Pancratia Bonfils ....1895—1903
Sister Mary Edith Loughran...1903—1910
Sister Mary Dolorine Morrison..1910—1911
Sister Mary Eulalia McFarland ....Sept., 1911—Feb., 1912
Sister Miriam Judd...Feb., 1912—June, 1912
Sister Mary Faber Wheat..1912—1913
Sister Mary Dolorine Morrison..1913—1919
Sister M. Francisca Engles...1919—1927
Sister Mary Urban McFarland..1927—1928
Sister Mary Edgar McCall..1928—1930
Sister Mary Modwena Doyle..1930—1334
Sister Helen Clare Fitzsimmons..1934—1935
Sister Mary Romula Dea..1935—1936
Sister Marie Lourde Conboy ....1936—1941

REGENTS, PRESIDENTS, DEANS, REGISTRAR
Regents

Mother M. Ann Francis McArdle...1938—1940
Sister Francis Marie Walsh...1940—

Presidents

Mother M. Clarasine Walsh...1918—1922
Mother M. Linus Maier..1922—1925
Mother M. Eustachia Elder...1925—1929
Sister M. Edmond Fern..1930—1934
Mother M. Ann Francis McArdle ....1934—1938
Paul J. Ketrick..1938—

Deans of Study

Sister M. Dolorine Morrison...1918—1934
Sister M. Frances Therese Halloran...1934—1937
Sister M. Francis de Sales McGarry...1937—

Deans of Women

Sister M. Ann Francis McArdle..1929—1932
Sister M. Francisca Engles...1932—1934
Sister M. Roberta Hardesty...1934—1937
Sister M. Frances Therese Halloran...1937—

Registrar

Sister Mary Vivian Edelen...1918—

LIST OF MOTHERS GENERAL
Loretto Motherhouse Archives

Name	Elected	In office to
Mother Ann Rhodes	June 29, 1812	Dec. 11, 1812
Mother Mary Rhodes	(Dec. 1812).	1822
⎧ Mother Juliana Wathen	Feb, 8, 1822	
	Installed March 25, 1822	1824
⎩ The first election held under Approved Constitutions Certificate of Election in Archives.		
Mother Isabella Clarke	1824	1826
Mother Sabina O'Brien	1826	1832
Mother Josephine Kelly	1832	1838
Mother Isabella Clarke	1838	1842
Mother Generose Mattingly	1842 (by Episcopal appointment)	1844
Mother Berlindes Downs	1844 (by Episcopal appointment)	1846
Mother Berlindes Downs	1846 (by election)	1852
Mother Bridget Spalding	1852—Aug. 15 (elected)	1855
Mother Bridget Spalding	1855—Aug. 15 (re-elected)	1858
Mother Berlindes Downs	1858—Aug. 15 (elected)	1861
Mother Berlindes Downs	1861—Aug. 15 (re-elected)	1864
Mother Bertha Bowles	1864—Aug. 15 (elected)	1867
Mother Bertha Bowles	1867—Aug. 15 (re-elected)	1870
Mother Elizabeth Hayden	1870—Aug. 15 (elected)	1873
Mother Elizabeth Hayden	1873—Aug. 15 (re-elected)	1876
Mother Dafrosa Smythe	1876—Aug. 15 (elected)	1879
Mother Dafrosa Smythe	1879—Aug. 15 (re-elected)	1882
Mother Ann Jos. Mattingly	1882—Aug. 15 (elected)	1885
Mother Ann Jos. Mattingly	1885—Aug. 15 (re-elected)	1888
Mother Dafrosa Smythe	1888—Aug. 15 (elected)	1891
Mother Dafrosa Smythe	1891—Aug. 15 (re-elected)	1893
Mother Catherine Connor (elected to fill	1893—Aug. 15 (for 1 yr.)	1894
unexpired term)	1894—Aug. 15 (elected)	March 1896
Mother Praxedes Carty (By Episcopal appointment—1896—March 21)		1898

By Election

Name	Elected	In office to
Mother Praxedes Carty	1898—July 16	1901
Mother Praxedes Carty	1901—July 16	1904
(First election according to newly approved Constitutions.)		
Mother Praxedes Carty	1904—July 26 (for 6 yrs.)	1910
Mother Praxedes Carty	1910—July 16	1916
Mother Praxedes Carty	1916—July 16	1922
Mother Clarasine Walsh	1922—July 17	1928
Mother Olivette Norton	1928—July 16	1934
Mother Olivette Norton	1934—July 16	1940
Mother Edwarda Ashe	1940—July 16	

PROGRAM OF FIRST EXHIBITION

Denver Republican, June 16, 1892

Program of First Exhibition **Denver Republican,** June 16, 1892
The evidences of culture in art are many, and the display is a creditable one, alike to scholars and teachers. Among the pieces of art work especially worthy of mention are the following:

Large panels in oil by Georgia Weinberg, Nellie Stockbridge, and Olive Fort; an oil painting by Emelia Gallegos, a little Spanish maiden of thirteen years; a dog's head in water color by Emma Bowen; plush table scarf by Henrietta Coghlan; donkey in crayon by Elsie Gustorf; "The Little Friar" by Maude Seek; "The Monarch of the Glen" and "The Victor of the Glen," two magnificent stag-figure crayons, by Emma Bowen and Olive Fort; piano scarfs in plush, oil painted and embroidered by Adelien Tynan and Olive Fort: fire screens by Nellie Stockbridge, Emelia Gallegos, and Rebecca Salazar; beautiful combination box in corn-colored silk, kid bound and hand painted, by Georgia Weinberg; oil painting by Stella McPhee.

Piano Recital ....Mendelssohn
    Misses E. Gallegos, E. Gusdorf, L. Wisch, T. Montague, M. Chamberlain, J. McPhee, J. McAdams, K. Brennan, N. Montague, B. Porter, M. Becker, and M. Seek

Everything's Laid on Me..Junior Vocal Class

Piano..Miss J. McPhee

Bestowal of Graduating Honors on...
          Misses Olive Fort and Katherine Casey

Sub-Graduating Honors on ....
          Miss Nellie Stockbridge

Loretto Heights Orchestra Recital..
    Organ: Misses K. Casey and E. Mullen
    Violin: Miss L. Fort
    Zither: Miss N. Stockbridge
    Guitars: Misses G. O'Neil, S. McPhee, M. Richards, L. Winstanley and M. Scott
    Mandolins: Misses O. Fort, G. Weinberg, A. Duffly, M. Miller and C. Mills
    Banjos: Misses J. McKinley, L. Becker, M. Seek, and N. Montague

Recitation, Robert of Sicily ....Miss G. Weinberg

Rondo All 'Ongarese Duet..Hayden
    Misses M. Thorpe, S. McPhee, A. Duffly, J. McKinley, L. Becker, C. Mills, L. Winstanley, and M. Richards

Vocal Duet, Voices of the Night.....................................Glover
        Young Ladies' Vocal Class; Piano, Miss M. Miller

March Sentimentale, Trio...Muller
    Misses S. White, J. McAdams, H. Coghlan, E. Gallegos, B. O'Neil, Stella Nelson, A. Reilly, M. Scott, J. McPhee, N. Montague, S. Scherrer and M. Seek

Fairy Revel Drill and Vocal Duet...................................H. Lotner
        Piano, Miss G. O'Neil
    Fairies: Queen, Miss M. Miller; Misses M. Wone, M. Ducey, N Montague, M. Seek, S. Nelson, K. Brennan, K, Stark, L. Winstanley, M. Scott, L. Becker, E. Gallegos, M. Weidman, A. Reilly, and S. White

PROGRAM OF FIRST EXHIBITION—(Continued)

Flower Girls: T. Montague, M. Reilly, J. McAdams, M. Becker, L. Fort, M. Smith, A. Summers, M. Lancaster, B. Porter, B. O'Neil, E. Gusdorf and K. White.

Archers: J. McPhee, S. Scherrer, H. Summers, B. McCabe, M. Chamberlain, L. Wisch, C. Palmer, F. O'Connor, P. Lowthian, B. Maloney

Aurora..Miss E. Mullen

Piano Recital, Norma Duo..Thalberg
      Misses G. O'Neil, O. Fort, N. Stockbridge, and H. Garland

Naughty Little Kittens..Little Girls' Vocal Class
               Piano, Miss B. Porter

Loretto Heights Orchestra Medley..Original

Essay—Self-Culture, the Reward of Labor..
             Miss Katherine Casey

Piano Recital, Die Italienerin in Algier....................................Rossini
    Misses G. O'Neil, S. McPhee, H. Gartland, C. Mills, K. Casey, E. Mullen, M. Miller, J. McKinley

Magnificat Quartet ....Mozart
        Vocal Class; Organ, Miss H. Gartland

Valedictory..Miss Olive Fort

The following medals were awarded by the Reverend Father Malone and Bishop Matz: Graduating prizes of laurel crown and gold medal to Miss Olive Fort and Katherine Casey. Half crown awarded to Miss Nellie Stockbridge. For good conduct, allotted to Mary Richards from Rev. P. A. Phillips. For diligence, presented by Thomas H. O'Neil, to Olive Fort, Katherine Casey, Nellie Stockbridge, Julia McKinley, Ursaline Nulint, Anna Riley, Ellen Mullen, Mayme Miller, Mary Richards, Georgia Weinberg, Stella McPhee, Caroline Mills, Laura Becker, Elizabeth Winstanley, Maud Seek, Emelia Gallegos, Stella Nelson, Nellie Montague, Jennie McAdams, and Elsie Gusdorf; drawn by Jennie McAdams.

Medal for neatness in work, presented by Thomas H. O'Neil. Allotted to Olive Fort, Katherine Casey, Nellie Stockbridge, Anna Riley, Helen Gartland, Laura Becker, Caroline Mills, Elizabeth Winstanley, Nellie Montague, Marie Wone, Georgia Weinberg, Stella McPhee, Maud Seek, Emelia Gallegos, Rebecca Salazar, Stella Nelson, Ella Mullen, Mayme Miller, and Mary Richards; drawn by Olive Fort.

Medal of Art Work, presented by J. G. Smith, allotted to Katherine Casey, Olive Fort, Georgia Weinberg, Ellen Mullen, Nellie Stockbridge, Maud Seek, Rebecca Salazar, and Emelia Gallegos; drawn by Nellie Stockbridge.

Prizes of books were awarded Cora Palmer for Christian Doctrine, Hattie Becker for diligence, Stella Scherrer for neatness, and Belinda Maloney for the greatest proficiency among the little girls of the school.

GRADUATES OF LORETTO HEIGHTS and PANCRATIA ACADEMY

Class 1892
Kate Casey
Ollie Fort

Class 1893
Mae Dahoney

Class 1894
Georgie Weinberg

Class 1895
Amelia Gallegos
Ella Mullen
Stella Nelson

Class 1896
Kate Gilgallon
Kizzie Mann
Minnanne McDonald
May Mullen
Christine Schintz

Class 1897
Mamie Carroll
Ethel Jordan
Blanch O'Neil
Emma Vizina

Class 1898
Lockey Fort (deceased)
Mamie Horrigan
Clara L'Abbe
Pauline Peyton
Mamie Ryan
Sara Salmon

Class 1899
Honor Breen
Nelle Gilgallon
Catherine Mullen

Class 1900
Nelle Finnerty
Rosamond Pryor
Eileen Sullivan

Class 1901
Louise Seeberger

Class 1902
Marie Berry
Margaret Fallon
Lucille Moore

Class 1904
Ethelle Corson
Marie Foley
Mabel Grimes

Class 1905
Mayo Bransom
Mamie Mackin
Elisa Salazar

Class 1906
Leonore Durkee
Marion Harwood

Class 1907
Estelle Desserich
Anna Dick
Marie Enneking
Grace Judge

Class 1908
Vina Fern Byron
Salina Casey
Irene Hartford
Rebecca Henrigues
Dora McCoy
Marie Murphy

Class 1909
Ethel Enright
Lottie Fowles
Ella Menke
Grace Warshauer

Class 1910
Margaret Connolly
Ida Heibler
Genevieve Morrison

Class 1911
Mary Cassell
Gladys Menke
Violante Rapson
Alma Redmond
Cassilda Salazar
Nora Schang

Class 1912
Dorothy Adams
Emma Archuleta
Nellie Bowles
Catherine Brady
Ruth Carroll
Angeline Durocher
Eulalia Loomis
Hazel Menke
Agnes Neuer
Elizabeth Prince
Ismena Roper

Class 1913
Alice Marie Davoren
Angelic Early
Helen Enright
Helen Howard
Frances Keefe
Teresa Loisel Lange
Frances Loomis
Orpha Ritter
Helen Ross

Class 1914
Gladys Browns
Helene Buehler
Doris Stuart
Olive Trail
Mildred Welch

Class 1915
Hazel Hewitt
Madeleine Keefe
Janet Matthews
Ina McMahon
Jeannette Speiss
Lotus Watts

Class 1916
Agnes Berry
Dorothy Besse
Josephine Casey
Vada Fennell
Anna Gill

ACADEMY GRADUATES—(Continued)

Emma Hill
Isabelle Horan
Elizabeth Keefe
Helen Lopez
Eva Toole

Class 1917

Nancy Van Deusen
Mildred Gireaud
Dorothy Hatch
Evelyn L'Abbe
Mary McDonald
Gertrude Norman
Anna Rittmayer
Genevieve Rittmayer

Class 1918

Grace Bransom
Wilhelmena Cordona
Alice Croke
May Guireaud
Irene Johnson
Helen Kehn
Lucille Mannix
Pauline Nelson
Mary P. Queen
Patrice Richards
Mary Shaw
Muriel Turnbull

Class 1919

Frances Conway
Claire Corning
Edna Ferris
Cecilia Gallegos
Hannah Gross
Martha Manty
Ruth McFarland
Dorothy Platt
Virginia Rice
Phyllis Udick

Class 1920

Erin La Bissoniere
Lucille Croke
Florence Donnelly
Helen Doyle
Marie Eaches
Corinne Espinoza
Marjorie Grimes
Pauline Hite
Frances McGarry
Mary McGregor
Elsie Mahoney
Virginia Paradise
Mary Reddin
Belinda Salazar

Class 1921

Kathleen Andrew
Georgena Burns
Margaret Dunn
Thelma Everitt
Maryette Fitch
Hester Holland
Elizabeth Offerman
Sara O'Keefe
Rose Marie McGinley
Catherine Rose
Margaret Smith
Lolalee Tomblin
Roslyn Vurpillat
Pauline Whitman
Vivian Wilson

Class 1922

Ida Chase
Helen Croke
Dorothy Doyle

Genevieve Funk
Marie Hamilton
Bernice Mecum
Alice O'Neil
Bernadine O'Neil
Louise Paggi
Anne Pendergast
Alice Powers
Katherine Ryan
Anna Scariano
Josephine Schneible
Treva Williams
Shirley Wood

Class 1923

Frances Blake
Margaret Brown
Loretto Delehanty
Mary Ford
Florence Henry
Doris Howes
Rosella Johnson
Virginia Porter
Helen Stahl
Dolores Strutzel

Class 1924

Queena Aulgur
Angela Ayola
Ursula Fagan
Juanita Hagan
Helene Hall
Theresa May Hample
Mary Keegan
Mildred O'Neil
Enaze Porter
Eulalia Reagan
Mary Tracy
Eileen Whisler

Class 1925

Corinne C. de Baca
Catherine Clements
Catherine Croke
Helen Doyle
Ruth Ellis
Ada Emerich
Bernice Garwood
Charlene Garwood
Mary Charlotte Hannig
Evelyn Kipferl
Eleanor McKelvey
Mary O'Loughlin
Elizabeth Swift
Charlotte Temple
Helen Tubbs
Evelyn Waldo
Julia Wooldridge

Class 1926

Margaret Barney
Ethel Beringer
Mary Cassidy
Marguerite Dolan
Marjorie Edman
Alice Jane Evans
Kathaleen Feeney
Sally Fisher
Elizabeth Gartland
Mary Elizabeth Gaule
Sidney Graybeal
Marguerite Hall
Bernice Lattin
Mary Ledford
Naomi Lilja
Emily McKeon
Madeline Milan
Lena Rogers
Alice Staunton

ACADEMY GRADUATES—(Continued)

Class 1927
Margaret Allen
Louise C. de Baca
Rachel Berry
Helen Chambers
Rose Doyle
Dorothy Duffes
Madelynne Erickson
Helen Fairfield
Hilda Gallagher
Paula Garcia
Mary Heffron
Catherine McMullen
Leanore Ostrander
Marie Pigeon
Isabel Ward

Class 1928
Prue Avery
Marguerite Baca
Mae Carney
Dorothy Coon
Dorothy Ennis
Mae Irene Gish
Helen Gallagher
Eunice Lopez
LuBerta McClung
Helen McGraw
Louise McMahan
Marquette Spence
Mercia Walker

Class 1929
Martha Berger
Rosemary Cassidy
Suzan Cassidy
Margaret Cole
Margaret Hesse
Trinidad Lopez
Welma Meyer
Clara Mueller
Laura Oswald
Marguerite Roy
Margaret Runsteller
Pauline Smith
Ruth Thomas
Josephine Wardell

Class 1930
(Last class from old
Building)
Helen Bugas
Marian Church
Catherine Eickhoff
Fay G. Hougham
Patricia E. Kenehan
Monta Irene Kohler
Grace L. Mahoney
Orpha June Mawher
Catherine McClure
Helen McKelvey
Julia L. Smead
Virginia A. Vyse

Class 1931
Leonore Carney
Edith Dunn
Ruth Hughes
Dorothy Karasiewic
Rose Nelson
Esther Thomas
Eileen Vezina
Edna May Weller

Class 1932
Lucille Allen
Charlotte Beeby
Florence Burke
Margaret M. Dahl
Eugenie Guindon

Rosalie McBride
Dolores McConnell
Marie Rosa Ortiz
Mary Margaret Tobin

Class 1933
Dorothy Aley
Mary Kate Bland
Ruth Church
Theresa Connelley
Helen Deutsch
Eleanor Esser
Mildred Hines
Marian Lower
Mary Kathryn Russell
Helen Tobin

Class 1934
Jean Baumer
Ellen Rita Milan
Genevieve Mollands
Cassilda Romero
Mary Elizabeth Schreiber
Eleanor Swezey

Class 1935
Laurette Allen
Elizabeth Jane Bent
Laura Mae Givan
Martha Jane Kaiser
Blanche Knights
Bernice Evans Lyon
Mary Agnes Milan
Lucila Ortiz
Mary Cecille Romero
Lina Beatrice Roybal

Class 1936
Louise Doherty
Margaret Durocher
Gladys Givan
Jennie Lege
Mary Josephine Lege
Kathleen McDonald
Magdalena Ortiz
Violet Roybal
Rafaelita Simpson
Shirley Marie Sullivan

Class 1937
Pauline Guindon
Dorothy Jean Stovall
Anna Margaret Zook

Class 1938
Lorraine Gasser
Helen Madeleine Gordon
Margaret Jean Irvin
Shirley Kalotta

Class 1939
Isabelle Gomez
Katherine Esther Gust
Bonnie Daisy Kolb
Betty Jo McConnell
Marie Amada Pena
Martha Adelena Yantarno
Betty Norine Zinn

Class 1940
Mary Katherine Brown
Peggy Jane Keown
Ana Avelina Pena
Bonnie Jean Meyers

Class 1941
Ruth Elizabeth Graber
Sara Jane Greer
Ophelia Gomez
Dixie Lee Howard
Constance Kanable

LORETTO HEIGHTS COLLEGE STUDENTS
WHO ENTERED RELIGION

LORETTO HEIGHTS COLLEGE GRADUATES WHO ENTERED RELIGION

Sister Agnes Regina, S.L...Regina Montgomery
Sister Mary Aquinas, S.C.L...Mary Elizabeth Haas
Sister Ann Rupert, S.C.L...Mary Clare Meek
Sister Bonaventure, O.S.F...Mary Elizabeth Hanson
Sister Bernadette Marie, S.C...Bernice McGroarty
Sister Mary Bernice, S.C...Loretto McGrath
Sister Mary Calixta, O.P...Clare Biglin
Sister Charles Helen, S.C...Dorothy Lonskey
Sister Celestine, R.S.M...Adelle Clements
Sister Celine of the Trinity, D.C...Mary Hayden
Sister Francetta, S.C.L...Mary O'Donnell
Sister Mary Gabriella, L.H.M...Margaret Bensberg
Sister Lucy Maurice, S.L...Mary Agnes Galvin
Sister Marie Clare, S.L...Claire Dunphy
Sister Mariella, S.L...Mary Collins
Sister Marineil, S.L...Isobel Mahoney
Sister Mary Martin, C.S.J...Margaret Fitzpatrick
Sister Miriam Jerome, S.L...Mary Stout
Sister Maura, S.L...Madonna Campbell
Sister Mary St. William, G.S...Anna McGlone
Sister Michaela, S.L...Helen Collins
Sister Naomi, S.L...Elizabeth O'Meara
Sister Pauline Marie, S.L...Pauline Smith
Sister M. Philibert, S.L...Marie Fuite
Sister Rose Patricia...Helen Doyle
Sister Mary Rosalie, S.L...Rosemary Elliott

LORETTO HEIGHTS COLLEGE STUDENTS WHO ENTERED RELIGION

Sister Mary Charleen, S.L...Mary Keaney
Sister Mary Charlesana, S.L...Mary B. Barbour
Sister Edward Mary, S.L...Mary Alice Ely
Sister Mary Elaine, S.L...Alice McLaughlin
Sister Esther Marie, S.L...Esther Goodrow
Sister Mary Flaget, S.L...Eve Waller
Sister Francis Cecille, S.L...Mary Hanrahan
Sister Francis de Sales, S.L...Frances McGarry
Sister Mary Geralda, S.L...Nellie Trainor
Sister Mary Luke, S.L...Ruth Tobin
Sister Richard Marie, S.L...Vivian Barbour
Sister Alice Catherine, S.C...Alice Vogt
Sister Charles Marie, C.S.J...Marjorie Reifsnyder
Sister David Marie, S.L...Agnes Lallamant
Sister Mary Esther, S.L...Mary Margaret Conter
Sister Mary Francella, S.L...Marcella Vollmer
Sister Mary Janice, C.S.J...Ruth Yeggy
Sister James Ellen, S.C...Eileen Ferriter
Sister Jean Patrice, S.L...Olive Golden
Sister Mary Charles, S.L...Betty Ward
Sister Margretta, S.L...Helen Doyle
Sister Miriam, S.L...Ruth O'Brien
Sister Marie Therese, S.C...Helen Darcy
Sister Matilda, S.C...Matilda Jaggers
Sister Teresa Ann, S.L...Catherine Reardon
Sister Mary Edmunda, C.S.J...Lucille Mulligan
Sister Catherine Marie, S.L...Catherine Pohndorf

LORETTO HEIGHTS COLLEGE STUDENTS WHO
ENTERED RELIGION—(Continued)

LORETTO HEIGHTS ACADEMY GRADUATES WHO ENTERED RELIGION

Sister Agnes Dolores, S.C.	Agnes Neuer
Sister M. Alma, S.L.	Mamie Carroll
Sister Ancilla Marie, S.L.	Florence Burke
Sister Ann Loretto, S.C.L.	Leonore Carney
Sister Anna Margaret, S.L.	May Carney
Sister Annetta, S.L.	Theresa May Hampel
Sister Athanasia, S.L.	Marie Hamilton
Sister Ceceille, S.L.	Mary Reddin
Sister M. Clement, S.L.	Eileen Whisler
Sister Marie Clyde, S.L.	Marie Murphy
Sister Frances Loretto, S.L.	Madeleine Keefe
Sister Mary Jane, S.L.	Jeanette McDonald
Sister Joan of Bl. Sac., Notre Dame de Namur	Mary Kate Bland
Sister Kathleen Marie, S.L.	Marie Foley
Sister Lorene, S.L.	Gladys Browns
Sister Martha, S.L.	Alma Redmond
Sister Menodora, S.L.	Kate Casey
Sister Michelle, S.L.	Marguerite Dolan
Sister Teresa, S.L.	Esther Thomas
Sister Mary Norbert, S.L.	Clare Personeault
Sister Pancratia, S.L.	Irma Madrasz
Sister Pancratius, S.L.	May Redmond
Sister Mary Susette, R.S.M.	Mary Kintzley
Sister Felician, O.S.F., R.I.P.	Loretto Owens
Sister Ann Dolores, S.S.J.	Florence Fuller
Sister Marcella, S.L.	Irene Valentian
Sister Alice Vincent, S.C.L.	Mary Downey
Sister Thomasetta, S.L.	Celestine Olivas
Sister Bernadette Marie, R.S.M.	Leona Coming
Sister Ositha, S.L., R.I.P.	Alphonsine Coming
Sister Macarius, S.L.	Anna Le Master

GRADUATES OF LORETTO HEIGHTS COLLEGE

1921

Mary Catherine Hayden

1922

June

Monica Elizabeth Hayden

August 2

Sister Mary Helen Denvir
Sister Marguerite Marie Donnelly
Sister Mary Aloyse Ellingson
Sister Mary Zilda Hammond
Sister Mary Linus Maier
Sister Mary Urban McFarland
Sister Mary Matthias Wall

1923

June 2

Catherine Cecelia Byrne (Mrs. Henry
  Humes)
Mary Lucille Mannix (Mrs. N. J. O'Dea)
Mary Margaret Stout

August 2

Sister Mary Aloysius Adams
Sister M. Bernice Cromwell
Sister Maureen O'Connell (China,
  Shanghai)
Sister Mary Grace O'Shaughnessy
  (Deceased)

1924

June

Sarah Delette Coy (Mrs. Charles
  Turnbull)
Helen Marie Doyle (Mrs. J. J. Johnson)
Marie Shane Eaches (Mrs. Marcus
  Travis)
Helen Cecelia Hyland
Bernice Catherine McGroarty
Mary Agnes Shovlin
Margaret Josephine Sullivan
Laura Surilda Wilson (Mrs. W. H.
  Closky)

August 2

Sister Rose Cyril Callahan
Sister M. Gerald Farrell
Sister Mary Brigid Fern
Sister M. Dafrosa Grimes
Sister Roberta Hardesty
Sister Mary Aimee Hynes (deceased)
Sister Ignacita Mulrennan
Sister Lilliana Owens
Sister Mary Jean Owings
Sister Mary Martha Redmond
Sister Antonina Ryan

1925

June 2

Mary Margaret Carrahar (Mrs. Gene
  McCormick)
Mary Adele Clements
Ethel Catherine Doss
Mary Madeline Gibbons
Margaret Lucille Lucy (Mrs. Henry
  Jacques)
Anne Delia New (Mrs. Walker)
Margaret Elizabeth Vinton

August 2

Sister Teresine Byrne
Sister Georgianna Ernst

1926

June 2

Clare Frances Biglin
Margaret Madonna Campbell
Bernadine Elma Hagan (deceased)
Iverne Cecilia Hickey
Mary Ellen Mitchell
Isabelle Agnes O'Drain
Mary Cecilia Sullivan (Mrs. Albert R.
  Spillman)
Ida Ann Uerling

August 2

Sister M. Florence Corrigan (deceased)
Sister Borromeo Hynes
Sister Frances Loretto Keefe
Sister Mary Thelma Nast
Sister Frances Jane O'Toole
Sister M. Orline Tepfer

1927

June 2

Eileen Joanna Barry (Mrs. Willis D.
  Nutting)
Margaret Bensberg
Mary Evelyn Campbell (Mrs. N.
  Lawrence, deceased)
Helen Irene Cannon
Mary Genevieve Fuite
Mary Margaret Kelly (Mrs. Frances
  Curtis)
Loretta Agnes McGrath
Patricia Fabiola Ross (Mrs. E. J.
  Connell)
Eileen Frances Solis (Mrs. Frieberger)
Mary Ann Taylor (Mrs. Dwyer Smith)

August 2

Sister M. Malachy Kerrnan
Sister Peter Joseph Lyons
Sister Ethelbert Owens
Sister Felicitas Quinliven
Sister Melissa Rourke
Sister Mary Frances Slattery

1928

June

Winifred Frances Corcoran (deceased)
Winifred Irene Friel (Mrs. F. Curran)
Nellie Mae Hunt (Mrs. Wm. Kelty)
Mary Ellen Keegan (Mrs. Ed. K. Bare)
Loretta Rose Kirk
Dorothy Marie Lonskey
Helen Elizabeth McDonald

August

Sister Francis de Sales McGarry
Sister Mary Rose Rodman
Sister Florita Thomas

1929

June

Catherine Mary Bailey
Regina Helen Black
Rosalie Helen Buchmann (Mrs. Martin
  Newhoff)
Marie Kathryne Coffey (Mrs. John
  Dinan)
Loretta Ann Cook
Rosemary Agnes Dolan
Bessie Driver (Mrs. Francis Tracy, Jr.)
Trinidad Garcia
Elizabeth Frances Haas

GRADUATES OF LORETTO HEIGHTS COLLEGE
(Continued)

Mary Tumpam Judge (Mrs. O'Neil Smith)
Hazel Anne Lindstrom (Mrs. John F. Meek)
Mary Ida Petros (deceased)
Mary Katherine Reardon
Evelyn Laura Taylor
Julia Ward Wooldridge (Mrs. Paul Dunn)

August

Sister M. Hilaria Alton
Sister Francetta Barberis
Sister M. Ursula Griffin
Sister M. Constantia Schaub (deceased)
Sister Fabiola Wood

1930
June

Mary Louise Black (Mrs. John Beeston, Jr.)
Rose Agnes Clinton
Norma Dearhamer
Mary Elizabeth Donnelly (Mrs. M. Campbell)
Helen Mary Finn (Mrs. Leo Boyle)
Muriel Eileen Fuite
Mary Elizabeth Gaule (Mrs. John Barry)
Olive Mary Horner
Margaret Mary Keaney
Jewel Dorothy Keating (Mrs. Lester Cowan)
Madeline Cecilia Milan
Mary Agnes O'Connor
Mary Evelyn Ryan (Mrs. Ed. J. Schiefen)

August

Sister Mary Matilda Barrett
Sister Mary Ricarda Blincoe
Sister Modwena Doyle
Sister Mary Hubert Hentzgen
Sister Frances de Chantal McLeese
Sister Ramona Marie Roberts
Sister Geralda Trainor
Sister Mary Flaget Waller

1931
June

Grace Agnes Bryan (Mrs. Glen Dickman)
Mary Patricia Cassidy
Rose Marie Doyle
Agnes Agatha Fladung
Hilda Mary Gallagher
Josephine Bernice Lattin (Mrs. Miles Milan)
Mary Elizabeth Leslie (Mrs. Tom Brady)
Alvena Alexander Leversedge (Mrs. T. Burnite)
Marie Elizabeth McNamara (Mrs. James Creamer)
Mary Margaret Moffit
Margaret Anne O'Connor
Helen Mary Sullivan (Mrs. P. Dowling)
Jane Winburn (Mrs. James Close)

August

Sister Mary Theodore Droney
Sister Frances Therese Halloran
Sister Lilliosa Kelly

1932

Sister Florian Duffy
Sister Lucy Marie James

June

Edith Bernadine Bensberg (Mrs. M. Taylor)
Regina Louise Bessler (Mrs. Cletus Charron)
Louise Marie Chesire
Mary Cecilia Collins
Helen Agnes Gallagher
Mary Agnes Galvin
Charlotte Mae Hamburger (Mrs. James Kelly)
Frances Margaret McCarty (Mrs. Patrick Callahan)
Anna Margaret McGlone
Helen Jane McGraw
Elizabeth Loretta O'Meara
Lucille Margaret Riede (Mrs. H. Montgomery)
Marie Helen Stillhammer
Claire Ellen Sullivan
Marie Julita Trenchak

August

Sister Mary James Dowd
Sister Helen Clare Fitzsimmons
Sister Fredric Glassmeyer
Sister Mildred Clare Grinsell
Sister Eileen Marie Heckman
Sister Rose Theresa Soran

1933
June

Marjorie Mary Cannon (Mrs. Frederick Vernon Murphy)
Laura Winifred Espy
Mary Frances Geraldine Gray
Mary Magdaline Klausner (Mrs. Martin Schoeneman)
Mary Ellen Maginnis (Mrs. C. E. Fleming)
Regina Isabelle McMindes (Mrs. Jeremiah Murphy)
Virginia Elizabeth McMindes (Mrs. Lymann Bagge)
Isabelle Martha McNamara
Regina Miriam Montgomery
Marcella Ann Murphy (Mrs. James Tuttle)
Mary Margaret O'Donnell
Mary Jane Peconi
Pauline Katherine Smith
Geraldine Margaret Sullivan (deceased)

August

Sister Dominica Gannon
Sister Matthew Marie Grennan
Sister Columba Higgins
Sister Ceciliana McDonald

1934
June

Marguerite Mary Bisbing
Rose Mary Bradasich
Elizabeth Evelyn Briggs (Mrs. Joseph Lewter)
Regina M. Coll (Mrs. Louis C. de Baca)
Helen Elizabeth Collins
Margaret Mary Connelly (Mrs. Tom Walsh)
Elizabeth Frances Cullen (Mrs. Mart Saya)
Catherine Agnes Floyd (Mrs. George Kelly)
Marie Gazzolo
Mary Elizabeth Hanson

GRADUATES OF LORETTO HEIGHTS COLLEGE
(Continued)

Patricia Jane Lucy
Mary Frances Nieters
Ruth Frances Peterson (Mrs. Joseph Budd)
Sarah Williams

August

Sister Leon Albin
Sister Elaine McLoughlin
Sister Mary Luke Tobin
Sister Imelda Wallace

1935
June

Claire Teresa Dunphy
Margaret Mary Dunphy (Mrs. Ed. Lowry)
Mary Katherine Fitzpatrick (Mrs. Louis D. Nelan)
Mary Alma Fregeau
Jeanette Mary Gies
Mary Evelyn Kirby (Mrs. E. K. Wilson)
Isobel Frances Mahoney
Lorraine Mary O'Meara
Agnes Piccoli (Mrs. Leo Donovan)

August

Sister Rose Celeste Block
Sister Mary de Pazzi Burns
Sister Harriet Condon
Sister Mary Elizabeth Haggerson
Sister Mary Sodelbia Hughes

1936
June

Ellen Mary Campbell
Jane Carroll (Mrs. Frank Lammerman)
Eugenie Guindon
Raphael Gwynn (Mrs. Anthony Campbell)
Kathryn Lewis (Mrs. Paul J. Foehl)
Mary J. O'Donnell

August

Sister Richard Marie Barbour
Sister Dorothy Ann Dunn
Sister Frances Aloys Hunleth
Sister Michael Marie Lyons
Sister Marie O'Flaherty
Sister Aquinata Mitchell
Sister Mary Norbert Personeault
Sister Ann Thomas Roach

1937
June

Joan Catherine Ayres (Mrs. P. O'Brien)
Marcella Eleanor Colburn
Lucille Anne Edwards (Mrs. Fred Kirk)
Irene Catherine Friel
Jewel Elizabeth McGovern
Gladys Golden O'Farrell
Mary Catherine St. John (Mrs. Joseph Krebs)
Anne Marie Sullivan (Mrs. Sven Reher)
Agnes Josephine Weber (Mrs. Tom Neal)

August

Sister Alphonsa Marie Boone
Sister Mary Gregory Maloney
Sister Gerald Marie O'Connor

1938
June

Margaret Colette Fitzpatrick
Marie Antonia Floyd (Mrs. R. Gushurst)
Leona Agnes Gallagher (Mrs. Thomas Wood)
Marjorie Ellen Gray
Mary Clare Meek
Jane Elizabeth Menten (Mrs. Cyril Elkins)
Ellen Rita Milan (Mrs. Robert White)
Clare Loretta Mooney
Mary Adeliade Morrow (Mrs. John Merkle)
Hazel Clare Murphy
Kathleen Elizabeth O'Hare
Mary Cecilia Pagano
Doris Jane Porter (Mrs. Stanley Hall, Jr.)
Maxyne Isabelle Rogers (Mrs. Charles D. Keller)
Catherine Teresa Thackrey
Anna Marie Wade (Mrs. Frank Gold)
Madaline Elizabeth Weber
Clare Margaret Werle (Mrs. T. Bach)
Genevieve Catherine Wilson (Mrs. Edward Lyons)

August

Sister Mary Charlesana Barbour
Sister Helen Therese Blum
Sister Virgil Marie Jagemann
Sister Margaret Loyola Scanlan
Sister Virgil Thomas
Ruth A. Yont

1939
June

Mary Maxine Davis (Mrs. Alvin Simms)
Martha Ellen Dea
Dorothy Ann Evers
Mary Elizabeth Gallagher
Madelyn Prudence Nickolds (Mrs. Hedrick Alex)
Theresa Elizabeth Pagano
Nancy Gregory Quintana
Patsy Ann Savage (Mrs. T. Verdieck)
Margaret Irene Toohey
Virginia Elizabeth Vollmar (Mrs. Thomas Shoncey)

1940
June

Frances Ann Childers (Mrs. Rawlings Poole)
Rosemary Elliott
Veronica Gegan
Gladys Givan
Helen M. Kelly
Rosalie Lawrenson
Geraldine Macauley
Margaret A. Mahoney
Ann Elizabeth Monaghan
Eva Sydney Monoghan
Margaret Anna Mullen
Mercedes Riordan
Dorothy L. Starbuck
Natale Swan
Gertrude Walters

August

Sister Edward Mary Ely
Sister Esther Marie Goodrow

GRADUATES OF LORETTO HEIGHTS COLLEGE
(Continued)

Sister Frances Cecille Hanrahan
Sister Charleen Keaney
Sister Marie Therese Koch
Sister Alice Carlene Roach
Sister Mary Clement Whisler

1941

June

Marie Anastasia C. de Baca
Sister Adella Brochtrup
Dorothy Ann Cudmore
Mary Ellen Green
Pauline Marie Guindon
Virginia Mary Hornig
Elizabeth Emma Kelley
Adelaide Benita Lachowsky
Rose Marie Lucy
Merylmarie McAvoy
Mary Irene McMahon
Flora Louise Meek
Helen Ann Nieters
Mary Catherine O'Byrne
Leah Ann Pape
Mary Margaret Qualkenbush
Margaret Rose See
Barbara Katherine Sparn
Ferne Vivian Tooke
Dorothy Jane Vogel
Marguerite Amelia Wathen
Elizabeth Germaine Woodman
Margaret Zook

August

Sister Rose Maureen Saunders
Sister Elvira Rogers

1942

June

Ellen Rita Abegg
Virginia Margaret Bailey
Kathryn M. Blodgett
Angela Alberta Eisenman
Mary Elizabeth Eisenman
Laura Mae Givan
Kathryn Glore
Helen Mary Haddican
Mary Kay Hagerty
Isabel Elaine King
Helen Marie Mahoney
Patricia Ann McLaughlin
Peggy Nieters
Catherine O'Donnell
Dorothy Marie Popish
Emma Madelene Romano
Betty Schroll
Adelaide Marie Semmelmann
Kathleen Creighton Sheil
Margaret Jean Singer
Josephine Walsh

August

Sister Rose Rita Bailey
Sister Marianna Harkins
Sister M. Monica Hughes

SISTERS OF LORETTO BURIED IN THE CONVENT
CEMETERY ON LORETTO HEIGHTS GROUNDS

January, 1943

Sister M. Augustina Chaves
Born, 1842; Died, June 15, 1870
In the 11th year of her religious life
St. Mary's Academy, Denver, Colo.

Sister M. Peter Joseph Benavedz
Born, 1844; Died, July 2, 1872
In the 4th year of her religious life
St. Mary's Academy, Denver, Colo.

Sister M. Ignatia James
Born, 1853; Died, June 13, 1884
In the 12th year of her religious life
St. Mary's Academy, Denver, Colo.

Sister M. Jerome Murphy
Born, 1834; Died, June 3, 1885
In the 26th year of her religious life
St. Mary's Academy, Denver, Colo.

Sister M. Joachim Houlehin
Born, 1852; Died, March 15, 1886
In the 16th year of her religious life
St. Mary's Academy, Denver, Colo.

Sister M. Olivet McLean
Born, 1868; Died, November 16, 1888
In the 2nd year of her religious life
St. Mary's Academy, Denver, Colo.

Sister M. Davina Burns
Born, 1854; Died, August 16, 1889
In the 14th year of her religious life
St. Mary's Academy, Denver, Colo.

Sister M. Nerinckx O'Neil
Born, 1846; Died, October 8, 1889
In the 23rd year of her religious life
St. Mary's Academy, Denver, Colo.

Sister M. Benigna Brady
Born, 1847; Died, November 17, 1890
In the 18th year of her religious life
St. Mary's Academy, Denver, Colo.

Sister M. Victorine Renshaw
Born, 1851; Died, March 23, 1891
In the 24th year of her religious life
St. Mary's Academy, Denver, Colo.

Sister M. Josefina Ortiz
Born, 1861; Died, February 12, 1896
In the 18th year of her religious life
St. Mary's Academy, Denver, Colo.

Sister M. Frances O'Leary
Born, May 3, 1854; Died, Nov. 5, 1898
In the 15th year of her religious life
Loretto Heights Academy, Loretto,
Colorado

Sister M. Teresa Augusta Owings
Born, Feb. 12, 1862; Died Apr. 20, 1899
In the 9th year of her religious life
Loretto Heights Academy, Loretto,
Colorado

Sister M. Paschal Doyle
Born, Aug. 6, 1858; Died, Dec. 9, 1903
In the 30th year of her religious life
St. Mary's Academy, Denver, Colo.

Sister M. Claudia McCauley
Born, Mar. 10, 1852; Died, June 8, 1904
In the 35th year of her religious life
St. Mary's School, Colorado Springs,
Colorado

Sister M. Agatha Wall
Born, Jan. 20, 1830; Died, July 9, 1907
In the 54th year of her religious life
Loretto Heights Academy, Loretto,
Colorado

Sister M. Carmelita Hodapp
Born, July 26, 1870; Died, Apr. 26, 1909
In the 14th year of her religious life
St. Mary's Academy, Denver, Colo.

Sister M. Eutropia Toolan
Born, 1840; Died, April 28, 1910
In the 42nd year of her religious life
Loretto Heights Academy, Loretto,
Colorado

Sister M. Lua Kelliher
Born, 1888; Died, December 23, 1912
In the 6th year of her religious life
Loretto Heights Academy, Loretto,
Colorado

Sister M. Columba Gallavan
Born, Dec. 22, 1857; Died, Nov. 25, 1913
In the 37th year of her religious life
Loretto Heights Academy, Loretto,
Colorado

Sister M. Bartholomew Nooning
Born, Dec. 13, 1849; Died, Jan. 29, 1915
In the 48th year of her religious life
Loretto Heights Academy, Loretto,
Colorado

Mother M. Pancratia Bonfils
Born, Sept. 24, 1852; Died, Oct. 12,
1915
In the 50th year of her religious life
Loretto Heights Academy, Loretto,
Colorado

Sister M. Stephana Courtney
Born, 1841; Died, September 8, 1918
In the 59th year of her religious life
Loretto Heights Academy, Loretto,
Colorado

Sister M. Euphemia Maloy
Born, 1842; Died, July 18, 1919
In the 39th year of her religious life
Loretto Heights Academy, Loretto,
Colorado

Sister M. Antoinette Logsden
Born, 1851; Died, October 28, 1919
In the 46th year of her religious life
Loretto Heights Academy, Loretto,
Colorado

Sister Mary Martin Camp
Born, Aug. 31, 1844; Died, Feb. 3, 1924
In the 61st year of her religious life
Loretto Heights College, Loretto,
Colorado

Sister M. Teresa Cummings
Born, 1852; Died, May 11, 1924
In the 50th year of her religious life
Loretto Heights College, Loretto,
Colorado

Sister Mary De Sales Hynes
Born, Mar. 25, 1845; Died, Apr. 12,
1925
In the 60th year of her religious life
Loretto Heights College, Loretto,
Colorado

Sister M. Flora McCauley
Born, Dec. 4, 1847; Died, May 18, 1926
In the 56th year of her religious life
Loretto Heights College, Loretto,
Colorado

SISTERS OF LORETTO BURIED IN THE CONVENT CEMETERY ON LORETTO HEIGHTS GROUNDS

January, 1943—(Continued)

Sister M. Ludmilla Lehritter
Born, Oct. 3, 1867; Died, Jan. 1, 1927
In the 39th year of her religious life
Loretto Heights College, Loretto,
Colorado

Sister M. Louise Romero
Born, 1846; Died, December 14, 1928
In the 64th year of her religious life
St. Mary's Academy, Denver, Colo.

Sister M. Agnes Patricia O'Hayre
Born, Aug. 3, 1897; Died, July 26, 1929
In the 3rd year of her religious life
Sacred Heart School, Pueblo, Colo.

Mother M. Eustachia Elder
Born, Mar. 11, 1865; Died, Aug. 20,
1929
In the 47th year of her religious life
Loretto Heights College, Loretto,
Colorado

Sister M. Eudocia Chacon
Born, Dec. 6, 1843; Died, Dec. 29, 1929
In the 69th year of her religious life
Loretto Heights College, Loretto,
Colorado

Sister M. Aimee Hynes
Born, Nov. 11, 1868; Died, Aug. 2, 1930
In the 42nd year of her religious life
St. Mary's Academy, Denver, Colo.

Sister M. Dominic Early
Born, Feb. 15, 1867; Died, Jan. 11,
1931
In the 35th year of her religious life
Loretto Heights College, Loretto,
Colorado

Sister M. Edwina Casey
Born, Sept. 18, 1877; Died, Aug. 8, 1931
In the 37th year of her religious life
Sacred Heart School, Pueblo, Colo.

Sister M. Florence Corrigan
Born, Oct. 30, 1891; Died, Apr. 24, 1932
In the 19th year of her religious life
St. Mary's High School, Colorado
Springs, Colorado

Sister M. Constantia Schaub
Born, Aug. 7, 1882; Died, Oct. 5, 1933
In the 33rd year of her religious life
Loretto Heights College, Loretto,
Colorado

Sister M. Lavialle Daly
Born, Apr. 6, 1854; Died, Nov. 10, 1935
In the 65th year of her religious life
Loretto Heights College, Loretto,
Colorado

Sister M. Rosaline Hutchins
Born, Aug. 27, 1858; Died, Dec. 4, 1936
In the 61st year of her religious life
Loretto Heights College, Loretto,
Colorado

Sister M. Theotine Thomas
Born, Mar. 13, 1904; Died, Mar. 7, 1938
In the 17th year of her religious life
St. Mary's Academy, Denver, Colo.

Sister M. Loretto McAuliffe
Born, 1855; Died, March 16, 1938
In the 52nd year of her religious life
Loretto Heights College, Loretto,
Colorado

Sister Miriam Judd
Born, July 10, 1874; Died, Oct. 2, 1939
In the 45th year of her religious life
Loretto Heights College, Loretto,
Colorado

Sister M. Floscella Keating
Born, Mar. 7, 1872; Died, Mar. 23, 1940
In the 46th year of her religious life
Loretto Heights College, Loretto,
Colorado

Sister M. Jovita Mills
Born, Sept. 7, 1846; Died, March 30,
1940
In the 71st year of her religious life
Loretto Heights College, Loretto,
Colorado

Sister M. Corona Griesbach
Born, May 7, 1870; Died, Aug. 14, 1940
In the 44th year of her religious life
Loretto Heights College, Loretto,
Colorado

A STUDENT GROUP, 1942-1943

Seniors

Suzanne Bell
Esther Therese Beneventi
Betty Jo Campbell
Margaret Mary Cronin
Mae Lorraine Dornbusch
Sister Thomas Marie Farris
Frances Finnegan
Frances Patricia Gallagher
Mary Alice Gorman
Sister Teresa Augusta Hagney
Shirley Horan
Grace James
Edna May Gutman
Jean Ann Kelley
Margaret Anne Madden
Mary Catherine Madden
Jeannette Mullen
Betti Rose NanKeville
Joan O'Byrne
Mela Ortiz y Pino
Regina Mary Reitemeier
Eva Adair Riley
Corinne Schultze

Juniors

Barbara Bindel
Alicia Butler
Mary Elizabeth Conway
Irene Bernadette Costello
Katherine Eileen Dean
Elizabeth Dikitolia
Gloria DeRose
Catherine Deus
Margaret Eileen Evert
Bernice Jonke
Barbara Elaine Murphy
Virginia Elizabeth Piccoli
Frances Pauline Quinn
Rosemary Reddick
Margaret Reidy
Sister M. Joella Revers
Drucilla Janet Richardson
Mary Elizabeth Taylor
Virginia Lee Thieler

Sophomores

Helen Josephine Austin
Betty Bader
Frances Brown
Ruby Catanach
Genevieve Cesario
Catherine Crisp
Stephena Custy
Eleanor Dant
Loretta Diodoslo
Catherine Dolan
Mary Virginia Duggan
Jeanette Esponda
Mary Louise Fick
Ophilia Gomez
Ruth Graber
Anna Louise Hahn
Caroline Haninger
Desneige Jane Harris
Mary Catherine Jaeger
Marie Catherine Jeffries
Ellen Kenehan
Margaret Lawrenson
Nancy Jane Maruca
Barbara Nieters
Martha Norris
Jane Offutt
Josephine Palaze
Catherine Pruisner
Edith Maureen Reidy
Josephine Salcetti
Mary Ann Schwab
Betty Spehar
Mary Louise Stephenson
Vivian Theresa Street
Sister M. Charlotte Zingg

Freshmen

Margaret Louise Abegg
Marian Ashe
Marilyn Anne Beckard
Beverly Bell
Geraldine Bindel
Madelene Bindel
Ollie Marie Blevins
Lola Brunacini
Barbara Cannell
Marion Campbell
Margaret Ann Carney
Peggie Chambers
Helen Marie Conhiser
Eileen Joe Dolan
O'Della Ann Dudley
Catherine Gertrude Duffy
Viola Fellin
Kathleen Friend
Catherine Frkovich
Irene Guise
Margaret Constance Hamilton
Elma Lois Hardin
Dorothy Harkins
Harriet Hubbard
June Jackson
Julia Catherine Job
Mary Martha Jones
Helen Kane
Patricia Lewis
Kathryn Mahoney
Alice Matson
Marian Elizabeth Mayer
Beulah Menhennet
Rose Morandin
Mary Oehrle
Rose Mary O'Leary
Rose Marie Palaze
Lillian Perko
Marie Porreca
Mary Lu Prendergast
Bess Riesenman
Mary Anne Russell
Eleanor Ryan
Frances Salas
Cathey Schrodt
Josephine Schram
Mary Jean Seeburg
Joan Shearman
Katherine Stimac
Loretta Sweeney
Margaret Jane Telk
Florence Marie Urizaga
Cecilia Waters
Rosemary Witherow
Sara Lee Yetter
Rosemarie Zegob

INDEX